Advising Student Groups and Organizations

Second Edition

Advising Student Groups and Organizations

Second Edition

Norbert W. Dunkel, John H. Schuh, and Nancy E. Chrystal-Green

JB JOSSEY-BASS™

A Wiley Brand

Cover design by Wiley
Cover image © fishbones | Thinkstock
Copyright © 2014 by John Wiley & Sons, Inc. All rights reserved.

Published by Jossey-Bass
A Wiley Brand
One Montgomery Street, Suite 1200, San Francisco, CA 94104-4594
www.josseybass.com/highereducation

Jossey-Bass books and products are available through most bookstores. To contact Jossey-Bass directly call our Customer Care Department within the U.S. at 800-956-7739, outside the U.S. at 317-572-3986, or fax 317-572-4002.

Wiley publishes in a variety of print and electronic formats and by print-on-demand. Some material included with standard print versions of this book may not be included in e-books or in print-on-demand. If this book refers to media such as a CD or DVD that is not included in the version you purchased, you may download this material at **http://booksupport.wiley.com**. For more information about Wiley products, visit **www.wiley.com**.

The Five Practices of Exemplary Leadership®, Leadership Practices Inventory®, LPI®, and Student Leadership Practices Inventory® are registered trademarks of John Wiley & Sons, Inc.
www.leadershipchallenge.com
www.studentleadershipchallenge.com

Library of Congress Cataloging-in-Publication Data has been applied for and is on file with the Library of Congress.
ISBN 978-1-118-78464-8 (pbk); ISBN 978-1-118-78490-7 (ebk); ISBN 978-1-118-78480-8 (ebk)

Printed in the United States of America
SECOND EDITION
PB Printing   10 9 8 7 6 5 4 3 2 1

The Jossey-Bass Higher and Adult Education Series

Contents

The Authors

Norbert W. Dunkel is associate vice president for Student Affairs, Auxiliary Operations at the University of Florida. His responsibilities include oversight of the Department of Recreational Sports, J. Wayne Reitz Union, and the Department of Housing and Residence Education. He serves concurrently as the chief housing officer and manages a comprehensive campus housing operation for ten thousand residents and their families including business services, residence life and education, administrative services, custodial, maintenance, personnel and payroll, marketing and public relations, and information technology. He oversees eighteen hundred full- and part-time employees with operational auxiliary budgets over $70 million annually. These one hundred seventy facilities encompass four million square feet. Mr. Dunkel holds an adjunct faculty appointment in the Department of Educational Administration and Policy.

Dunkel is the author, coauthor, or editor of over ninety-one publications, including eighteen books and monographs, twenty-nine book chapters, and over forty-five articles. His books include *Campus Housing Management* (six volume set edited with James Baumann), *Campus Crisis Management* (edited with Gene Zdziarski and Mike Rollo), *Advice for Advisers: Empowering Your Residence Hall Association* (3rd edition) (edited with Cindy Spencer), *Foundations: Strategies for the Future of Collegiate Housing* (edited with Beth McCuskey), *Advising Student Groups and Organizations* (with John Schuh), *Campus Housing Construction* (with Jim Grimm), *Peak Experiences* (edited with Paul Jahr). He was editor of the *Journal of College and University Student Housing* and associate editor of the *College Student Affairs Journal*. Dunkel has made nearly one hundred presentations and speeches to various conferences and institutions including twice testifying before United States Congressional Committees. He has served as a consultant to twenty-three universities and colleges.

Dunkel has served as president for the Association of College and University Housing Officers-International (ACUHO-I) and twice previously served on the executive board. He cofounded and codirected (for ten years) the ACUHO-I James C. Grimm National Housing Training Institute, now in its twenty-second year. He is the current founding codirector of the Roelf Visser Student Housing Training Institute in South Africa, now in its fifth year. He hosted the Global Housing Summit in Hong Kong with over seventeen countries in attendance.

Dunkel came to the University of Florida after holding administrative positions at South Dakota State University and the University of Northern Iowa. He holds Bachelor of Science and Master of Science degrees from Southern Illinois University in Carbondale. At the University of Florida, Dunkel is a member of the UF Budget Advisory Council, Crisis Response Team, University Counseling Resources Network, Emergency Policy Group/Executive Management Team, Food Service Advisory Council, and Land Use and Facilities Planning Committee.

Dunkel has received the ACUHO-I Foundation Parthenon Society Award and Foundation of Excellence Award. He has received the Leadership and Service, Presidential Service, and Research and Publication Awards from ACUHO-I; the Dr. Kenneth Stoner Distinguished Service Award and Dan Hallenbeck Service Award from the National Association of College and University Residence Halls (NACURH); the Charles W. Beene Memorial Service Award from the Southeastern Association of Housing Officers (SEAHO), and the James E. Scott Bridging the Gap Memorial Award from the University of Florida.

John H. Schuh is director of the School of Education at Iowa State University. As such he is responsible for the educational program of the School including all degree programs and other educational experiences offered by the School. He assumed this position on July 1, 2013. He also is the director of Iowa State University's Emerging Leader's Academy.

John Schuh also is distinguished professor of Educational Leadership and Policy Studies at Iowa State, where he was department chair for six and one-half years. Previously he held administrative and faculty assignments at Wichita State University, Indiana University (Bloomington), and Arizona State University. He received his Master of Counseling and PhD degrees from Arizona State. He served for more than twenty years as a reserve officer in the United States Army Medical Service Corps, being assigned to the retired reserve with the rank of major in 1991.

Schuh is the author, coauthor, or editor of over 235 publications, including 29 books and monographs, 80 book chapters, and over 110 articles. Among his books are *Assessment Methods for Student Affairs, One Size Does Not Fit All: Traditional and Innovative Models of Student Affairs Practice* (with Kathleen Manning and Jillian Kinzie), *Student Success in College* (with George D. Kuh, Jillian Kinzie, and Elizabeth Whitt). Currently he is associate editor of the *New Directions for Student Services* Sourcebook Series after serving as editor for thirteen years. He was associate editor of the *Journal of College Student Development* for fourteen years and was book review editor of *The Review of Higher Education* from 2008 to 2010. Schuh has made nearly three hundred presentations and speeches to campus-based, regional, national, and international meetings. He has served as a consultant to more than eighty institutions of higher education and other educational organizations.

Schuh has served on the governing boards of the American College Personnel Association, the National Association of Student Personnel Administrators (twice) and the Association of College and University Housing Officers (twice), and the Board of Directors of the National Association of Student Personnel Administrators Foundation. He is a member of the Evaluator Corps of the Higher Learning Commission of the North Central Association of Colleges and Schools where he also serves as a Team Chair for accreditation visits.

Schuh has received the Research Achievement Award from the Association for the Study of Higher Education, the Contribution to Knowledge Award from the American College Personnel Association, the Contribution to Research or Literature Award and the Robert H. Shaffer Award for Academic Excellence as a Graduate Faculty Member from the National Association of Student Personnel Administrators, and the S. Earl Thompson Award, Association of College and University Housing Officers-International. The American College Personnel Association elected him as a Senior Scholar Diplomate. Schuh was chosen as one of seventy-five Diamond Honorees by ACPA in 1999 and as a Pillar of the Profession by NASPA in 2001. He is a member of the Iowa Academy of Education. He has received a number of institutional awards including the Distinguished Alumni Achievement Award from the University of Wisconsin-Oshkosh, his undergraduate alma mater.

Schuh received a Fulbright award to study higher education in Germany in 1994, was named to the Fulbright Specialists Program in 2008, and had a specialists' assignment in South Africa in 2012. In 2013 he was named to the Peer Review Committee for the Fulbright Specialist Program. He has been engaged with institutions of higher education in Scotland, England, Germany, Syria, Ukraine, Bulgaria, Hong Kong, Ireland, Macau, Malaysia, South Africa, and Saudi Arabia.

Nancy E. Chrystal-Green currently serves as the director of Student Activities and Involvement at the University of Florida having responsibility for Sorority and Fraternity Affairs, advising student government, campus programming, event management, student organization advising, and the Travel and Recreation Program. She is also an adjunct faculty member in the Department of Educational Administration and Policy. Chrystal-Green received her bachelor's degree in Political Science from McMaster University in Hamilton, ON, Canada (1993), a master's degree in Recreation Administration from Georgia Southern University (1996), and a doctorate in Student Affairs Administration from the University of Georgia (2004).

Chrystal-Green has spent her twenty-year career advising students and student organizations as a student affairs administrator in the fields of residence life, campus recreation, and student activities. Prior to joining the Division of Student Affairs at the University of Florida, she held administrative positions at Coastal Carolina University, Oxford College of Emory, and the University of Georgia. She has been recognized for her service to national student affairs organizations for a variety of capacities including chairing the faculty for the School of Recreational Sports Management. Chrystal-Green has also been recognized by students by being awarded the James E. Scott Bridging the Gap Memorial Award from the University of Florida and being inducted into Florida Blue Key Leadership Honorary. She has presented over thirty sessions at regional and national conferences, facilitated dozens of skill development sessions with student leaders, been a keynote speaker for many awards banquets and leadership retreats, and served as an external reviewer. Her research interests include staff supervision, leadership development, cocurricular learning, and legal and ethical issues in student affairs practice.

Preface

IN WRITING THE second edition for this book, we reviewed the changes in advising over the past fifteen years. The exponential increase in the use of technology, the evolving legal landscape, and the increasingly challenging financial environment are just a few of the broad, contextual areas that advisers have had to stay abreast of in providing the information, materials, and support needed by student organizations.

We continue to be amazed by the energy, excitement, and drive that each year's new class of students brings to our campuses. We know many of them will develop into mature, sophisticated leaders by the time they graduate while a few will at times challenge our patience. Most important, we take pride in their development and have a renewed sense of energy when our new students walk through the door to attend their first student organization meeting.

Over the years higher education has continued to receive criticism for not putting student learning first (for example, Wingspread Group on Higher Education 1993; Association of American Colleges and Universities 2002), and, at times, that criticism could be justified. Sometimes other priorities get in the way of student learning, but we need to continue to analyze how faculty and staff use their time (see Boyer 1990). Many of us continue to draw our vision in part from *The Student Learning Imperative* (American College Personnel Association 1994) and *Learning Reconsidered* (National Association of Student Personnel Educators and the American College Personnel Association 2004), which proposed that faculty and educational leaders in higher education, including student organization advisers, need to develop conditions that motivate and inspire students to devote more time and energy to educationally purposeful activities both in and outside the classroom. Student organization advisers have the opportunity to link classroom learning to practical applications through the experiences students have in their organizations. Although the role of adviser is different from that of classroom instructor, Love and Maxam (2011) point out "Group advising also involves the role and skills of a teacher" (419).

This book was written to help student organization advisers have the information to perform their essential role and assist students to obtain the best educational experience possible from their membership in a student organization.

For student affairs professionals, serving as an adviser to a student organization often is a job expectation and having the opportunity to advise key student organizations is sought out, in part, to broaden one's array of professional experiences for future advancement. Student affairs staff, as a consequence of their graduate education, typically recognize the amount of student growth and development that takes place with their involvement in a student organization. These staff have a foundational understanding of the students' lives, the fads and practices that students engage in, and know the music and social networking that attract students. For many advisers, this is why they keep coming back year after year to advise an organization. For advisers outside of student affairs, their role may have been undertaken with little training or understanding of the substantial responsibilities that are part of advising a student organization. They may not understand that they have little authority over the organization they advise. We believe that being an adviser requires specialized knowledge and skill to understand the difficult legal situations, financial considerations, and travel and transportation circumstances. We hope these negative aspects of advising are counterbalanced when one considers the advantages that advisers accrue from working with students in organizations.

The value to students of belonging to a student organization is well established in the literature. Astin (1993) asserts that student-to-student interaction, including participation in student clubs and organizations, produces positive outcomes for students. Pascarella and Terenzini (2005) concluded that students involved in diversity experiences positively affected their student learning. They also state that "the more the student is psychologically engaged in activities and tasks that reinforce the formal academic experience, the more he or she will learn" (119). Van Etten, Pressley, McInerney, and Liem (2008) identified college seniors who listed extracurricular activities as an important factor in their college persistence. The National Survey of Student Engagement (NSSE 2012) found that students who are involved in the life of their college or university by participating actively in student organizations will devote more time and energy to academics, spend more time on campus, and have more positive interactions with faculty and staff.

Many large campuses now have hundreds or even thousands of different student organizations in which students can become involved. Considering that membership in student organizations has such tremendous value for students in terms of contributing to their growth and development, institutions of higher education are obligated to provide advisers with the tools they need to enhance the development of the organizations with which they work. McKaig and Policello (1987) underscore this point: "The role of the adviser can be an integral element in the success of the student organization and in ensuring that the educational potential of the extracurriculum is realized" (45). Kuh, Schuh, and Whitt (1991) identified examples of organizational advisers playing roles in their study of the factors and conditions that lead to high-quality out-of-class learning experiences for students. Kuh, Kinzie, Schuh, and Whitt (2010) found that accessible faculty contribute in numerous ways to student learning. Serving as an organization's adviser is one way for faculty to be accessible to students and influence their educational experiences.

To summarize, we draw three important conclusions: (1) students benefit from participating in student organizations; (2) advisers can play a key role in advancing student organizations, and (3) advisers, too often, are not well equipped for their role. We have written this second edition to address the concern implied by the third conclusion.

Audience for This Book

This book was completed for several targeted audiences. Our priority audience includes the tens of thousands of faculty and staff who serve as organization advisers but who assume these roles with limited background. These faculty and staff may be at four-year universities and colleges, two-year colleges, or community/junior colleges. They include faculty who may have teaching, research, service, outreach, and economic development as their primary assignments; institutional staff working in numerous campus offices who do not have advising as a primary job priority; and new student affairs staff who have recently started their positions with little advising experience as a graduate student or entry-level professional staff member in student activities, leadership and service, campus housing, multicultural affairs, and sorority and fraternity affairs.

The secondary audience includes staff members who possess responsibility for training and providing consultation to student organization advisers. Typically, these staff have worked for several years traditionally in the area of student activities and sorority and fraternity affairs. We believe these staff will benefit from the materials provided, examples and samples of forms and documents, approaches to training, and the like. These are also the staff who should call regular meetings of student organization advisers to discuss issues and concerns they are experiencing as advisers.

An additional audience for this book includes senior administrators who provide supervision and oversight for student affairs areas including student activities, campus housing, sorority and fraternity affairs, leadership and service, student government, recreational sports, and multicultural and diversity affairs. These administrators include directors, assistant and associate vice presidents, vice presidents, provosts, and even the president. Increasingly, the senior student affairs officer reports to the provost, who likely has limited student affairs experience. We believe it is important for provosts with limited student affairs experience to read this book as a useful approach to becoming familiar with campus organizations. Although we understand that provosts may not read the book from cover to cover, it would be reasonable for them to read those parts of the book that address the challenges advisers face in their daily work with student organizations, and to understand that good advising is no different than good teaching or good research. This book emphasizes the connections between curricular and cocurricular learning by showcasing opportunities for students to demonstrate both cognitive and psychosocial development. We hope that one of the learning points from this book is that work with student organizations helps institutions produce individuals who are well educated and skilled in working with others in a complex community.

Finally, we believe this book will be a useful resource for graduate students who are preparing for a career in student affairs. Most graduate students will advise a student organization such as a hall government, programming board, spring break trip, or speakers' bureau.

We must emphasize that this book was not prepared to provide information on academic advising, nor has it been prepared for staff who serve as counselors or who provide other forms of educational or personal assistance. It is written solely for faculty and staff who advise student organizations on college and university campuses. There are many other sources available on academic advising and counseling for persons interested in learning more about how to assist students to develop their careers or providing help with student development problems.

In addition, we would like to briefly clarify a few terms. We will use the terms "institution," "college," and "university" interchangeably in this book to mean all institutions of higher education. We also use the terms "student organization" and "student group" synonymously; by these we mean student organizations that are recognized, sponsored, or registered on campus. We also occasionally use "faculty" adviser because of its historic roots to describe the person who directly advises a student organization. However, a more inclusive term that is more representative of current practices is "student organization adviser" as there are many people in nonfaculty positions working with student organizations.

Purpose of the Book

This book was written to provide advisers with the knowledge, skills, and materials necessary to effectively advise a student organization. Our specific purposes are as follows: (1) to provide advisers the foundational knowledge and basic concepts of working students and student organizations, (2) to provide the day-to-day details that advisers need to accomplish their assignments, and (3) to provide information on ensuring quality in advising.

Overview of the Contents

The book can be divided into three general sections. The first four chapters of the book provide advisers with foundational knowledge. Chapter 1 identifies the rewards and challenges of advising student organizations from the individual, institutional, and community perspectives. Chapter 2 provides advisers with an overview and history of student organizations. The chapter reviews the many types of student organizations present on college campuses and how advisers may have to adjust their approach in working with these organizations. This chapter also includes a history of when and where the categories of student organizations began. Chapter 3 is dedicated to Greek organizations. This chapter discusses the history and taxonomy for the various types of Greek chapters and provides details on the organizational structure, funding, and relationships Greek organizations have with their institutions. Chapter 4 includes information and several theories and models on group dynamics, leadership development, and learning. We include practical examples of working with student organizations in different stages of organizational development.

The next six chapters in the book provide information on the day-to-day details that advisers need to accomplish their roles. Chapter 5 includes the knowledge, skills, and qualities essential to advisers. Position descriptions, constitutions, roles, the motivation of students, and understanding mission and purpose of an organization are identified. Chapter 6 discusses how an adviser can provide academic and career assistance to students. This chapter also presents information on the academic nature of the institution, how to refer students, what basic academic information to know, and performance as a student. This chapter also supplies numerous materials to assist students in understanding values, morals, and ethics as well as their level of involvement in the organization. Chapter 7 provides information on representing institutional and organizational needs. This information includes policies and procedures, service learning, and traveling. Chapter 8 introduces budget management to advisers. The chapter provides essential information on budget development, software available to track budgets, types and sample budgets, funding sources, audits, and tax information. Chapter 9 offers rudimentary information to advisers on legal issues and strategies for managing risk. Understanding the Clery Act, hazing, dealing with issues related to alcohol, managing money, and the like are essential knowledge for advisers of student organizations. Chapter 10 describes how to work with students and organizations when issues and conflicts arise. The chapter provides approaches and tools to use to minimize these difficulties.

The final three chapters provide information on ensuring quality in advising, approaches to training, and development of adviser personal effectiveness. Chapter 11 introduces how to ensure quality in advising. This chapter offers information on how to evaluate adviser and the organizational effectiveness. Chapter 12 discusses detailed information on training advisers and on advisers training students. This chapter shares training topics, approaches, and schedules. Chapter 13 introduces recommendations for professional practice, keeping advising activities rewarding, and suggestions for continuing education and professional development.

How to Use This Book

We believe the book captures important elements of advising a student organization. Reading the book in its entirety will provide you with the foundational information you need in developing a yearlong approach to advising a student organization. The information also will provide you with strategies and approaches to use when issues and concerns arise, as well as helping you to understand potential legal and financial problems before they arise, and describing how to work with and better understand your students.

The book includes numerous case studies, checklists, examples of forms, sample letters, and many other materials to support your work as a student organization adviser. We encourage you to meet with other student organization advisers on your campus. We have found that regular meetings with other advisers to discuss issues and concerns, recognition, schedules, institutional procedures and processes, and the amount of time spent on the organization is incredibly beneficial to those advisers. No one adviser should be without a group of colleagues on campus. You may want to bring your copy of this book with you and pick various aspects of the book to discuss openly among your colleagues. Better approaches and methods always come from discussions about challenges, solutions to problems, and how to help students advance their organization.

Acknowledgments

FROM THE AUTHORS: We thank all the faculty and staff who have dedicated time to advise a student organization. You have assisted thousands of students in their leadership development. Special thanks go to Erin Null, senior editor; Alison Knowles, associate editor; Joanne Clapp Fullagar, senior production editor; Shauna Robinson, senior editorial assistant; and Hunter Stark, marketing coordinator from Jossey-Bass who assisted us throughout the publishing process. We would like to thank Mr. Jack Causseaux, director of Sorority and Fraternity Affairs at the University of Florida, who used his fifteen years of experience to explain to us Greek Life. His description was invaluable to us.

Norb Dunkel wishes to recognize Quincy Chapman for research assistance. He also thanks his colleagues John Schuh and Nancy Chrystal-Green for committing their time and knowledge to coauthor the second edition. Norb also thanks Dave Kratzer, vice president for Student Affairs at the University of Florida, for his enduring work to support, encourage, and advocate for our students. Norb wishes to thank his wife, Kim, and son, Nicholas. They have always supported his professional development involvements when it meant evenings, weekends, and travel abroad.

John Schuh would like to recognize all the students he has worked with over the years, particularly those who served as leaders in organizations he advised. He'd like to thank his family for putting up with lots of evening meetings and weekend events that were part of his work with student groups. Special thanks go to Norb Dunkel and Nancy Chrystal-Green for being wonderful colleagues.

Nancy Chrystal-Green would like to acknowledge the support of her husband, Gregg, who understands the time and energy it takes to be successful in this profession and her daughter, MacKenzie, who reminds her daily of what is really important in life. Nancy would also like to thank John Schuh and Norb Dunkel for being willing to share this experience and their wisdom. Nancy wants to extend a special thank-you to all the student leaders she has worked with over the years. Advising students is both inspiring and challenging, and each interaction has contributed to how she approaches her work.

April 2014

Norbert W. Dunkel
Gainesville, Florida

John H. Schuh
Ames, Iowa

Nancy E. Chrystal-Green
Gainesville, Florida

Advising Student Groups and Organizations

Second Edition

Chapter 1

Challenges and Rewards of Advising

STUDENTS BENEFIT SUBSTANTIALLY from being involved in campus organizations. Astin (1985) states that "students learn by becoming involved" (133). He defined a highly involved student as "one who . . . devotes considerable energy to studying, spends a lot of time on campus, participates actively in student organizations, and interacts frequently with faculty members and other students" (134). The Student Learning Imperative adds that "serving as an officer of a campus organization or working offer opportunities to apply knowledge obtained in the classroom and to develop practical competencies" (American College Personnel Association 1994, 2).

Involvement in student organizations also provides challenges and rewards for you as the adviser. On the one hand, some advisers are actively involved with their students and enjoy their interaction immensely. Some advisers work with debate teams and travel every weekend to various contests; others enjoy white-water rafting with their organization or having lunch at the dining center with the executive officers. On the other hand, some advisers have such a negative experience that after one term they refuse to advise another student organization.

Regardless of why you have become an adviser—be it a role freely chosen or one thrust upon you—an understanding of the benefits gained by student involvement and the challenges and rewards of advising will help you fulfill your responsibilities more effectively.

This chapter summarizes Astin's Theory of Involvement (1984) and how various institutions have utilized the research to promote student involvement in organizations. The chapter then identifies the challenges and rewards—for the community, the institution, the organization, the adviser, and the student—of being involved in and working with student organizations, and at several points directs your attention to other chapters for in-depth discussion of specific issues.

Astin's Theory of Involvement

The core of any student group or organization is the student. The student's time, commitment, and energy to be involved in the organization helps drive the organization's membership, excitement, and interest by other students. Students gain a number of benefits from being involved in a student organization. Astin's Theory of Involvement provides evidence of these benefits. Hutley (2003) has provided an excellent summary of Alexander Astin's Theory of Involvement:

> The most basic tenet of Astin's Theory of Involvement is that students learn more the more they are involved in both the academic and social aspects of the collegiate experience. An involved student is one who devotes considerable energy to academics, spends much time on campus, participates actively in student organizations and activities, and interacts often with faculty (Astin, 1984, p. 292). . . .
>
> Astin states that the quality and quantity of the student's involvement will influence the amount of student learning and development (Astin, 1984, p. 297). True involvement requires the investment of energy in academic relationships and activities related to the campus and the amount of energy invested will vary greatly depending on the student's interests and goals, as well as the student's other commitments. The most important institutional resource, therefore, is student time: the extent to which students can be involved in the educational development is tempered by how involved they are with family, friends, jobs, and other outside activities (p. 301).

Montelongo (2002) summarized in his review of literature as follows:

> Participation in college student organizations promotes affective and cognitive changes within college students. Involvement in extracurricular activities, especially in college student organizations, has benefits extending beyond classroom learning. Participation in extracurricular activities contributes to the intellectual, social, and emotional changes in a person over time. Outcomes associated with participation in college student organizations includes cognitive development or higher intellectual

processes such as critical thinking, knowledge acquisition, synthesis, and decision-making, as well as personal or affective development of attitudes, values, aspirations, and personality disposition. . . . Participation in college student organizations has been shown to have an influence on affective outcomes of the college experience, such as cultivating a student's sense of satisfaction with the college experience and in increasing participation and involvement within campus and community. College student organization participation also was an influential component in a student's total co-curricular experience as shown by enhancing intellectual development and by allowing students to become aware of and involved with the educational environment. Students were able to assess campus resources to achieve their educational goals. (61–62)

Institutions have drawn from the considerable research to promote the benefits of student organization involvement. At the University of Nebraska at Omaha (2013), the student activities and leadership programs office website includes a list of benefits: "academic enhancement, communication skills, scholarship incentives, personal/professional growth, career development, community service, leadership skills, self-confidence, and life-long friends."

At California State University San Marcos (2013), the student life and leadership website states that as a result of getting involved leaders "develop a campus support network, grow their leadership skills and plan fun activities for their group. . . . Current student leaders report their communication, interpersonal and social skills have improved as a result of being involved on campus and in the San Marcos community."

The website of Bethany College (2013) in West Virginia lists benefits of joining a student organization that include "making new friends, career exploration, career information, getting involved, gaining a sense of being, a chance to share common interests, learning to work in a group, learning to manage your time, an opportunity to learn and practice leadership skills, learning to organize meetings, events, and programs, and recognition for achievement."

At Rutgers New Brunswick (2013), the website's list of benefits to students includes "providing students with an opportunity to explore interests, sharpen skills, and learn about themselves and others while enhancing the academic mission of the college. Organizational involvement allows students to develop those skills that will prepare them for their career and civic responsibilities beyond the University."

The RedbusUS site (2013) identifies eight reasons why students should join a student organization. These include networking, social skills, professional experience, personality development, leadership skills, alumni networking, organization and management skills, and friendships and fun.

Whether an institution selects to identify student benefits gained based directly on a theory or model, by using institutional values or mission, or by using anecdotal or testimonials from students, student activities and involvement offices will commonly couch these benefits and publicize them through their student organization registration processes, student and adviser training, and leadership development programs. We believe it is important to select and promote a list of benefits that students will gain through their student organization involvement.

Challenges

The community, institutions, organizations, advisers, and students face a variety of challenges related to student groups. We look at each of these challenges in detail.

Community

There are few challenges to the local community from student organizations. Most of the challenging situations in the community are from the result of individual student behavioral issues. The community may also be challenged by student celebrations following final examinations or winning a championship sports game. These issues are typically remedied by local city codes and standards, law enforcement, or the institution's off-campus housing or dean of students offices.

Student organizations whose activities run counter to the local community environment can be seen as challenging. Some examples of such activities include a student organization creating a farmer's market to occur at the same time as a local farmer's market, a student organization protesting local restaurants whose practice or purchasing of materials may be viewed as against their wishes, or a student organization speaking to the city or county commission about their political position or decisions made.

Institutions

Faculty and practitioners in student affairs units know the benefits students experience by being involved in campus organizations, but it is nevertheless an institutional challenge to educate the greater campus community about the benefits of student involvement in organizations. We strongly recommend that you read *Achieving Educational Excellence* (Astin 1985), *How College Affects Students, Volume 2: A Third Decade of Research* (Pascarella and Terenzini 2005), and *What Matters in College? Four Critical Years Revisited* (Astin 1993). These three books are central to understanding the rewards and benefits that an institution can gain from having involved students. Consequently, the first challenge faced at an institutional level is to ensure that the knowledge of the benefits and rewards described in these books is distributed widely among faculty and staff.

A second institutional challenge is to develop and maintain a legal safety net for organizational activities, programs, and travel. Student organizations work with contracts and agreements, travel extensively throughout the country and world, and participate in such higher-risk activities as skiing, skydiving, caving, white-water rafting, and mountain climbing. The institution must have staff assigned to assist organizations with complex contractual agreements, to assist in providing safe transportation, to discuss the issues of risk management, and so on. Colleges are facing increasingly complex liability and risk management questions; the campus legal counsel can assist in many aspects of this institutional challenge. Texas A&M University provides a risk management team as part of their division of student affairs and student activities unit. This risk management team "strives to help student leaders and advisors facilitate experiences that are developmental, educational, safe, and successful. Risk Management is the process of advising organizations of the potential and perceived risks involved in their activities, providing education about the guiding boundaries established for organizations, and taking corrective actions and proactive steps to minimize accidental injury and/or loss" (Texas A&M 2013b). Chapter 9 provides detailed information on selected legal issues of advising.

A third institutional challenge is the increased need to find the supplies and the meeting and office space to enable student organizations to function. Student activity fees enable many institutions to construct and maintain a central suite of offices for students. Typically this suite is located in a student union, student center, or leadership and service building. Student committees typically allocate the student office space. Student organizations, in turn, will usually provide their own office equipment and supplies. Some campuses have identified a requirement that these student offices must be staffed by members of the student organization and open for minimum periods during the week, such as 15–20 hours.

Meeting space for student organizations is increasingly difficult to find. Institutions are struggling during difficult funding periods to balance assignment of meeting rooms, conference rooms, and ballrooms for conferences and other revenue-generating activities against the needs of student organizations. Institutions have reviewed other campus space to use for student organization meetings and are increasingly using vacant classrooms, residence hall common spaces, or covered outdoor space. In other circumstances, student organizations are finding it necessary to move their meetings to off-campus facilities such as students' houses, conference or convention centers, churches, restaurants, or parks.

Many chapter houses for sorority and fraternity members are well-maintained with significant reserve funds available. The conditions of the aging facilities of some Greek chapter houses, however, have increasingly become an institutional challenge. As some of the houses have fallen into disrepair due to the lack of funds or ability to coordinate the repairs, the institution has stepped in on several campuses to offer assistance. In some cases the institution has provided low-interest loans for chapters to install fire sprinklers; provided consultation to house corporations on what is necessary to upgrade their facilities; or provided project coordination to ensure work is completed on time and within budget. Other campuses have worked to assume full control of the chapter houses by financing the construction or renovation of the houses and then provided oversight for all financial, facility, and staffing issues.

Another institutional challenge has been to clarify for the public the distinction between registering versus recognizing student organizations. Members of the general public often complain with letters to the editor, phone calls to the president, letters to the local governing board, or social media remarks about student organizations that appear to run contrary to the mission of the institution. Whereas private institutions can take a more restrictive position regarding which student organizations may be allowed to be "recognized" by the institution, public institutions tend to follow a procedure of "registering" student organizations. At times some members of the public consider the mere existence of a particular organization an affront to the use of tax dollars (e.g., a white student union organization or atheist student organization, and so on). The general public may not possess a clear understanding that the institution only registers the organization and does not recognize (or approve) the organization. We explain the registration process in detail in chapter 2. The challenge for institutions is to communicate with the public regarding the educational mission of the institution. For example, this mission may include providing a means of dialogue, debate, and free speech, thus allowing students an opportunity to explore the value of an organization that appears to offend others.

The fifth institutional challenge is to bring campus leaders together for discussions of events, problems, and the life of the institution. Institutional leadership should understand that the students are some of the best sources of feedback and insight for the institution. Students can provide valuable information on academic advising, campus safety and security, career planning, and parking.

Many institutions have invited students from select student organizations to provide this information. The presidents, vice presidents, and directors at these institutions have discovered the value of establishing relationships with a student constituency that can later be helpful when a campus crisis occurs and students are needed to assist in distributing information, making public statements, or sharing a podium during a press conference. They have found value in gaining student support for needed fee or tuition increases, securing funding for building construction, or voicing support for a policy, statute, or law change. Chapter 7 discusses the relationships that student organizations have with the institution. Thus, another institutional challenge is to understand the ongoing value and resources that student organizations, their leadership, and their membership can provide to the institution.

A final institutional challenge is to educate the members and officers of student organizations about the requirements for holding an elected position and the priority the institution places on students' academic success. Institutions, primarily through the student activities office, maintain the information necessary for determining officer eligibility. As the number of student organizations has swelled to over one thousand on some campuses, institutions face increasing difficulty in reviewing records for eligibility. Some campuses have specific eligibility requirements for students to be members or to serve as officers (or both). These requirements may include students maintaining a minimum grade point average, students enrolling in and maintaining a minimum number of course credits to hold a position, or that students show academic progress to graduation. In these cases, it is the institution's responsibility to review the officers' or members' grade point averages and class loads, because student records cannot be revealed to student organizations under current privacy laws.

Organizations

One of the greatest challenges facing a student organization is to recruit and retain an adequate membership base. Recruiting is less of a concern for some organizations because of the nature of their activities. For example, military or recognition organizations may have a direct academic linkage that serves as an organization's entry point. Others, such as intramural sports groups or sports clubs, experience substantial student interest and may have to limit the number of participants. Still other organizations, such as fraternities and sororities, have an extensive process of recruitment and a comprehensive orientation into the organization. The recruitment process may involve many hundreds of interested students.

For many special-interest student organizations, recruitment and retention are vital, ongoing concerns. The organization may spend time at student organization program fairs, spend money on ads, identify student members to utilize social media sites to promote their organization, or they may produce video pieces to publicize their organization. Because so few students may be interested in a particular special interest, the organization must publicize to the broader student body to attract members. These organizations work with media outlets to share information about their successes, projects, and the benefits membership provides.

Securing funding to meet the organization's needs is another challenge. Some organizations receive direct funding from student activity fees, student government allocations, fundraising efforts, membership dues, private donations, or foundational accounts and trusts. Most student organizations, however, spend time raising funds and soliciting for money to operate on even the most frugal budgets. Successful student organizations will identify multiple reoccurring funding sources to support their efforts versus relying on one funding source. Chapter 8 provides a number of suggestions about fundraising to support student organizations.

Auditing financial records and maintaining fiscal responsibility also are organizational challenges. Providing oversight for the budget is crucial. Many institutions require audits of accounts through a student government or student activities general accounting office. More often, this responsibility is assigned to the organization's treasurer, with additional oversight provided by the adviser. Some large student government operations may be audited by the institution's office of audit and compliance on an annual basis due to budgets well over $1 million. Again, chapter 8 provides guidance for this challenge.

Another organizational challenge is to identify and train individuals to advise student organizations. To be recognized, registered, or sponsored on most campuses, an organization must have an adviser. Granted, most organizations select their adviser on the basis of the interest or previous involvement the person has with the organization. Other organizations inherit advisers who serve in that capacity due to the responsibilities of their positions. These organizations may have little or no input into the selection of their adviser. Still other organizations have great difficulty finding a faculty or staff adviser due to the perceived amount of work the adviser must contribute to the student organization, the nature of the organization or its values, the travel required, or the embarrassment an adviser might experience by being associated with a controversial student organization. Due to the continually changing landscape of liability and regulations—which includes Clery Act reporting, Title IX, and protocols related to minors—fewer faculty and staff are eager to serve in an advising role.

Another challenge for the organization is to make an active effort to involve the adviser in its meetings and activities. For many organizations this is never an issue as advisers are fully engaged and attend all meetings and activities. Other organizations appear to work in a vacuum, failing to communicate with their adviser on any matter including the dates and times of meetings. In order for advisers to be effective, they must be able to attend and, to a certain level, participate in organizational meetings and activities.

A difficult challenge for some organizations is understanding that the act of registering their organization comes with the responsibility of complying with policies and procedures of the institution. Often these policies and procedures require organizations to submit timely and proper paperwork to maintain organizational eligibility, budget oversight, or officer rosters. Student organizations travel internationally, work with food purveyors, manage complex contracts, and purchase materials and equipment. Many of these processes may require the adviser's signature for approval. These organizations work closely with the institutional staff to manage the processes necessary for any oversight. This challenge is especially difficult for disorganized or unorganized student groups. Organizations not receiving funding from the institution may have the perception that they do not owe the institution anything and consequently do not need to submit anything to the bureaucracy of the institution. An adviser can always assist in these matters by providing direction for the organization and clarity of purpose.

A final challenge facing organizations relates to one mentioned in our discussion of institutions. The organization must monitor activities and events for liability and risk management implications. In many cases, as an institutional representative, the adviser serves an important function by reviewing planned organizational activities and events. An adviser's knowledge of the details of the activities and events is of even more importance when contracts, travel, large purchases, or other potential risks to students are involved. The institution and organization must provide adequate training to the adviser. Much of this training will be the responsibility of the campus student activities office.

Advisers

In your work as an adviser, one of your greatest challenges is managing your time and not becoming overcommitted to the organization. The students and the organization can be very demanding of your time. Attending weekly meetings with the student organization president, the executive board, and the organization itself; attending a couple of activities or events each week; traveling to conferences, meetings, and events; making phone calls; attending individual meetings with students in the organization; and writing letters of reference and recommendation—these activities collectively can take a considerable amount of time. You need to set expectations early as to your ability to attend meetings, events, and activities. Meeting with the organization's executive board soon after their election or selection is important to discuss your level of availability and attendance. Your personal and professional situation (e.g., work requirements, family obligations, and so forth) may require you to openly discuss your availability. Discussing and setting expectations early will help prevent a later misunderstanding. Chapter 5 provides additional information on the demands placed on advisers.

The typical training of the adviser can be minimal to elaborate. Some advisers refine their skills by taking advantage of professional organizations and associations to attend programs and listen to speakers. Others will use the organization's manuals or notebooks to provide advising information. Still other advisers have developed a proven advising technique over many years of experience or have applied their knowledge of supervision to the role of advising. Some student activities and involvement offices provide intentional adviser training on behalf of the institution. This training might include legal and financial topics, processes and procedures to purchase materials and equipment, processes to reserve space, and the like. Chapter 5 provides detail on the skills common to both supervising and advising.

Graduate courses continue to emerge that focus on advising student groups and organizations. Colorado State University's graduate degree in student affairs in higher education lists advising student groups and organizations within their portfolio of professional practices competencies. Arkansas Tech University offers an elective course in advising student groups as part of their Master of Science degree in college student personnel. The campus student activities office and the central office of an organization's national association are excellent places to start in identifying adviser training opportunities to overcome the challenge of lack of training. Colgate University utilizes a guide to advising student organizations through their center for leadership and student involvement. Baylor University uses a student organization adviser summit held every semester to train their advisers. The National Association for Campus Activities (NACA) includes adviser training within their annual national convention.

Another challenge for you is to clarify for members what your role is in the organization. Students will have their own ideas; your role should be discussed as soon as possible following the election or selection of officers. Following a discussion of everyone's expectations, it is also important to discuss what you and your office staff can provide, how to communicate effectively among the members, the executive board, and yourself, and the time and stress management of the member, executive board, and adviser positions. Chapter 5 provides some activities to assist in the discussion of these issues.

Another challenge for you is to avoid becoming overly controlling in the organization's matters. The organization is for the students, and decisions should be made by students. An adviser who begins to take control by making decisions or running meetings takes the risk of having the students vote with their feet by leaving the organization or ostracizing the adviser. Most faculty and staff advisers play supervisory roles, and their practice and experience as supervisors is helpful for providing direction, assisting in the decisions, and facilitating meetings. Advisers must step back and allow the students the opportunity to run their organization. Some circumstances can arise in which you should take more directive action. Chapter 9, on legal issues, provides detailed information on the matters in which the institution might be liable and it would be necessary for you to intervene. Chapter 8 discusses circumstances in which the financial integrity of the institution would be at risk, necessitating your taking action. In most situations, these matters can be worked out with the organization's president or executive board in advance of the program, activity, or meeting.

Another challenge for you is to be aware of decisions and action taken by the organization. Some advisers are not able, for a variety of reasons, to attend the organization or executive board meeting and therefore will miss some of the decisions being made by the organization. It is nonetheless the responsibility of the adviser to be aware of the decisions that are made in order to respond to questions, to ensure that financial and legal issues are properly addressed, and to better understand the climate and attitude of the organization and its members. You can stay informed about decisions by meeting on a weekly basis with the organization's president, by reading minutes, or by communicating via e-mail or social media with the president or secretary.

Finally, you can be challenged to be patient in the growth and developmental processes of students. It may seem easier simply to make decisions for the organization and quickly provide solutions and results. You need to ask yourself, however, in what ways membership in the organization will augment the students' education. If you allow students the opportunity to discover answers themselves and to attempt different approaches or techniques to group development, the students will benefit. Doing so entails patience and the ability to sit back and allow the process to take its course. Trial and error can be a valuable approach to student and organizational development without harm to the students, organization, or institution.

Students

Astin's research (1993) found several challenges for students related to their involvement in campus organizations. He determined that involvement in a social fraternity or sorority has a negative effect on liberalism; participating in intercollegiate sports has a negative effect on students' performance on three standardized tests (GRE Verbal, LSAT, and NTE General Knowledge), and requires a substantial amount of time for competition at the intercollegiate level; and working on class group projects has a negative effect on students' performance on the GRE Verbal test. Kuh and Lund (1994) found that "participation in student government was negatively correlated with the development of altruism" (11).

Another challenge to students, whether they are members of the executive board or members of the organization, is for them to make an active attempt to establish a relationship with you. You may be new to the organization, or you may have been involved as an adviser for many years. In any case, the student's challenge is to work with you to identify expectations and roles. This relationship building is a process that continues throughout the year. Chapter 4 provides detailed information on the relationship- and team-building processes.

Students are challenged to establish a system of communication that benefits and provides information to the organization. Student organizations thrive on continuous communication among the executive officers and members, the adviser and executive officers, the organization and institution, and perhaps the members and their constituency. Communication can be facilitated through technology (e.g., Facebook, Twitter, e-mail, text messaging, voice mail, and the like), the distribution of agendas and minutes of the meetings, and discussions during meetings. Students are challenged to develop an effective means of communication in order that all members and other interested parties receive proper and timely information.

A difficult challenge for students is to balance the time needed for their academic responsibilities and for the extracurricular activity of a student organization. You should be in a position to provide the information, resources, and referrals necessary to assist students in achieving this balance. Some advisers work individually with students to complete a time management analysis. Chapter 6 provides information and activities for you to use with your students.

A final student challenge is to be patient with the institution's decision-making processes. Colleges and universities, whether public or private, all have complicated systems of accounting for funds, submitting paperwork for travel, and making room reservations. You can help students work their way through these institutional procedures. In addition, you are in a position to provide information and clarification on these lengthy procedures. You can identify the faculty or staff on campus who will visit with students to hear about their needs or who might help to accelerate the administrative processes. However, students should not rely on you for all the answers or shortcuts in solving their problems. Nor should student leaders look for shortcuts for fast-tracking institutional procedures.

Rewards

Let us turn now to the wide variety of rewards that the community, institutions, organizations, advisers, and students can enjoy as part of their experience with student groups.

Community Rewards

The local community realizes a reward from the leadership and service provided to the greater community. Many student organizations have within their mission to provide community service. These student organizations focus on providing service for after-school students; mentoring for at-risk elementary, middle, and high school students; holding volunteer fairs to provide information on social issues and service opportunities; painting, repairing, or building homes and apartments; providing healthy lifestyle information to community members; judging local science fairs; or cleaning up local creeks and parks.

The Independent Sector (2013) provides an estimated value of volunteer time. In 2012 this time was valued at $22.14 per hour. Many colleges and universities use this calculation to quantify their student organization and members' service hours. The Center for Leadership and Service at the University of Florida (2013) in their most recent report calculated 115,963 student and student organization service hours valued at $2,163,870 for the State of Florida and $2,526,833 nationally. The University of Tennessee (2013) allows students to self-log their service hours. In 2012–13 over 12,000 service hours were performed by students and student organizations.

College students make a significant contribution to their communities through volunteering and service, according to the most recent Volunteering and Civic Life in America 2012. According to the Corporation for National and Community Service (2013), in 2012, 3.1 million college students dedicated more than 118 million hours of service across the United States—a contribution valued at $2.5 billion.

Institutional Rewards

An institution's ability to attract and recruit new students may be greatly increased by the visibility and involvement of students in organizations. Some of the more visible student organizations lead summer orientation programs for new and prospective students and their parents and families. Other organizations work throughout the academic year as student diplomats and ambassadors to host tours and speak to prospective students and their parents. These student organizations have as their primary purposes advancing the institution and providing information to campus visitors for the recruitment of students. Many other student organizations (such as military, collegiate sports, and special interests) use their visibility or connection to academic programs to recruit students to the institution. Involvement in recruitment programs can be found in many other student organizations' purpose statements. The array of cultural organizations on your campus allows institutions to demonstrate the diversity of their student body.

Improved retention is another institutional benefit of students' involvement in organizations. We know that "learning, academic performance, and retention are positively associated with academic involvement, involvement with faculty, and involvement with student peer groups" (Astin 1993, 394). Academic involvement includes time allocated to studying and doing homework, courses taken, and specific learning experiences. Involvement with faculty includes talking with faculty outside of class (for example, as part of involvement in student organizations), being among a group invited to a professor's home, or working on a research project. Involvement with student peer groups includes "participating in intramural sports, being a member of a social fraternity or sorority, . . . being elected to a student office, and hours spent in socializing or in student clubs or organizations" (385).

Improved retention has also been demonstrated through the National Survey of Student Engagement (NSSE) (Hughes and Pace 2003). Students who participated in a community-based project, participated in cocurricular activities, and students who planned to have an internship or field experience were less likely to withdraw from the institution. Another NSSE study (2001) indicated that two-thirds of all minority senior students were "involved in community service and volunteer work" (3). In addition, a 2008 study (Kuh, Cruce, Shoup, Kinzie, and Gonyea) concluded that "student engagement in educationally purposeful activities is positively related to academic outcomes as represented by first-year student grades and by persistence between first and second year of college" (555). Educationally purposeful activities were from a scale of 19 NSSE items including participating in a community-based project as a part of a regular course and working with faculty members on activities other than coursework (i.e., committees, orientation, student life activities, and so on).

Another benefit to the institution is to have students serve on various advisory boards and committees to provide feedback for institutional events and projects. Many institutions request that students from various organizations serve as representatives on search committees, athletic advisory committees, student union boards, concert committees, recreational sports advisory boards, budget advisory committees, or even as voting members of institutional and state governing boards. The feedback and insight that students provide the institution come directly from the consumer through a student organization.

A similar reward is to have key student organization leaders meet with campus administrators, faculty, and staff during times of crisis to provide feedback and assistance to the institution. In the past few years, serial killings, major fires, natural disasters, and terrorist activities have occurred on college campuses. The individuals who have lost their lives included students, faculty, and staff. These events and their aftermaths are difficult periods for the campus. The director of the counseling center on a campus that experienced multiple homicides observes, "The absolutely outstanding cooperation of our student leaders, particularly the student body president, enabled us to get valuable student feedback and perspectives, and provided strong leadership for students" (Archer 1992, 97). Involving key student leaders from such organizations as the residence hall association, fraternities and sororities, student government, the Hispanic-Latino student association, or the black student union can help the institution plan memorial ceremonies, improve educational approaches to safety and security, or publicize enhanced services. In addition, student organizations can be involved in press conferences to help reassure students and answer questions.

Organizational Rewards

Naturally, the primary organizational reward is in providing students with an opportunity to participate in an enjoyable activity or to achieve a valuable purpose. Students participate in organizations, in part, to gain a sense of acceptance by their peers. Astin (1993) asserts that the peer group is the most potent source of influence on students' growth and development during their college careers. If students discover an organization that provides a common interest or academic theme to their liking, they may feel a greater sense of acceptance. The organization's reward is a group of students with common interests, enjoyment, or goals.

Another organizational reward is the opportunity to contribute to the tradition and history of the institution and organization. Many student military, sports, Greek letter, and honorary organizations have a rich history within an institution. The organizations may sponsor homecoming events, such as the student-produced Gator Growl at the University of Florida, a comedy, concert, and fireworks show pep rally in the football stadium, which attracts over thirty thousand students and alumni; career expositions; or major institutional events, such as VEISHEA at Iowa State University. "VEISHEA is an acronym for each of the colleges in existence at the time the festival was founded [in 1922]" (Schuh 1991, 40). Another example of a campus event is the Great Cardboard Boat Regatta at Southern Illinois University in Carbondale, originally developed by Richard Archer, a professor of art and design, as a final examination for his freshman design class. These types of events provide some student organizations with the opportunity to contribute to the tradition and history of the college.

Another organizational reward is in the fulfillment of the organization's purpose. Some organizations advance an area of study or research, provide feedback to the institution, prepare students for military service, provide recreation, or represent students of a particular constituency. A student organization that fulfills its purpose provides one of the greatest rewards possible. When student leaders can keep their organization involved in matters within its stated purpose, the organization maintains strong leadership and meets its goals. This improves the legitimacy of the organization on campus as being recognized for good work and increases its sphere of influence. When a student organization finds it necessary to pursue other meaningful purposes, the students must know and understand how to revise their constitution, adjust purpose statements, or redirect the resources available to them.

Adviser Rewards

One of the several rewards for you as an adviser is being able to observe the development of students during their college matriculation. You have the opportunity to work with incoming students and, in many cases, observe them in and out of classroom environments over the course of several years. You can feel the students' excitement as they too discover an organization. It is rewarding to observe the students as they move from membership to leadership roles, or from being reserved to participating fully. When seasoned advisers are asked why they continue to serve, the majority of answers include the idea of being in a position to make an impact on the growth and development of students.

Another reward for you, one that is seldom sought, is to be recognized by the institution, organization, and students for a job well done. Letters from students ten years after they graduate, a plaque from the executive board at the conclusion of the year, a distinguished service award from the institution, an advising award from the organization's national association, or a thank-you from a student—all these are possible (usually unexpected) rewards for your involvement in a student organization.

You should feel flattered in serving as a reference for students. When a student approaches you for a reference, it means that in the student's eyes, a relationship exists between you and the student. At certain times of the year the request for references can be inordinately heavy; however, the reward in being asked to complete a reference far outweighs the work involved in providing it.

A very fulfilling aspect of being an adviser is in serving as a mentor for students. Either you or the student can initiate the mentor relationship. Maintaining contact with certain students during their academic career or providing them assistance following their graduation can be very rewarding to a mentor in an advisory capacity. Chapter 5 provides detail about the mentoring role and also identifies activities that you and students can undertake.

Another reward for you is the opportunity to be able to observe the fads, cultures, and subtle changes that occur in student life. You sometimes are among the few individuals on campus who possess a sense of campus activities and attitudes. In the course of attending meetings, going on trips with the organization, or attending evening activities, you will find it easy to observe and note the language, dress, and nonverbal communication of the students along with the various messages and nuances of their interaction. Your being able to relate enables better understanding of students, which in turn helps you as you work with the organization, academic department, or institution on student problems and concerns.

Advising also provides an opportunity to teach, lead, and coach students involved in student organizations. You may present programs to the organization's membership or executive boards, facilitate leadership development programs for members, take members and executive boards on retreats and workshops, or involve the members in community service or volunteer service. These types of activities allow you to practice your teaching, leading, and coaching skills. Chapter 5 provides detailed information and activities for each of these advising roles.

Another reward is an opportunity to form networks with colleagues involved as advisers of similar organizations. Traveling to professional or student-oriented conferences allows you the opportunity to visit with colleagues with similar interests. These trips and collegial relationships not only rejuvenate you but also help create a network to rely on for resources and information. Some organizations have highly developed regional, national, or international associations for advisers, separate from the students. These organizations provide you a forum in which to openly discuss problems and present views. Similarly, an increasing number of online discussion groups are available for advisers of different organizations. These groups provide a more global opportunity to discuss topics and access resources without even leaving the office. Chapter 2 provides summary information on different types of student organizations as well as on the professional organizations available to you.

The opportunity advising provides to serve the institution is yet another reward. Many faculty in large, research-oriented institutions are evaluated on the basis of their teaching, research, and service. Serving as a faculty adviser to an organization enriches the service component of a faculty member's annual dossier. This reward is peripheral to the many others you will realize as an adviser, but is nonetheless important for those faculty who have tenure or other related compensation considerations tied, at least in part, to institutional service. In community colleges the faculty evaluation process will emphasize teaching and service. Advising a student organization as a faculty member at a community college is an excellent way to provide services and is rewarded accordingly.

A final reward for you is the opportunity to participate in an organization whose purpose you enjoy. For many faculty and staff, the work of their profession leaves little time for additional special interests. However, among the wide variety of student organizations that exist, you can often find one whose activities or purpose complements your interests.

Student Rewards

As we have already discussed, the rewards or benefits students gain through involvement in extracurricular activities have been studied extensively.

Astin (1993) reports that membership in a social fraternity or sorority has positive effects on leadership abilities; participating in intramural sports has a positive effect on physical health, alcohol consumption, and attainment of the bachelor's degree; and participating in collegiate sports has positive effects on physical health, leadership, and satisfaction with student life. Pascarella and Terenzini (2005) conclude that learning and personal development are enhanced when students are involved in educationally purposeful extracurricular activities. Kuh and Lund (1994) observe that involvement in student government "was the single most potent experience associated with the development of practical competence" (10). Practical competence in this case is defined as skills that employers are seeking, in such areas as decision making, leadership, cooperation, and communications. Kuh and Lund also report that participation in student government contributes to the development of self-confidence and self-esteem. Student skill development can be greatly increased through their building self-confidence and self-awareness. "Students with an awareness of their weaknesses were better equipped to challenge themselves to apply new skills and improve themselves through practice" (Fincher 2009, 303). Involvement in student organizations provides students an opportunity to become better listeners, manage problems, and expand their motivation.

Student rewards include being recognized by the institution, organization, or adviser; meeting new people and discovering new friends; gaining new skills that can be transferred to their careers; networking with faculty, staff, and employers through contacts gained in the student organization; enjoying the personal satisfaction of completing tasks and projects that have received a positive evaluation; and the sense of giving back to their institution by serving as a campus resource to parents, faculty, staff, and other students.

Students also benefit when they learn skills while working with the organization that can be transferred to their career. Chapter 6 provides an exercise in identifying these transferable skills.

· · ·

You will find tremendous gratification in advising a student organization. The few challenges are always manageable. The following chapters will provide you numerous resources to prepare you to realize the many benefits.

Chapter 2

Overview of Student Groups and Organizations

AS AN ADVISER you should understand the mission and purpose of the specific organization with which you work; you will also benefit from an overview of the many types of organizations, their purposes, and the role advisers play in each type.

Tens of thousands of different groups and organizations involving millions of students exist on college and university campuses. In this chapter we identify various types of college and university student groups and organizations. We have developed the following taxonomy of organizations: student government, Greek letter, residence hall, honors and recognition, military, sports, departmental or academic, and special interest. Our description of each category includes its purpose and history, the type of person who typically advises that kind of organization, and the various associations that provide services and direction. We look first at the purpose and role of the student activities office; on most campuses this office coordinates the registration of student groups and organizations. In addition, we provide the general requirements for sponsoring, registering, or recognizing an organization.

The Role of the Student Activities Office

Extracurricular activities typically are coordinated by an office of student activities or by similar administrative units. These activities range from listening to speakers, building homes, riding horses, to playing rugby, Quidditch, or chess; they provide students an opportunity to volunteer, participate, and lead. Student activities normally will provide students with an opportunity to continue the socialization process, participate in group interaction and relationships, and develop leadership skills (Mueller 1961).

The history of student activities can be traced to the American colonial period, prior to the development of the first Greek letter organizations. Early student activities were based on religious themes and strong discipline. They evolved to include literary organizations, debating societies, and athletic clubs that organized social events, debates, or sporting contests. As the Greek letter organizations, honors organizations, recognition societies, student government associations, and intercollegiate athletics developed, so did the view that institutions needed to employ professionals to advise student activities. "The student affairs staffs now included such titles as director of student activities, director of counseling, as well as the original title of dean of women, dean of men" (Saddlemire and Rentz 1988, 264).

The National Association for Campus Activities (NACA) was formed in 1960 to help increase the buying power of campus programming dollars and has evolved into the nation's largest organization of campus activities programmers. At first, NACA conferences were held so that colleges could collectively book performers and attractions. Throughout the years this organization has expanded to keep pace with current educational and student needs. NACA's purpose (National Association for Campus Activities 2013) is "to advance campus engagement" (1). Working with over 950 college and university members, NACA's mission is to "be the recognized leader in higher education for providing members with innovative practices and access to programs that support campus engagement" (1). The Association accomplishes its mission by ensuring that campus engagement is essential for student success, that they are the recognized knowledge source for campus engagement, that there are established vibrant business opportunities, that membership is diverse, that meaningful volunteer experiences are fostered, and that they promote excellence in association management (NACA 2013).

The NACA national conference and seven regional conferences are developed to support the service and resource aspect of this mission. The conferences include three different elements: showcase, education programs, and exhibit marketplace. First, the showcase provides a stage for bands, comedians, and other performing artists to perform in front of students and staff who might wish to contract their act. The national conference showcases over eighty acts. Second, there are numerous education programs presented by faculty, practitioners, and students. These programs provide information on how to work with agents, do publicity, and turn a cafeteria into a performance site. Third, there is an exhibit marketplace where vendors, agents, and businesses meet with conference participants.

NACA has bolstered these conferences with a series of institutes and online webinars to expand their professional development efforts to reach colleges and universities. In addition, the national conference provides an opportunity for institutions to block booking, cooperative buying, and discounted booking rates. These collective opportunities lead to cost savings for the individual institution when seeking entertainment and services.

The Association for the Promotion of Campus Activities (APCA) (2014) was founded in 1994 and serves the programming needs for all campus operations in the United States. Many community colleges and regional institutions have found excellent resources by attending the APCA programming conferences, leadership workshops, showcases, and adviser institutes throughout the year. APCA publishes the monthly *Student Activities Journal* which carries a theme for each issue (i.e., leadership, advising student programming boards, learning outcomes, and so on). APCA has five regions in the United States and each has a regional coordinator and one state coordinator from each state in the region. Each region holds a campus events planning conference where participants are provided information on schools and talent buyers, artists and agents, and the like. The APCA website also provides comprehensive information and resources (http:// www.apca.com).

Many student activities offices across the country are responsible not only for the development of a calendar of events for the campus but also for providing structure for campus organizations. The student activities office provides services and support to the organizations while allowing them the freedom to fulfill their purposes.

The process of identifying the type of student organization is one that may raise legal ramifications for the institution and should involve the institution's legal office to determine appropriate qualifications for a group or organization to be registered, recognized, or sponsored. Many campuses register their student groups and organizations. Registering the student groups and organizations ensures consistency to the institution (Craig and Warner 1991). Providing institutional consistency throughout the registration process usually requires that each proposed student group or organization (1) submit a constitution, complete with mission statement, membership requirements, and voting procedures; (2) provide a list of the executive board officers, who must meet the institution's minimum academic and disciplinary standards; and (3) report the name of the organization's adviser. A student group or organization fulfilling the registration process may then be eligible to reserve institutional space for meetings and events, be eligible to receive money from the student government association (usually this funding is provided by activity fees), be eligible to secure office space in a student activities center, and the like. Typically, private institutions may not only register student groups and organizations but also recognize the group or organization as one that supports and sustains the institutional mission. If the group or organization is determined to not support the institution's mission then it may not be recognized as a student group or organization on that campus. Institutions may also identify groups or organizations as sponsored. These are groups or organizations that may be created by an academic department (i.e., geology club, electrical engineering club, and so forth) or by an administrative unit (i.e., hall council, residence area government, and the like). In these cases, these groups or organizations likely receive funds from their sponsoring department, assign an adviser from the sponsoring unit (a staff member with advising as part of his or her job description), and have space reserved for them to meet in the academic or administrative unit. The sponsoring departments are encouraged to maintain the same requirements for groups or organizations being registered (i.e., constitution, executive officer listing, name of adviser, and so on) and may also be registered at the institution.

Student activities centers, also known as offices of student engagement, student involvement, or student life, often provide training for students and advisers, resources for program development, personnel to handle institutional contract management for performers and attractions, oversight for maintaining the minimum institutional standards for students to remain eligible to serve in leadership positions in student organizations, facilities for office and meeting space, and staff with experience to assist student organizations with the health and well-being of the group, including group dynamics, conflict management, membership recruitment, apathy, and officer transitions.

Characteristics of Typical Student Organizations

As mentioned in the introduction to this chapter, there are several categories of student organizations: student government associations, Greek letter organizations, residence hall organizations, honors and recognition organizations, military, sports, departmental or academic, and special-interest organizations. We discuss each type individually in the following sections.

Student Government
"Beginning at Amherst College in 1828, undergraduate students have sought to be involved with the governance of their institutions. While their

'House of Students' was short lived, this early organization ushered in the student government movement in American higher education" (Keppler and Robinson 1993, 36). These early forms of student government were centered around issues of disciplinary control and maintenance of residence halls; they also held a consultative role with faculty to structure student government organizations. These organizations had elected officers but were not empowered with decision-making ability (Horowitz 1987). From the austere beginnings of student government evolved today's organizations, which deal with such major issues as student apathy, rising tuition, budget cuts, campus parking, and multicultural awareness (Keppler and Robinson 1993).

Some highly visible student governments are involved in numerous aspects of college and university life and have oversight of millions of dollars. Cuyjet (1985) surveyed student government presidents and advisers to determine the role that student government plays on campuses. The presidents and advisers reported that student government provides the official representation of the student body to the administration and faculty. However, they indicated that student government has little influence on the major decision-making councils on campuses.

The purpose of student government varies from campus to campus. For example, the purpose statement of the student government at the University of Florida reads:

> We, the Student Body of the University of Florida, in order:
> Represent and defend the rights and interests of students to the
> university, the community, and government; Provide a forum
> for the expressions of student views and interests; Promote the
> academic freedom and responsibility and high standards of
> education; Provide services and organize events for the benefits
> of students; and Help promote understanding and recognition of
> the responsibilities of students to the university, the community,
> and humanity, do hereby establish this Constitution. (Student
> Government 2010, 1)

The organizational statement is that of a highly complex organization with a wide variety of purposes, interests, and activities.

Student governments can be highly complex organizations that include a student body president; a vice president overseeing cabinet directors; a treasurer supervising financial assistants, auditors, and general accounting office personnel; a chief of staff who coordinates various central office staff and campuswide projects and programs; an honors court chief justice overseeing academic dishonesty procedures; a senate president coordinating the senate proceedings; and other agencies that contract with a student government, such as performers, attractions, yearbook staff, and so forth.

Student governments will also represent community colleges. The responsibilities of the student government at Sauk Valley Community College (SVCC) include representing the student body to the SVCC administration, sponsoring campuswide activities, serving on collegewide committees, recognizing new student organizations, allocating programming money to new and existing student organizations, and completing community service activities (Sauk Valley Community College 2014).

Campus business services, student affairs, and auxiliary services have traditionally been viewed as the campus service providers. Student government also is an important service provider. Cuyjet (1994) examines student government issues and services and finds that in student government, the most important issues and services are general student apathy, allocation of student activity fees, activities programming, availability of classes, participation in college or university governance, race relations on campus, representation on campuswide committees, rising tuition, safety on campus, and recycling and the environment. Cuyjet also observes that even though the preceding list included the most prevalent issues and services, students also addressed administrative and faculty salaries, organizing national lobbies, drug use and testing, enrollment ceilings, faculty and staff collective bargaining, admissions standards, legal aid, day care for student families, graduation standards, and community homelessness. The breadth of involvement of student governments on campuses reflects a strong interest in wanting to evaluate and influence both contemporary issues and services as well as being instrumental in planning for the future. For example, listening to student senate meetings will give you a sense of the issues that students of today are concerned about on campus and in the community (and what is not of concern to them). Speaking to the president of the student government association will provide you insights into the things students will be advocating for in the future.

Boatman (1988) identifies four essential components of a strong student government. The first component includes being party to information similar to that which the faculty and employees receive, having information that provides clarity to the institutional structure, and receiving information regarding the relationship of other campus student organizations to the student government. The second component includes access to high-level administrators, involvement of students on all levels of committees and boards, and provision for general social interaction with faculty and staff. The third component is a shared respect between student government and faculty and staff, between student government and the press, and between student government and the general student body. The final component of a strong student government includes an organizational structure that allows for proper representation throughout the various forms of campus governance, a clear system of student leadership development, and an atmosphere in which students and staff communicate as colleagues.

Advisers to student governments include the vice president for student affairs, the dean of students, the student activities staff, faculty, and graduate students. Boatman (1988) identifies some of the characteristics and skills of an ideal student government adviser: (1) having the ability to develop a relationship with students (for example, appreciating students, being supportive and sensitive); (2) being an informed resource person (for example, having information regarding home and peer institutions, being involved in associations and aware of current issues); (3) having institutional credibility (for example, having access to and credibility with high-level decision makers, being a skilled advocate, and having time in the midst of his or her responsibilities to advise); (4) being a positive role model (defined as modeling creative problem solving, demonstrating a positive approach, modeling a balanced life, and modeling an appreciation of diversity); and (5) having adaptive skills (for example, patience and tolerance). Advisers have the challenge of working with diverse students possessing numerous motives for their involvement in student government. Students within student government associations are often well positioned on campus, serving on influential university committees and governing boards. Advisers must also be cognizant of university politics to best support the student government's agenda, especially when it may run counter to that of the institution's agenda.

The American Student Government Association (ASGA) is an organization founded in 2003 that provides networking, research, and information services to various student governments. ASGA has 1,226 member institutions from all fifty states (ASGA 2014). They offer members free consulting, research, and nationwide networking through their ten student government training conferences nationwide each year and their comprehensive website (http://www.asgaonline.com).

Greek Letter Organizations

The American college and university fraternity system has been established for over two hundred years. It represents hundreds of sorority and fraternity chapters in which tens of thousands of students are members. The fraternity system makes up one of the largest categories of student organizations represented on college and university campuses today. Phi Beta Kappa, founded at the College of William and Mary on December 5, 1776, was the first Greek letter organization on an American campus. Two years later, Phi Beta Kappa founded chapters at Yale University and Harvard University (Owen 1991). Since the founding of Phi Beta Kappa, chapter membership in other fraternities continued to expand with chapters for men and women; African American, Hispanic-Latino, and Asian students; honor students; students involved in civic affairs; and students who are campus leaders. See chapter 3 for detailed information on Greek organizations.

Residence Hall

Campus housing accommodations have been provided for students since Oxford and Cambridge developed residential colleges in the thirteenth century. Male students living in the early residential colleges were to be educated as gentlemen scholars (Rudolph 1962). In American higher education, residential components accompanied the founding of institutions across the country. In 1890, for example, President Eliot of Harvard University split classroom responsibilities from the student relations outside the classroom and created the first dean of men position (Cowley 1937). This development and the growth of student government organizations allowed students in residence halls increased opportunities for beginning residential governing bodies.

Campuswide residence hall associations (RHAs) were established at many colleges and universities in the early twentieth century. In 1954, the Midwest Dormitory Conference was founded at Iowa State University by Iowa State University, the University of Colorado, the University of Missouri, and the University of Northern Iowa, to encourage the exchange of ideas and information (Coleman and Dunkel 2004). In 1961, the Inter-Mountain Residence Hall Association (IMRHA) affiliated with the Association of College and University Residence Halls to form the National Association of College and University Residence Halls (NACURH). Its purpose is to "design and facilitate programs and informational services to promote the educational goals of residence hall students through discussion groups, seminars, and speakers at the annual conference and other means of information exchange throughout the year" (Stoner, Berry, Boever, and Tattershall 1998, 182).

Today, NACURH has over 450 affiliated member institutions from six countries, hosts an annual conference of approximately 2,300 delegates, has eight regions, and is the largest student-operated organization in the country. NACURH offers a variety of services to institutions, including several publications; honorary recognition to students through the National Residence Hall Honorary (NRHH); access to their electronic Resource File Index of programs from member institutions; peer substance abuse programs delivered by the Student Action Teams (SAT); and central resources from the National Information Center (NIC) and NACURH Services and Recognition Office (NSRO). All of these services are located on university and college campuses and staffed by student leaders and volunteers.

There are also many statewide residence hall organizations. These state organizations are similar to the eight NACURH regional organizations in that they have a state board of directors, various committees, and an adviser from a member institution. One example of a typical mission statement of a state association is "to coordinate state residence hall association activities and represent and serve collective interests of all residents as decided upon by member institutions. FARH will further serve as the liaison between housing operations, housing related conferences, residence halls, various universities, and outside interests" (Florida Association of Residence Halls 2013, 1). State associations typically host an annual conference, and in some cases hold a leadership mini-conference for the residence hall associations' executive board members.

Institutionally, RHAs traditionally are predominantly organized with a bureaucratic structure. "The use of the bureaucratic model as a single approach apparently results from one of three choices: first, students may be unaware of alternative structures or models for RHAs or are unable to access information about alternative organizational models; second, students may not have been challenged by advisers to consider alternative models for organization; and third, students may be convinced that current organizational structures best meet the needs of students and the purpose of campus RHAs (McCluskey-Titus and Paterson 2006, 104–105). Most bureaucratic structures include an executive board consisting of a president, vice president, secretary, treasurer, and adviser. The RHA may be structured in one of three ways: (1) centralized RHA with building or area representation, (2) building or area governments with no central RHAs, or (3) blended buildings or area governments with central RHAs (McCluskey-Titus and Paterson 2006). The RHA often is responsible for creating programs, forming policy, addressing quality-of-life issues for the residence hall program, allocating money, and recommending contracts and vendors (Verry 1993).

The advisers of the hall, area, institutional, state, regional, and national organizations are exclusively from campus housing staff. The advisers may hold positions as chief housing officers; senior, midlevel, or entry-level professionals; or graduate staff. Osteen (1988) recommends an advising model in which the campuswide RHA is advised by a central housing office staff member, the area governing body is advised by an area staff member, and the hall-level governing body is advised by a hall staff member. Komives and Tucker (1993) confirm the validity of this approach in their national study of successful RHA themes. They also find that to be successful, RHAs must establish a system of leadership training and have a clearly focused purpose, staff committed to student involvement, several sources of funding, and a system of recognition and rewards. Tucker (2006) further went on to develop a study in 2001 examining the effectiveness of RHAs. His study proved that effectiveness may be defined and measured as effects, housing relationships, and formal processes.

Because advisers to RHAs are exclusively housing staff, many of these advisers belong to the Association of College and University Housing Officers-International (ACUHO-I). This association, founded in 1950, provides professional development; policy assistance; and resources through the annual conference, publications, drive-in workshops, institutes, and consulting services. Close to one thousand institutions are members of ACUHO-I. The ACUHO-I central office is located in Columbus, Ohio.

Honors and Recognition

Honors and recognition societies have a rich history on college and university campuses. The number of honors and recognition societies rapidly grew in the early 1900s. In 1925, a meeting held in Kansas City was the first formal gathering of eighteen such organizations (Owen 1991). This early meeting provided the platform upon which the Association of College Honor Societies (ACHS) was formed. Today, approximately seventy honor societies and forty recognition societies are members of the ACHS. The association archive has been established at Muhlenberg College in Allentown, Pennsylvania.

The Association of College Honor Societies defines its purpose as follows:

> To act as the coordinating agency for college and university honor societies . . . ; to provide facilities for the consideration of matters of mutual interest, such as administrative problems, establishment and maintenance of scholastic and other standards, membership costs, functions of honor societies, and prevention of undesirable duplication and competition among honor societies; to define honor societies of the several types and to classify existing societies into their proper categories under these definitions; to

cooperate with college and university faculty and administrative officers in developing and maintaining high standards and useful functions within honor societies which are organized or seek to be organized; and to collect, publish, and distribute information and data of value to honor societies, colleges and universities, and publishers of directories and journals. (cited in Owen 1991, I-52)

The ACHS draws a distinction between honor societies and recognition societies. An honor society is "an association of primarily collegiate chapters whose purposes are to recognize and encourage high scholarship and/or leadership achievement in some broad or specialized field of study" (cited in Owen 1991, I–51). A general honor society is defined as "one which receives into membership individuals from one or all schools and colleges of an institution who have achieved high scholarship and who fulfill such additional requirements of distinction in some broad field of study, research, and culture or in general leadership as the society has established" (cited in Owen 1991, I-51). Examples of honor and general honor societies are Mortar Board Senior Honor Society (service, scholarship, and leadership), Phi Kappa Phi (scholarship), Order of the Coif (law), Gamma Theta Upsilon (geography), Tau Beta Pi (engineering), Alpha Lambda Delta (freshman scholarship), Phi Alpha Theta (history), and Phi Theta Kappa (international honors society of community colleges).

A recognition society is defined as one that "confers membership in recognition of a student's interest and participation in some field of collegiate study or activity, with more liberal membership requirements than are prescribed for general and specialized honor societies. Accordingly, recognition societies are not eligible for membership in the Association of College Honor Societies" (cited in Owen 1991, I-54). Examples of recognition societies are Blue Key (student activities), Scabbard and Blade (military), Sigma Delta Psi (athletics), and Beta Beta Beta (biology).

The advisers of the honors and recognition societies generally are from the faculty and staff of the college. Often these advisers are alumni or alumnae of the society or are faculty in the department the society represents, or they are inducted as honorary members of the society they advise.

Military

Student military organizations were founded over two hundred years ago, when the concept of military training was integrally linked to institutions of higher education. These organizations "within degree-granting institutions of higher learning" possessed the underlying mission "to educate citizens in the principles and fundamentals of war" (Army ROTC 1996, I–1). As these organizations evolved from earlier missions and structures, the Reserve Officer Training Corps (ROTC) emerged. Today's ROTC is organized with three separate branches: the Army ROTC, Air Force ROTC, and Navy ROTC (includes students under the Marine Option).

Advisers to the individual programs at institutions are military officers who serve as instructors in the ROTC program. The advisers generally are assigned an incoming class, and work with the class members during their four-year undergraduate education. The advisers work closely with the students, assisting them with personal, career, academic, and military service concerns. Students involved in these programs also may be involved in civic volunteer activities, color guard and drill teams, intramural sports, student government, or any other university and college student organization.

Navy-Marine ROTC The Navy-Marine ROTC (NROTC) was established "to develop midshipmen mentally, morally and physically and to imbue them with the highest ideals of duty, and loyalty, and with the core values of honor, courage and commitment in order to commission college graduates as naval officers who possess a basic professional background, are motivated toward careers in the naval service, and have a potential for future development in mind and character so as to assume the highest responsibilities of command, citizenship and government" (Navy–Marine Corps ROTC 2013, 1).

As of June, 2013, seventy-four universities and colleges were hosts to NROTC programs in thirty-seven states and the District of Columbia. Students who begin an NROTC program enter as midshipmen appointed to the U.S. Naval Reserve. During the four-year college matriculation, midshipmen take courses in military science and tactics, and in the history and traditions of the Navy. In the summer, midshipmen take part in one or more cruises. On completion of the four-year program, a graduate receives a commission in the Navy or Marine Corps.

The battalion is the organization for the freshmen through senior classes. The battalion is further organized into companies commanded by a midshipman or officer candidate (OC) with the rank of midshipman captain, assisted by an executive officer and staff. These students are responsible for all battalion events and activities.

The NROTC program was founded in 1926 and the Marine Corps entered the NROTC program in 1932, and since 1946 more than eighty thousand men and women have received their commissions through the Navy-Marine ROTC (NROTC 2013).

Air Force ROTC The Air Force ROTC is "designed to recruit, educate and commission officer candidates through college campus programs based on Air Force requirements" (United States Air Force 2013). The first Air Force ROTC units were established between 1920 and 1923 at the University of California at Berkeley, Georgia Institute of Technology, the University of Illinois, the University of Washington, Massachusetts Institute of Technology, New York University, and Texas Agricultural and Mechanical College. Following World War II, General Eisenhower signed General Order No. 124 in 1946, establishing Air Force ROTC units at seventy-eight colleges and universities throughout the nation. Women were enrolled in the commissioning program in 1956. The 1964 ROTC Vitalization Act established scholarships (United States Air Force 2013).

As of June 2013, there were Air Force ROTC units in 145 colleges and universities in the United States. Additionally, 1,100 additional institutions of higher learning participate in cross-town agreements supported by one of the host institutions. Students beginning the program enroll as cadets attending courses in general military science. After completing the first two years of course work, and upon being selected, students may enter the professional officer course, continuing with attendance at a four-week summer field training program and leadership laboratory. Upon graduation, "the cadets are commissioned as Air Force officers with a four-year active-duty service commitment" (United States Air Force 2013, 1).

Army ROTC The Army ROTC maintains a philosophy that "dates back to the colonial times when the colonial frontiersman accepted responsibility to take up arms for his own and his neighbors' common defense. Since the emergence of our nation we have been dedicated to the proposition that national defense is a responsibility of citizenship and that those men and women to whom our society has offered a higher education incur the responsibility of leadership. It is through the Army ROTC program that this philosophy is formalized and implemented" (Army ROTC 2013a, I-1).

Army ROTC began when the concept of military training was introduced into institutions of higher education in 1819; Captain Alden Partridge, a West Point graduate, founded the American Literary, Scientific and Military Academy (now Norwich University). He is regarded as the "Father of AROTC." The Virginia Military Institute in 1839 and the Citadel in 1842 were the next degree-granting institutions established. In 1908, Congress authorized the appointment of doctors as reserve officers in the Medical Corps. In 1916, President Woodrow Wilson signed the

National Defense Act formally established the Army ROTC for emergency duty. Since 1916, two other acts have affected the Army ROTC: the 1955 Reserve Forces Act establishing reserve commissions and the 1964 ROTC Vitalization Act establishing scholarships (Army ROTC 2013b).

Army ROTC programs are found at 273 colleges, universities, and junior colleges in all fifty states, the District of Columbia and Puerto Rico (Army ROTC 2013b). There are also 1,100 partnership and affiliate schools across the country. Students enter the program as cadets. Typically, cadets take four years to complete their program. The combined cadet corps of freshmen through senior classifications represents the battalion. The cadet corps is further organized into companies, platoons, and squads, each with a student commander or leader.

Over two hundred institutions participate in Scabbard and Blade, an Army ROTC national honorary society. Founded in 1904 by five cadets at the University of Wisconsin, Scabbard and Blade raises the standards of education and encourages good leadership and fellowship among the detachments (Army ROTC 2013b).

Sports

Student involvement in organizations providing leisure, fitness, and sports has exploded on college and university campuses in the past twenty years as evidenced in the increased number of types of student sports organizations and clubs on campuses. Student interest has been the impetus for the funding of multimillion-dollar facilities, extensive graduate and professional staffing, transportation systems, and equipment purchases in order to support the wide variety of sports organizations available to students.

During the eighteenth century, members of the upper class on the East Coast developed club sports in the European tradition, representing such interests as bridge, chess, rugby, and sailing. In 1734, the Jockey Club was formed in Charleston, Virginia, marking the founding of the first recognized recreational sport. During the nineteenth century, as the working class found additional time for recreation, sports clubs such as baseball, archery, and track and field were organized. In 1814, Georgetown University permitted students to swim, box, fence, and play handball. The YMCA was founded in 1851 and the YWCA in 1866, to provide facilities and activities for informal sports such as bike riding, roller skating, and "early bird" swimming (Bayless, Mull, and Ross 1983).

Interest in physical education grew as public education became established. By the end of the eighteenth century, teacher training for physical education was institutionalized. In 1913, "the first organized intramural sport program with a faculty adviser began when the University of Michigan and the Ohio State University offered intramural competition in various sports. Dr. Elmer Mitchell, the 'Father of Intramurals,' authored the first intramural textbook in 1925" (Bayless, Mull, and Ross 1983, 135). During the twentieth century, sports proliferated on college and university campuses.

Sports programs were established by students to meet the varying needs of traditional and special-interest groups. Student organizations involved in sports is a collective term comprising four different types of sports: (1) instructional sport, or the teaching of skills and strategies for the purpose of educating participants; (2) recreational sport for the participation and fun of involvement; (3) athletic sport for achieving excellence in performance further defined as winning; and (4) professional sport, which places a higher priority on entertainment and financial rewards (Bayless, Mull, and Ross 1983).

Recreational sports are further divided into four separate categories: informal sport, a self-directed activity; intramural sport, which involves structured contests and tournaments limited to the institution from which it was originated; extramural sport, which involves structured contests and tournaments between different institutions; and club sport, which involves groups organized because of a common interest in a particular sport (Bayless, Mull, and Ross 1983).

One other way of classifying student sports is by the type of competition. Team sports include soccer, rugby, and basketball. Meet sports include track, swimming, and gymnastics. Dual sports include tennis, handball, and racquetball. Individual sports include skiing, fencing, and target shooting. Special event sports are represented by activities such as new games or superstar competitions (Bayless, Mull, and Ross 1983).

An example of a purpose statement for a sports club is that of the University of Michigan's Women's Rugby Club (2013): "The University of Michigan Women's Rugby Football Club aims to become an elite rugby program in the Midwest and a premier club sport within Michigan. We will provide all committed and hard-working teammates the opportunity to grow as rugby players, athletes and individuals. We are devoted to building a competitive team and program focused on athletics, teamwork, dedication and camaraderie."

Another example of a purpose statement for an informal club is from the Radford University Clogging Team (2013). Its purpose is to "expose all students and the city of Radford to the form of dance known as clog dancing. This club will achieve these goals through performances at various events held on campus and events and/or festivals held by the city of Radford" (2013, 1).

An example of a purpose statement for the golf club at Santa Fe College (2014) is "to practice the sport of golf with other SF students who are interested in learning and improving their games" (1).

As the demand for trained personnel increased, so too did interest in forming a collective organization. In 1950, the National Intramural Association was formed; in 1975, the organization was renamed the National Intramural-Recreational Sport Association (NIRSA). In 2012, that moniker changed to NIRSA: Leaders in Collegiate Recreation. The vision of NIRSA is "to become the premier association of leaders in higher education who transform lives and inspire the development of healthy communities worldwide" (NIRSA 2013a).

NIRSA now represents nearly eight hundred colleges and universities, four thousand professional and student members, serving an estimated 7.7 million students (NIRSA 2013b). The NIRSA national center office is located in Corvallis, Oregon.

Advisers of student club sports organizations may be involved in a variety of capacities. Some may work with a specific student organization. These advisers generally have a special interest as a participant or proponent of the sport that the organization addresses. Others may be part of an advisory council or board that conducts studies; serves as a liaison between staff, students, administrators, and participants; makes recommendations regarding policy and procedure; or serves as a sounding board to influence decisions (Bayless, Mull, and Ross 1983).

The roles and responsibilities of advisers vary widely in sports organizations. For example, the adviser of the Ball State University Country Kickers Dance Club serves in an advisory capacity to the executive and does not have voting rights (Country Kickers Dance Club 1997). The head coach and two forwards coaches of the University of Michigan's Women's Rugby Football Club have tremendous experience as former players and coaches. The players are also involved in numerous community service learning projects from Freedom House and Relay for Life to Camp Kesem (University of Michigan Women's Rugby Football Club 2013).

Students continue to create new sports organizations to explore their interest areas. Across the country more than four hundred uniquely different sports organizations are registered on campus organization lists.

Departmental or Academic

Numerous student organizations are associated with academic departments. There exists a mutual benefit for the academic department and student organization to flourish. Institutions benefit because the existence of these organizations helps in fundraising efforts, accreditation, and to recruit new students. Students benefit from the existence of these organizations because of the practical application of the curriculum, leadership development within their field of study, and career networking opportunities. These student organizations can be traced back to the literary and debate clubs of the early nineteenth century. Throughout the years, students became increasingly invested in their academic departments as sources of academic assistance, career planning information, and conferences and meetings. Students within departments have a common course of study and naturally associate with one another in class. The various departmental student organizations that have been founded and registered on campuses range from geology and botany clubs to public relations societies and theater troupes.

Departmental or academic student organizations may belong to regional, national, or international organizations. The student organization may have a direct linkage to the larger, parent organization. The student organization may follow strict membership guidelines, funding directions, recruiting outlines, and the like from the parent organization. Advisers will play a larger role with these organizations to fully understand the linkage to the parent organization. These parent organizations and associations may host conventions. These larger gatherings provide students with opportunities to improve their leadership skills, develop networks with companies and agencies, listen to keynote speakers, and present papers and programs to colleagues.

An example of a purpose statement for a departmental or academic student organization is the Public Relations Student Society of America (PRSSA) at Appalachian State University. Its purpose is "to advance the public relations profession by nurturing generations of future professionals. We advocate rigorous academic standards for public relations education, the highest ethical principles, and diversity in the profession" (ASU PRSSA 2013).

The American Marketing Association chapter at the University of Wisconsin-LaCrosse is another example of a departmental/academic student organization. Its purpose is as follows:

> To provide students with the opportunity to be part of an
> on-campus group interested in current marketing practices, issues,
> and events. We promote networking among students, faculty,
> alumni, and business people through participation in group
> activities, events, and projects. Our main goal is to provide opportunities to apply classroom knowledge, thus enhancing members'

marketing skills and career opportunities after college, along
with leadership experience. (University of Wisconsin-LaCrosse
American Marketing Association Collegiate Chapter 2013)

Another example is from the University of Florida Geomatics Student
Association constitution (2013): "We, the students, the faculty, the staff and
the alumni of the Geomatics program at the University of Florida, believing that a mark of distinction should be placed on the undergraduate who
has upheld the honor of the program by high scholastic ability, and believing that a society with the broad principles of scholarship, character, practi-
cality, and sociability would be an incentive to greater achievements in the
Geomatics/Surveying and Mapping profession, do adopt this constitution
as a guiding instrument for this organization."

Advisers to departmental student organizations almost exclusively
come from departmental faculty. The responsibilities of the adviser can
be quite different from one departmental student organization to another.
In the case of the Public Relations Student Society of America, the faculty
adviser

> shall act as the official link between the student Chapter and PRSA
> [Public Relations Society of America]. To be eligible for election,
> a Faculty Adviser shall be a teacher of at least one of the pub-
> lic relations courses required for the establishment of a PRSSA
> Chapter. Faculty Advisers shall be PRSA Members or Associate
> Members. The professional adviser shall be Members of PRSA,
> at least one of whom shall be a Member who has at least five (5)
> years of professional public relations experience or is Accredited,
> interested in participating in the development of the student
> Chapter. Professional Advisers must be members in good standing
> of the PRSA Chapter sponsoring the Chapter application and may
> not be associate members. To facilitate the students' election of
> Professional Advisers, the officers of the sponsoring PRSA Chapter
> shall nominate eligible members of their Chapter annually as pos-
> sible Professional Advisers and submit the names to the student
> group for ratification. While the PRSSA Chapter is not obliged to
> choose the submitted nominees, any Professional Advisers elected
> annually must be a Member of PRSA and must agree to volunteer
> his or her time for the betterment of the students and the student
> Chapter. Professional Advisers shall not counsel more than one
> PRSSA Chapter at the same time. (Public Relations Student Society
> of America 2011, 13)

The PRSSA at Appalachian State University additionally requires one or two professional advisers "who are members of the PRSA, at least one of whom must be a member who is accredited, who shall represent the practice rather than the academic" (ASU PRSSA 2013).

The person advising the University of Wisconsin-LaCrosse American Marketing Association Collegiate Chapter (2013) "must be a professional member of the Association; will serve for at least one full school year, shall attend the meetings of the collegiate chapter, and shall aid and advise the group on matters under consideration; shall be responsible for the continuity of records and other property of the collegiate chapter; . . . and shall be the official contact with the AMA Headquarters" (3).

The University of Florida Geomatics Student Association (2013) requires the adviser to "act in an advisory capacity to the chapter, and is morally obligated to make the chapter officers aware of their duties. The adviser shall serve as the custodian of the chapter's rituals and paraphernalia."

Special Interest

The special-interest category comprises the greatest number and diversity of student organizations. Throughout the years, students exposed to fads, subcultures, new games, media, and new ideas formed a wide variety of new student organizations. A few examples of special-interest student organizations are Humans versus Zombies, Club Quidditch, Dance Marathons, Student for Peace in the Middle East, Habitat for Humanity, Students Supporting Environmental Action, and Campus Kitchens.

A number of spiritual and religious student organizations work closely with various campus ministries. Students participating in the New Center, Hillel, Inter-Varsity Christian Fellowship, and so forth bring a common spiritual goal to their organizations. The support provided through these student organizations helps satisfy students' religious and spiritual needs. Advisers may be clergy from the community, or faculty and staff from the campus who have similar spiritual interests.

Ethnic and cultural organizations are an important segment of student life on campus. Hispanic and Latino student associations, African American student associations, Asian student associations, Caribbean student associations, and the like provide students with similar racial and ethnic heritages the opportunity to enjoy common interests. These student organizations have been able to identify their issues and concerns and to work collectively in securing the necessary resources to support academic centers, museums, retreats, programming, and activities. These groups receive funds allocated from the student government association or campus general operating accounts in addition to funds contributed by members or raised by the group. Advisers to student ethnic and cultural organizations commonly share the racial or ethnic identity of the members. Campus administrators, faculty, or staff usually serve as advisers. These organizations play an increasingly important role in the life of their college. The organizations assist campus officials in identifying student academic and social needs. Moreover, they often are able to assist in student recruitment and retention. It is likely that new student organizations will be formed in the future in part "because of the growing awareness that no set of categories can adequately reflect the full array of students. Further subgroups will emerge, both in regard to student background and situational differences" (El-Khawas 1996, 74).

An example of a special-interest student organization is Ball State University Medieval Recreations, formerly known as the Society for Creative Anachronism. The organization's purpose is "to provide and promote active study and recreation of portions of pre-16th Century Western European history and activities" (Medieval Recreations 1997, 1).

Another example of a special-interest student organization is the Science Fiction and Fantasy Club. Their purpose is as follows: "to promote interest in and knowledge of science fiction and fantasy at the College and to provide a forum for their discussion and enjoyment" (SKIFFY: The Science Fiction and Fantasy Club of the College of William and Mary 2013a, 1).

An example of a special-interest student organization at Santa Fe College is the Biotechnology Club. Their purpose is: "to give students an idea of what can be done with a biotechnology degree after school. We tour local businesses, bring speakers to campus, and perform experiments outside of the classroom. We also do community service" (Biotechnology Club 2013, 1).

The role of the adviser and the range of the adviser's responsibilities in these organizations vary. For the Science Fiction and Fantasy Club, the adviser is not mentioned; however, in their constitution no less than a hundred elected officers, SKIFFY representatives, senators for life, and other officers (i.e., Ambassador to Tentacles, Ruthless Optimizer, SKIFFY Fashion Designer, and so forth) are notably identified (SKIFFY: The Science Fiction and Fantasy Club of the College of William and Mary 2013b).

Many campus student organizations may be members of larger state, regional, national, or international associations; these larger associations will have an adviser working with them. Advisers of the campus organizations and larger associations tend to be campus faculty members, administrators, or staff members who have a specific interest in the organization. The adviser can play an integral role in officer and member training and other programming of the special-interest group. For instance, in a religious student organization, the adviser may be a campus minister. The campus minister not only advises the executive board on institutional matters but also may instruct the organization in spiritual matters. The level of involvement required and responsibility assumed by the adviser is likely to come from the organization's constitution or purpose statement, or may be negotiated with the organization's leaders and members.

Many of these organizations are well funded and are woven tightly into the institution's fabric. Special interest organizations have an essential part in the extracurricular programs offered to students. For example, at the University of Florida, the programs offered during cultural month celebrations and Homecoming are the responsibility of special-interest groups. Attending to the advising responsibilities of these organizations is paramount to the success of both the organization and campus events.

Chapter 3

Greek Letter Organizations

> Let's be what we say we are . . . a fraternity, not a club . . . made-up
> of men, not boys . . . based on ideals, not expediency.
> —Ralph D. "Dud" Daniel of Phi Kappa Psi
> Baird's Manual of American College Fraternities

GREEK LETTER ORGANIZATIONS have been part of the landscape of North American higher education since the late 1770s. They have both shaped, and been shaped by social structure, world politics, and the changing role that higher education played in the lives of students. This chapter gives a brief explanation of a few terms associated with sororities and fraternities, their history, their structure, and what advising Greek letter organizations may look like on a college campus. This chapter is not intended to be a detailed discourse on everything fraternity and sorority. It is intended to help our audience understand that these are complex organizations which, with the support of excellent advising, have a lasting, positive impact on students who affiliate as "Greek."

Taxonomy

Defining and explaining terms related to Greek letter organizations could take pages. However, based on the scope of this book, there are a few that warrant attention.

Fraternity

According to the *Merriam-Webster Dictionary*, a fraternity is "a group of people associated or formally organized for a common purpose, interest, or pleasure" (2013). And though this seems a very simple definition, it does represent the foundation of the fraternal movement. A fraternity is usually comprised of two to four Greek letters that represent a motto which is supposed to be known only to the fraternity (Owen 1991) and is considered by most to be male-only organizations. Most higher education professionals would agree that a fraternity, in a general sense, is an organization of college student men or women that proclaim to live by a defined set of values, typically stressing excellence in scholarship, leadership, service to the community, and lifelong bonds of friendship. As Anson and Marchesani state, "fraternities have thrived because of their ability to unite in common purpose students from different backgrounds" (1991, ix).

For the purposes of this chapter, we will occasionally use "fraternity" interchangeably with "Greek letter organizations."

Sorority

As fraternity is used to describe at least all men's-based organizations, the term "sorority" is often used to describe women's-based organizations. This word did not exist until 1882 when a Latin professor at Syracuse University, who was advising a group of female students interested in forming their own fraternity, suggested that "sorority" may be a more feminine-sounding term (Turk 2004). The term "sorority" quickly received widespread acceptance and is used today as the descriptor of women's Greek letter organizations although some of the original chapters are chartered as "fraternity" (Turk 2004).

Ritual

The rituals used by fraternities and sororities are actions that display the organization's values, usually within the privacy of its membership. According to Owen (1991), "a ritual is used in conducting fraternity business, initiating new members, conducting formal chapter meetings, in ceremonies for installing officers and in memorial services" (I-13) and stems from the first fraternal secret society, Phi Beta Kappa. This secret society had a secret ritual, motto, grip, and password. Almost every fraternity founded since has followed that example (Owen 1991). In more recent times, the public has often incorrectly associated an organization's ritual with illegal and immoral hazing activities, while in fact, "a fraternity ritual is the solemn and historical rationale for an organization's existence" (Anson and Marchesani 1991, x).

Recruitment

Informally known as "rush" for predominantly white fraternities and sororities or "intake" for historically black and culturally based Greek letter organizations, recruitment is a complex, lengthy process to which chapters devote significant resources. Greek letter organizations are selective and the success of a recruitment class (or sometimes called a "line" for historically black and culturally based Greek letter organizations) will have an impact on the chapter's finances, the chapter's reputation on campus and within their national organizations, and the interpersonal dynamics within the organization.

Types of Greek Letter Organizations

There are many types of organizations who use Greek letters. From the onset of the first secret society, "the evolution of the system has created a number of different kinds of fraternities" (Owen 1991, I-3). Many people are unable to see a difference between these groups, but the differences are significant and have a major influence on how they are advised. According to Owen (1991), one of the simplest ways to differentiate the types of Greek letter organizations from each other is to look at the conferences or associations to which they belong. Therefore we used that framework to offer a description of three types of Greek letter organizations.

General Fraternity

More often called social fraternities, this type of group offers membership that is not dependent on what field students are studying, what class, year, or grade point average beyond a minimum standard. Students are elected to these organizations by mutual choice and are able to be initiated by only one in this category. As Owen (1991) explains, these organizations are "commonly called 'social' which refers to social development not social functions" (I-9). This concept of "social" is worth illuminating as it is a common misconception that general fraternities value social activities above all else when, in fact, "social" is the shortened term for a founding value of developing men and women to be contributing members of society. The majority of this chapter is focused on advising this type of Greek letter organization.

General fraternities are single-gendered organizations: men's fraternities and women's fraternities (or sororities). General fraternities are allowed to exist as single-gendered organizations under the United States Constitution. According to the North American Interfraternity Conference website, "Title IX of the Educational Amendment of 1972 provides that sexual discrimination shall not apply to membership practices of a social fraternity or social sorority that is exempt from taxation under section 501 of the IRS Code of 1954, the active membership of which consists primarily of students in attendance at an institution of higher education" (North American Interfraternity Conference 2013).

Professional Fraternity

The main distinction of this type of Greek letter organization comes from the membership eligibility which is determined based on a student's field of study. For example, premed and prelaw students would be invited to join different professional fraternities. These are coeducational organizations and like general fraternities, a student would be initiated by only one; however, students can be members of a general fraternity and a professional fraternity simultaneously (Owen 1991).

Honor Society

The purpose of these organizations is to "encourage and recognize superior scholarship and/or leadership achievement" (Owen 1991, I-9). They are coeducational and not necessarily dependent on field of study.

Service Fraternity

Service fraternities are also typically coeducational and focus primarily on community service activities and philanthropic efforts. Although other types of fraternities also share a similar value service, it is not the predominant or sole purpose of the organization.

History

Literary and debating societies are the earliest example of students developing their own groups outside of the classroom. The impetus for this was the desire students had to share their own writing and focus on their academic interests (Harding 1971, as cited in Dungy and Gordon 2011). Historian John Robson, cited in Turk (2004) argues that fraternities "found their basis in the Greek tradition of wisdom and human struggle for intellectual, physical, and spiritual betterment" (2).

The Phi Beta Kappa chapter at the College of William and Mary, founded in 1776, was not only the first Greek letter organization on an American college campus but also the first scholarly organization for men (Owen 1991). Though considered a literary society, it had all the modern traits of how we view fraternities today: secrecy, a motto, a handshake, and ritual. By the 1850s many New England and Midwestern state colleges had fraternal organizations. These were small, self-selected groups of men who pledged their loyalty, secrecy, and support of their hierarchical organizations. The faculty was leery of fraternities, believing that their purpose was counterproductive to the education a young man should receive at college. In fact, a number of college presidents tried to ban fraternities, but, according to Lucas (1994, as cited in Dungy and Gordon 2011) the organizations remained because students would not identify who were members. With the founding of fraternal organizations, individuals in college and university administration began to realize that there was more to campus life than the academic classroom (Owen 1991).

As Turk points out, "despite the proliferation of such societies for men, few clubs for women existed on college campuses in the mid-nineteenth century, a reflection in part of the fact that few women attended college at this time" (3). Few institutions accepted women and those that did often took a very paternalistic view of women. They were allowed to attend class but very little else and there was not much in the way of support for these women pioneers (Turk 2004). Therefore, with the proliferation of male fraternities, it was only a matter of time that women used that model as a basis for their own societies.

Women's fraternities began with Alpha Delta Pi, founded as the Adelphean Society in 1851. Pi Beta Phi, founded as I.C. Sororsis, came into being in 1867 as the first organization of college women established as a national college fraternity. Kappa Alpha Theta was organized in 1870 as the first Greek letter society for women (Owen 1991, I-12). Gamma Phi Beta, founded in 1882, was the first women's organization named as a sorority. According to Turk (2004), "the founding female Greek-letter organizations based their societies on ritualized vows of loyalty and used the familial language of 'sisterhood' to reflect the potency of their commitments to one another" (3). Even as the term "sorority" became the norm, a few of the original female Greek letter organizations, especially those which had been incorporated early on (Owen 1991), are proud to continue to use "fraternity" in their name.

Just as women were marginalized at institutions of higher education in the mid-1800s, so too were students of color. Owen (1991) states that "the Black Greek letter movement commenced in 1906 on a predominantly white campus as a means by which cultural interaction and community service could be maintained" (I-41). However, when young black men were excluded from white fraternal organizations they created a "parallel structure of their own" (Dickinson 2005, 12). Through this they found a shared experience; a safe place; a brotherhood. Torbenson (2005) proposed that black students on black colleges were active in clubs and student organizations; however, black students on predominantly white campuses were not only excluded from out-of-class experiences, but were "isolated and segregated from the general student population, resulting in an abysmal African American retention rate" (Ross 2001, 6). The first black Greek letter fraternity, Alpha Phi Alpha, was established in 1906 at Cornell University at first as a study group but very quickly the founders realized the value in finding permanency and defining purpose (Ross 2001). The first black sorority, Alpha Kappa Alpha, was founded at Howard University in 1908 followed by Delta Sigma Theta in 1913.

More recent history has seen a rise in culturally based Greek letter organizations. Although there are indications that Latino-oriented fraternal organizations date back to the late 1800s and early 1900s when Hispanic students of the privileged class were attending colleges, these organizations were unable to thrive (Kimbrough 2003). A resurgence of student interest in these organizations happened in the 1970s and 1980s as the numbers of minority students on college campuses increased. Latino-oriented Greek letter organizations were founded as a way for students to support each other, develop community, and find their voice (Smalls and Hernandez 2009). These organizations serve as a home away from home for Latino/Latina students and though they focus on Latino community issues they are open to all students (Smalls and Hernandez 2009).

Similarly, students who identify as Asian, or Asian Pacific Islander, have been involved in the Asian American fraternal development for a number of decades. Kimbrough, as cited in the NAPA Guide (Smalls and Gee 2009), says that between 1916 and 1930 the first Asian Pacific Islander fraternities and sororities were formed. As the Asian population exploded on college campuses in the 1980s and 1990s so too did the number of Asian-oriented fraternities. Previously localized to California, there are now more than fifty organizations across the country that are based on the values of friendships, leadership, scholastic achievement, cultural awareness, and community service (Smalls and Gee 2009).

According to the National Multicultural Greek Council website, the "1980s and 1990s saw the emergence of a multicultural fraternity/sorority movement" which celebrated the inclusion of all cultures, races, religions, and creeds. The proliferation of these organizations can be attributed to an increased discussion of an acceptance of multiculturalism as well as an increasing number of multi-identity students attending college who were looking for a place to call their own.

Those that advise Greek letter organizations will attest to the fact that we are often asked why are today's students interested in "going Greek."

It's a fair question considering that some of the reasons many of these organizations were founded are no longer relevant. Or are they? Anecdotally, this decade has seen an increase in recruitment participation. As Sandeen (2003) stated about male fraternities, though they were "founded on lofty academic, civic, and moral ideals, these groups have provided support and friendship for large numbers of young men" (17). They still do. Just as sororities and culturally based organizations do for their members. The reasons fraternities exist, according to the National Panhellenic Conference website (2011), is to "provide a good democratic social experience; give value beyond college years; create, through their ideals, an ever-widening circle of service beyond the membership; develop the individual's potential through leadership opportunities and group effort; and fill the need of belonging." Fraternities and sororities provide the personal connection that is missing from this tech-savvy generation. They can be fun with a ready-made schedule of events and activities that cater to a variety of interests from intramural sports, to community service to social functions. They offer students opportunities for personal development "students can test their skills as leaders, public speakers, community servants and good citizens" (Anson and Marchesani 1991, ix). This coupled with the fact that most organizations are competitive with one another, Greek students "are among the most visible student organizations on their campuses, and often have an influence in student life out of proportion to their numbers [which] has resulted in some impressive achievements" (Sandeen 2003, 17).

Structure of General (Social) Greek Letter Organizations

The purpose of this section is to give a quick synopsis of the structure surrounding social fraternities and sororities. Professional organizations exist on a national level to represent the interests of their member organizations. And while you may be familiar with the Greek chapters on your campus, you may not be familiar with the national or international central office (headquarters) for each chapter or the student-based governance councils on campus.

Professional Associations and Governing Organizations
North American Interfraternity Conference (NIC) Founded in 1909, the NIC is the association representing seventy-five international and men's fraternities on over 800 campuses with 350,000 undergraduate members (North American Interfraternity Conference 2013). According to the NIC website it, "serves to advocate the needs of its member

fraternities through enrichment of the fraternity experience; advancement and growth of the fraternity community; and enhancement of the educational mission of the host institutions" (North American Interfraternity Conference 2013).

National Panhellenic Conference (NPC) Beginning in 1902 as the Inter-Sorority Conference, the NPC represents twenty-six international sororities/women's fraternities (Owen 1991), at 655 campuses with more than 4 million women as members of local chapters (National Panhellenic Conference 2011). The NPC is "the premier advocacy and support organization for the advancement of the sorority experience"(National Panhellenic Conference 2011) and provides support and guidance to its members and advocates for sorority life on a national level.

The National Pan-Hellenic Council (NPHC) NPHC, the governing council for historically black Greek letter organizations, was formed in 1930 and is comprised of nine member organizations known as the Divine Nine. According to the NPHC website, "NPHC promotes interaction through forums, meetings and other mediums for the exchange of information and engages in cooperative programming and initiatives through various activities and functions" (National Pan-Hellenic Council 2014).

National Association of Latino Fraternal Organizations (NALFO) According to Smalls and Hernandez (2009), NALFO was established in 1998 to "promote the advancement of Latino/a fraternities and sororities" (6) It is an umbrella council for twenty Latino/a fraternities and sororities with over 850 undergraduate chapters across the country with the purpose of providing support and community for Latinos and a founding principle is community service (Smalls and Hernandez 2009).

National Asian Pacific Islander American PanHellenic Association (NAPA) Composed of twelve member organizations, the NAPA began in the summer of 2004 (Smalls and Gee 2009). NAPA serves to advocate the needs of its member organizations and provides a forum to share ideas and resources with its members at its website (www.napa-online.org). And, according to Smalls and Gee (2009) NAPA "promotes and fosters positive interfraternal relations, communications, and the development of all Asian Pacific American Greek Lettered Organizations through mutual respect, leadership, integrity, professionalism, academic achievement, cultural awareness, and community involvement" (6).

National Multicultural Greek Council (NMGC) The concept of the NMGC began in 1998 with the intention to "unite Greek-letter fraternities and sororities under one national entity" (National Multicultural Greek Council 2008). The NMGC serves in an advisory capacity to the twelve member organizations and its goals are: to provide a forum that allows for the free exchange of ideas, programs, and services between its constituent fraternities and sororities; to promote the awareness of multicultural diversity within collegiate institutions, their surrounding communities, and the greater community-at-large; and to support and promote the works of its member organizations.

Association of Fraternity/Sorority Advisors (AFA) Campus advisers to men's and women's fraternities and other fraternity/sorority professionals may belong to AFA. Founded in 1976, AFA has over one thousand regular and affiliate members (Owen 1991). The purpose of the AFA is to provide "exceptional experiences, a vibrant community, and essential resources for the success of fraternity/sorority advisors" (Association of Fraternity/Sorority Advisors 2013). AFA's website states that they have an "ongoing commitment to the professional development of our members, a deep appreciation of both academic and applied research that examines the entire spectrum of the fraternity/sorority experience and the advising profession, and a commitment to collaborations within and between the higher education and interfraternal communities" (Association of Fraternity/Sorority Advisors 2013).

Central Office (Headquarters)

According to Owen (1991), "the rapid increase in chapters and members coupled with a greater need for accountability caused central offices, or headquarters, and supervisory staff to be essential" (I-15). With a few exceptions of solely campus-based, "local" fraternities and sororities, the vast majority of Greek organizations on campuses are chartered chapters of an international fraternity or sorority. These fraternities and sororities have national structure that governs its chartered chapters. The professional staff that make up a fraternity or sorority Central Office or Headquarters are typically accountable to the national governing structure or board of directors. Headquarters of organizations handle the maintenance of membership records, develop and issue the organization's publications, preserve historical documentation, support the financial operations of the undergraduate chapters, and arrange regular conventions and conferences for professional development (Owen 1991). The staff of central offices are often involved in professional associations and partner with institutions to appropriately advise campus chapters.

Campus Greek Governing Councils

Institutions hosting fraternities and sororities will almost certainly require a structure in which each fraternity and sorority belongs to a Greek student-led governing council. The purpose of these councils is to provide structure, pooled resources, and self-governance to the member chapters on the respective campus. The concept of self-governance is important to the Greek letter organizations, but simultaneously the university wants "accountability on the part of the Greek community to adhere to university, federal and state laws, policies on racial equity and sexual harassment; expectations of safety of housing; responsible fiscal and property management; and sustained effort to promote student growth" (Baxter Magolda 2001, 299).

Governing councils can be challenging to work with because of the diverse needs, priorities, and goals of the chapters that make up the councils. Councils should function in the best interest of the chapter members and are concerned with standards, accountability, advocacy, and managing common programs (i.e., recruitment). These councils are typically advised by professional staff from the host institution and, in fact, the structure of the governing councils can be determined by the institution.

Each college or university may structure its councils differently. For example, some institutions may have just a fraternity council and sorority council, some may have councils for just the general Greek organizations, and others may include councils for the professional fraternities. The most typical structure on campuses is to have governing councils for at least the general Greek organizations, often separated by the chapters' corresponding national professional associations, or umbrella organizations:

> *Interfraternity Council (IFC).* This governing council typically hosts the NIC men's fraternities, or more traditional fraternities.
>
> *Multicultural Greek Council (MGC).* This council will host the culturally based fraternities and sororities. These organizations are often supported by NALFO, NAPA, or the NMGC. Some campuses may even have separate governing councils for the Latino- and Latina-based groups, Asian-based groups, and so on.
>
> *National Pan-Hellenic Council (NPHC).* Taking the same name as the host professional association, this council at the campus level governs the nine historically black Greek organizations represented on a particular campus.
>
> *Panhellenic Council (PC).* This governing council typically hosts the NPC women's fraternities and sororities.

These governing councils are extremely important for a number of reasons. First, they have the ability to develop community standards for all student members of Greek letter organizations and to hold their member chapters accountable to those standards. Second, these councils, more than individual chapters, represent the voice of the Greek community to the greater campus community. Third, the councils can mobilize the whole Greek community in ways individual chapters may be unable. For example, when all of your councils work in concert on a joint project, Dance Marathon for example, the sky is the limit on what they can accomplish.

Providing Advising to Fraternities and Sororities

Greek organizations are high-functioning, complex student organizations with an undeniable element of inherent risk. Advising Greek organizations can also be complex, as the college or university is just one of several stakeholders in the overall success of Greek organizations. Others include the national charter organization or headquarters staff, regional governing persons (as representatives of the national organization), and local chapter advisers. For those fraternities or sororities that reside in designated housing, you also often have house corporations, or boards, that manage or own the house and take responsibility for advising the Greek organization mainly as it pertains to the living, working environment. Greek organizations find themselves being accountable to all entities.

Today, colleges or universities that host Greek organizations are certain to have professional staff dedicated to supporting and advising those organizations. The number of staff assigned to work with Greek organizations varies with each institution, but the general responsibilities of these staff members, often simply called the campus Greek advisers, are the same: to support and educate all organizations on a variety of topics; to ensure compliance with policies, laws, and ethical standards, and to help mitigate risk and manage crises both at the university level and within chapters.

As discussed earlier in this chapter, the Greek community is composed of individual chartered chapters of national organizations, solely campus-based (or local) chapters, and the governing council to which the chapters belong. Campus Greek advisers work closely with council leadership to set the strategic vision for the whole community while helping craft chapter and council goals and hold chapters accountable to community standards. Advising the Greek community at a host institution is truly a partnership between the host institution staff, the local chapter advisers, the national staff, and other support personnel such as house directors. The campus Greek advisers are the liaison between all of these stakeholders.

Most host institutions have expectations or policies requiring local chapter advisers for their Greek organizations. These advisers can be local or regional alumni of that particular fraternity or sorority, or they may be a faculty or staff member from the host institution. Some Greek organizations favor a model in which there is a team of advisers for the chapter with a main, official chapter adviser. Where the professional staff of the host institution tends to focus on more on Greek community–wide issues and initiatives, the local chapter advisers are expected to focus more on the specific chapter needs and support. For example the chapter advisers can advise or educate chapters on how to conduct chapter business, recruit new members, manage risk within the chapter, and support leadership development.

Those Greek organizations that have an official, formal house or residence associated with the chapter will likely have professional house managers, or house directors. On some campuses these house directors may report to the institution, whereas at other campuses they report to housing board or corporation separate from the institution. These house directors can play a vital role in providing support, management, and even oversight into the chapter activities and operations that occur in the chapter facility.

As stated earlier, it is the headquarters staff who are often responsible for the management of the chartered chapters. The working relationship between the host institutions and the national staff is critically important and both should work hand in hand in supporting the chapters on campuses.

A healthy working relationship between the Greek organizations and its host institution is an essential ingredient of success for the Greek organizations and the institution alike. Greek organizations have come a long way from their early days when they were forced to operate in secret or when colleges and universities tried to ban them from their campuses. Still, negativity toward the Greek experience exists within the academy. Though some of this is warranted, as Sandeen (2003) states, "It [is] frequently awkward for those of us in student affairs to find ourselves as the sole supporters of fraternities, as these groups have essentially been dismissed by most faculty and academic administrators as antithetical to the educational mission of the institution. The fraternities will only be as good as the faculty, staff and others at the institution expect them to be" (18–19). It is fair to say, however, that most institutions have recognized the benefits that being a member of a fraternity or sorority provides to students.

Whether you are a campus Greek adviser, a faculty member who has been asked to advise a local chapter, or an alumnus or alumna who is reengaging in the organization, there are many skills and competencies that advisers of Greek organizations need to be successful. We discuss these competencies throughout the following chapters, but here we would like to highlight a few in terms of advising the Greek community. The first is to be present. For Greek letter organizations to be successful they need active advisers who will let them learn and grow as they succeed and fail. These organizations are too complex for advisers to be missing from the picture. You also need to be able to deal with conflict and hold students accountable to their decisions and behaviors. Having developed your own multicultural competency is also important. The Greek community struggles on many campuses to balance being selective with the problems of being homogeneous to the point of being myopic. In addition, many Greek advisers are Greek themselves. In these cases it is paramount that the advisers learn as much as they can about all chapters, what makes chapters similar and different, to be better able to support the Greek community as a whole. Also, having well-developed interpersonal skills, including communicating with different populations, is necessary. On a regular basis, Greek advisers will work with chapter alums, chapter advisers, parents, national office staff, and chapter house staff in addition to students. Working with these different stakeholders requires finesse. For example, explaining the process to a father who wants to know why his daughter did not receive an invitation to a sorority she wished to join requires one set of skills. Working with a chapter who is struggling to break ties with alumni who insist that hazing is an essential part of the fraternity experience relies on wholly different skills.

Case Vignettes

Will You Be My Adviser?

You are a staff member of Shores University who has been asked by a student to advise her chapter. She tells you that they are an Asian sorority and have just received a charter from a national organization. After she explains the values of the organization you are interested in providing support, but not having been

(continued)

(*continued*)

Greek yourself, you are hesitant. You are especially concerned when the student says they are in the middle of their first-ever intake process.

- Where can you find additional information about the organization?
- Who can you talk with both on and off campus regarding the time commitment, health of the organization, role of a chapter adviser, and so forth?
- What about this situation raises some concerns for you?

Define Social . . .

You have been an adviser to a chapter for a number of years. Lately you have become concerned with the behavior of the membership. They seem to be all about throwing parties instead of being engaged in activities with positive outcomes aligned with the organization's outcomes. What steps will you take to see how far from the values of the organization the members are? What options do you have to hold the chapter and individual members accountable?

Chapter 4

Understanding Individual and Group Development

A REOCCURRING THEME throughout this book is the impact that an effective adviser can have on the health of an organization and on the development of the student leaders with whom he or she works. The topics found within this chapter illuminate this quite clearly. A discussion about "development" can take many forms, especially in the context of working with college students. During these transformative years, students are developing a sense of self, a set of values and beliefs, independence and interdependence, skills and competencies, and learning how to make meaning of their relationship to the world around them. We believe that advisers need to pay special attention to, and have a responsibility to be engaged in, leadership development and student learning as it relates to individual students within organizations and group dynamics as it relates to the development of the organization.

Throughout this chapter we use the terms "group" and "organization" interchangeably. Although some will take exception to this, it works within the context of this book. The chapter is divided into three sections: leadership development, student learning, and group development. There are a number of thought-provoking examples and case vignettes to provide the opportunity for practice.

Leadership Development

As Komives (2011b) states, "one cannot taste, touch or see leadership" (354) but experienced advisers know when an organization has effective leadership and when it does not. Ask yourself questions like the following when you reflect on the leadership of and within the organization you advise:

- How does the executive board demonstrate effective leadership?

- What happens in a meeting when someone disagrees with the president?

- How is a differing opinion shared?

- Is the membership empowered to take responsibility for aspects of the organization?

Organizational development and leadership development have been intertwined throughout history and, therefore, the "perspectives on leadership and views of organizational dynamics interact and have changed over time" (Komives 2011b, 354). Just as the belief that leaders were born and not made has evolved, organizations have evolved to be more about influence and relationships than positional authority.

An example of how leadership is, at its core, predicated on relationships between individuals is demonstrated by the concept of servant leadership. In the 1970s Greenleaf introduced this concept by advocating for a new view of leadership. "The servant-leader *is* servant first . . . it begins with the natural feeling that one wants to serve, to serve *first*. Then conscious choice brings one to aspire to lead. That person is sharply different from one who is leader *first* . . . for such it will be a later choice to serve—after leadership is established. The leader-first and the servant-first are two extreme types" (Greenleaf 2002, 27). Servant leadership describes the desire of the positional leader to serve the group and empower individuals to contribute, develop, and lead themselves (Dugan and Komives 2011). From this emerged the thought that leadership can be a shared experience and that anyone engaging in leadership, whether positional or not, is a leader; these ideas became a research interest of scholars. Kouzes and Posner's research (2008) is a widely used framework which focuses on all people involved in the leadership process (Dugan and Komives 2011). *The Leadership Challenge* (Kouzes and Posner 2012) identifies five exemplary practices of ordinary leaders when they are at peak performance, as follows:

1. *Model the Way* is the ability to establish principles regarding how goals will be attained and how people interact, characterized by role modeling appropriate behavior and aligning actions with shared values.

2. *Inspire a Shared Vision* is the ability to envision, passionately communicate, and enlist support for future possibilities.

3. *Challenge the Process* is a willingness to examine and change the status quo, and to look for innovative ways to improve.

4. *Enable Others to Act* is the capacity to engage others in shared processes, to foster collaboration and develop confidence in others.

5. *Encourage the Heart* is the capacity to recognize and celebrate individual and group accomplishments by creating a spirit of community.

The Leadership Practices Inventory (LPI), was developed based on research generated through interviews from people's personal best leadership experiences and is described as "a 360-degree instrument assessing how frequently leaders engage in The Five Practices" (Kouzes and Posner 2012, 25). The authors have more recently developed an assessment tool specific to students called the Student Leadership Practices Inventory which was created to "measure their leadership behaviors and take action to improve their effectiveness as a student leaders" (Kouzes and Posner 2012). As Dugan and Komives (2011) state, "this can serve as a powerful personal learning tool regarding one's leadership behaviors and how they are perceived by others" (44). Exhibit 4.1 shows excerpts from the Greek Leadership retreat at the University of Florida. Chapter presidents and council leadership took the LPI during the weekend and retreat sessions were themed after the five exemplary practices. Student leaders were able to experience how to put their leadership competencies to practical use.

EXHIBIT 4.1
Greek Leadership Retreat Agenda

Friday, January 4, 2013

11:30 A.M.–12:00 P.M.	*Greek Speed Dating*	Youth Pavilion Gym
	Outcomes: Chapter presidents will learn five things about each other, including chapter, home town, and major.	
1:15 P.M.–2:45 P.M.	*The Student Leadership Challenge*	Youth Pavilion Gym
	Outcomes: Student leaders will understand Kouzes and Posner's five exemplary leadership practices and what their strengths and weaknesses are as leaders.	
3:00 P.M.–4:30 P.M.	*Enabling Others to Act:* The Privilege Line	Youth Pavilion Gym
	Outcomes: Student leaders are exposed to the concept of privilege and how they can create an inclusive, supportive environment for all students.	

(continued)

EXHIBIT 4.1 (*continued*)

4:30 P.M.–6:00 P.M.	*Leadership Challenge in Action:* Team Building	Ropes Course
	Outcomes: At the end of the experience students will reflect on the roles they played in challenging and supporting their peers and how this applies to their positions within the Greek community.	
7:00 P.M.–8:00 P.M.	*Challenging the Process:* The Great Greek Debate	Dining Hall
	Outcomes: Students will discuss the dichotomy between what they believe are the benefits from being Greek and public perception of the Greek experience. Student leaders will be able to articulate how they contribute to negative stereotypes.	
830 P.M.–10:00 P.M.	*Inspiring a Shared Vision:* Council Breakout	Various Locations
	Outcomes: Each council will determine five values that are shared by each chapter within that council that they would want to build upon as a community.	

Saturday, January 5, 2013

9:00 A.M.–10:30 A.M.	*Modeling the Way:* Living Your Ritual	Youth Pavilion Gym
	Outcomes: Chapter presidents will be able to articulate two ways in which the actions of the chapter are not reflecting its values and determine how to correct this.	
11:00 A.M.–1:00 P.M.	*Modeling the Way/Enabling Others to Act:* FL Greek Community	Various Locations
	Outcomes: Student leaders will learn how they are positioned to be positive influencers on campus and how to support each other's initiatives and those of the campus community.	
1:00 P.M.–2:00 P.M.	*Leadership Challenge in Action:* Team-builder	Ropes Course
	Outcomes: Student leaders will learn about setting an unachievable goal and reflect on what impact that has on their group and how they cope with "failure."	
2:30 P.M.–3:30 P.M.	*Inspiring a Shared Vision:* Goal Setting	Various Locations
	Outcomes: Council leadership will develop, with chapter presidents, measurable goals that all agree to achieve for their term in office.	
4:00 P.M.–5:00 P.M.	*Inspiring a Shared Vision:* Goal Setting and Accountability	Various Locations
	Outcomes: Councils share their goals and determine what three goals the Greek community needs to hold them accountable to achieving.	

8:00 P.M.–10:00 P.M.   *Encourage the Heart:* Wrap-Up Session   Campfire

Outcomes: All chapter presidents will be able to articulate three leadership practices they want to implement within their chapters to have a positive impact on the experience of the membership.

As an adviser, it is important to remember that any comprehensive leadership development program will begin with the institutional mission as it relates to developing leadership among students and that it is imperative to involve students in the process. Use their words to describe what leadership is and what skills they would like to develop. Enable the students to determine what activities and conversations they need to have. And, of the upmost importance, encourage students to reflect on their leadership, during both high-performing and turbulent times, so that they can make meaning of their leadership practices when they are successful and when they are not.

The Social Change Model of Leadership Development (SCM), designed by the Higher Education Research Institute (1996), can be applied to individuals, groups, and communities and is a widely used model in cocurricular programs (Dugan and Komives 2011). It is especially useful with student leaders because there are specific factors found within the college environment that can enhance this type of leadership development. According to Renn and Reason (2013), these factors include opportunities for increasingly complex leadership responsibilities, exposure to diverse others, and effective mentoring.

SCM is based on the approach that leadership is a "purposeful, collaborative, values-based process that results in positive social change" (Komives, Wagner, and Associates 2009, xii, cited in Dugan and Komives 2011). The SCM (Komives et al. 2011) is based on two principles: that leadership is tied to social responsibility and the model is intended to increase an individual's level of self-knowledge and ability to work with others. There are three dimensions (individual, group, and societal) that have seven critical values. There are three values within the individual domain: consciousness of self (awareness of beliefs, values, attributes, and emotions that motivate one to take action); congruence (acting in ways that are consistent with one's values and beliefs); and commitment (having significant investment in an idea or person and the energy to serve the group and its goals). Adapted from *The Handbook for Student Leadership Development* (Komives et al. 2011) the values found within the group domain are: collaboration (working with others in a common effort, sharing responsibility, authority, and accountability); common purpose (having shared aims and values); controversy with civility (recognizing that different viewpoints are inevitable and differences must be aired openly). The value within the societal domain is citizenship (believing that individuals and groups are responsibly connected to the community). These critical values contribute to the eighth, and central value, change (the belief in the importance of making a better world and better society for oneself and others).

What is especially applicable to the work of student organization advisers is that the SCM can be used to diagnose how an organization is functioning and if the individuals within the organization are progressing developmentally. As Dugan and Komives (2011) state, "as students experience group-level values, who they are as individuals may inherently change, causing the need to revisit previously understood values . . ." (47). An excellent example of putting the SCM into practice is the UCLA Bruins Leaders Project (2013). Participants can earn a leadership certificate through participation in seminars and service projects that are all based on the seven values of the SCM.

According to Dugan and Komives (2011) the Social Change Model is an example of a model that addresses how leadership may be practiced. Researchers have also studied how leadership may be learned. The Leadership Identity Development Model explores six developmental stages "that describe the increasingly complex ways in which individuals define leadership and identify themselves as leaders" (Wagner 2011).

Using *The Handbook for Student Leadership Development* (Wagner 2011) as a guide, how students make meaning of leadership in each stage is a result of five components: (1) the broadening view of leadership; (2) a developing self; (3) group influences; (4) a changing view of self with others; and (5) developmental influences. How students make meaning of leadership in each stage uses what they have learned in the previous stages; however, students moving to a new stage have a "new way of conceptualizing leadership that has real implications for interpersonal behavior and interpretation of leadership experiences" (Wagner 2011, 97). The six stages are: (1) awareness; (2) exploration/engagement; (3) leader identified; (4) leadership differentiated; (5) generativity; (6) integration/synthesis. Two of the stages are worth discussing in more detail as many of the students with whom advisers work are developing within these stages. In stage 3, leader identified, the actions and beliefs of students demonstrate a hierarchical structure whereby the positional leader is the only leader and that others are followers (Komives 2011b). Leaders in this stage feel a strong sense of responsibility to accomplish tasks and attempt to motivate followers to help. The shift to stage 4, leadership differentiated, comes as students recognize the interdependence of group members where students demonstrate shared leadership and practice "a philosophy that he or she can be a leader even if not the leader" (Komives 2011b, 368).

As an adviser, having conversations with student leaders about how they view leadership and the specific role they have as a leader will allow them to reflect on their own development. Because of that interaction, you can identify which stage a student leader may be in and provide the appropriate challenge and support to allow for movement to the next stage. Typically you will find the students in the organization to be in different stages of leadership development. Having reflection activities designed for students will allow them to challenge their current definition of leadership. These activities do not need to be complicated. You could have student leaders reflect individually through a journaling exercise that asks them to respond to questions like the following:

- As a leader, what am I good at?

- As a leader, what do I think the roles and responsibilities of other members are?

- What actions have I taken when there is a conflict within our group?

- What skills do I need to be a more effective leader?

- What can I do to improve the leadership abilities of those around me?

Student Learning

Historically student learning has been viewed as the responsibility of faculty, but recent research argues that there should be intentional linkages between cognitive and affective learning, that they should be integrated and viewed as parts of one process (King and Baxter Magolda 2011). Student organization advisers have the unique opportunity to tie together curricular and cocurricular learning, answering the call for transformative educational practices. In this section we will discuss, in simple terms, what learning outcomes are, how advisers can help shape the learning experience for students, and some examples of putting learning theory into practice.

Learning Outcomes

Learning outcomes are the product of an intervention that an individual experiences. The purpose of higher education is to provide students opportunities for knowledge acquisition and application and to put this learning to good use. Another expectation of higher education is to demonstrate how experiences, both in and outside the classroom, affect learning. So how do we know that the product of an experience has any impact on learning? We structure interventions intentionally to derive the outcomes we hope students will gain. We use our resources—time, energy, and money—on programs, services, and experiences that are purposely designed to elicit certain outcomes. And we measure those outcomes to demonstrate the learning that occurred and to improve the intervention in the future. There are examples of connecting competencies to learning outcomes and formulas for writing measureable outcomes. *Learning Reconsidered 2: A Practical Guide to Implementing a Campus-Wide Focus on the Student Experience* (Keeling 2006) is an excellent resource for this.

Being engaged in organizations offer students a wealth of learning opportunities. Student organization advisers have the opportunity to help shape experiences for these students so that the intended outcomes can be achieved. As Love and Maxam (2011) state, "advising is the practice through which a student's learning and development can be directly encouraged" (413). In addition to the learning to which students in organizations are exposed, organizations are able to have an impact on the learning of others. Advisers are well aware of the vast amount of programming organizations do. Asking student leaders if a particular program has any value can help determine whether it's an appropriate use of resources. Exhibit 4.2 is a simple worksheet you can have student leaders fill out to help them clarify the point of a specific program.

EXHIBIT 4.2

Program Outcomes

What program or service does the organization want to do?

What resources does the organization need to provide for the program/service to be successful?

Who is the intended audience?

What does the organization hope the audience will learn due to participation?

Why is there a need on campus for this particular program/service?

How would the organization measure whether or not the audience learned what was intended?

Learning Theory

Current learning theory argues that it is the responsibility of higher education to provide students with opportunities to experience the world and make meaning of these experiences in a way that allows students to reframe their perspectives (King and Baxter Magolda 2011). This is called transformative learning and is defined as "the process by which we transform our taken for granted frames of reference . . . to make them more inclusive, discriminating, open, emotionally capable of change, so they may generate beliefs or opinions that will prove more true" (Mezirow 2000, as cited in King and Baxter Magolda 2011, 208).

The concept of transformative learning is based in part on experiential learning theory. According to Johnson and Johnson (2013), "experiential learning involves reflecting on one's experience to generate and continually update an action theory that guides the effectiveness of one's actions" (46).

The research done by David A. Kolb in the 1970s and 1980s offered a fundamentally different view of the learning process. Prior to this time, theorists argued about how learning occurred. Cognitive theories emphasized knowledge acquisition and memorization, while behavioral theories denied "the role of consciousness and subjective experience in the learning process (Kolb 1984, 20). Kolb was clear that he was not offering a third alternative, but an "integrative perspective on learning that combines experience, perception, cognition and behavior" (Kolb 1984, 21). According to Kolb, effective learners need four different competencies:

- *Concrete Experience* (CE) focuses on being involved in experience; emphasizes feeling as opposed to thinking; takes an intuitive approach as opposed to a scientific approach to problem solving; values relating to people.

- *Reflective Observation* (RO) focuses on understanding the meaning of ideas and situations by observing them; emphasizes understanding as opposed to practical application and reflection instead of action; appreciate different points of view.

- *Abstract Conceptualization* (AC) focuses on using logic and ideas; emphasizes thinking as opposed to feeling; problem solving is from a scientific approach; values systematic planning, precision, and discipline of analyzing ideas.

- *Active Experimentation* (AE) focuses on actively influencing people and changing situations; emphasizes practical applications; pragmatic approach to what works; emphasis on doing as opposed to observing.

Kolb sees learning as a process involving a four-stage cycle where a concrete experience provides an opportunity for a student to reflect on the experience. This reflection allows the student to create his or her own meaning, or theories, which can be applied to other experiences. From these theories a student can determine appropriate actions to test in a new concrete experience (Saunders and Cooper 2001).

Kolb found that people develop some of these competencies better than others which leads them to prefer certain methods of learning (Saunders and Cooper 2001). Therefore, along with his learning style theory, Kolb developed a typology of four distinct learning styles which is applicable to advisers. Stage and Muller (1999) describe Kolb's learning styles succinctly.

- *Convergers* use abstract conceptualization and active experimentation because they prefer practical application of ideas and dealing with technical tasks rather than social and interpersonal issues.

- *Divergers* are most comfortable with concrete experience and reflective observation as they have a vivid imagination, the ability to offer alternative solutions to problems, and are interested in people.

- *Assimilators* learn through abstract conceptualization and reflective observation. They use inductive reasoning concerned with ideas and can integrate different ideas into logical theoretical models.

- *Accommodators* use concrete experience and active experimentation most naturally. They are doers more so than thinkers, solve problems intuitively, and rely on information from others as opposed to theories.

As Saunders and Cooper (2001) state, "[those] who wish to maximize learning and developmental outcomes need to recognize differential patterns and preferences in student learning" (315). Kolb's learning styles provide a framework for advisers to think about when developing learning experiences for students in organizations. The important thing to remember is that not all students learn the same way so using different methods to share knowledge or opportunities for students to acquire information will be more effective than if the group only employs lectures as a means to learn new material.

The *Learning Partnerships Model* (LPM) developed by Baxter Magolda is another helpful tool for advisers to use when strategizing ways to help students learn through their experiences in a student organization. The premise behind this model is a concept that Baxter Magolda, using research by Robert Keegan, refers to as "self-authorship." As a result of her seventeen-year study of young adult learning and development, Baxter Magolda determined that young adults go through stages of learning as they begin to balance their personal needs within the community with the responsibility for contributing to the learning environment (Baxter Magolda and King 2004). Self-authorship is the belief that young adults need to determine their own reality for themselves based on the way they make meaning and the experiences they have as they develop. The LPM demonstrates environments that promote self-authorship and operates on three key assumptions and three key principles (Baxter Magolda and King 2004) that are grounded in the familiar constructs of challenge and support. The three key assumptions used in environments to challenge learners to move towards self-authorship are: knowledge is complex and socially constructed; self is central to knowledge construction; and learners must share authority and expertise (Baxter Magolda and King 2004). Meanwhile, educators support a learner's ability to develop internal authority by practicing three principles: "validating learners' capacity as knowledge constructors, situating learning in learners' experience, and defining learning as mutually constructing meaning" (King and Baxter Magolda 2011, 217). Using the assumptions and principles intentionally allows for the creation of learning partnerships between educators and learners that emphasize the movement of the learner along the meaning making spectrum.

So how does this apply to our work as student organization advisers? In chapter 5 we discuss the roles of advisers in more depth, but for now consider an adviser to be an educator. Advisers have the opportunity to establish environments where the principles of self-authorship can come to life. King and Baxter Magolda (2011) discuss the relationship between educator and learner as one where the learner is in the driver's seat, determining both speed and direction, while the educator is in the back seat providing guidance and support while also appropriately challenging the learner about the decisions he or she makes.

Also, advisers are positioned to know a student's capacity for meaning-making and they can use the appropriate amount of challenge and support to cause dissonance in a way that promotes development without causing a student to shut down. For example, the adviser to the student body president is uniquely positioned to publicly support the decision he or she made in regards to appointments made to university-wide committees, but in private can challenge the president on his or her decision-making process and the ramifications of public perception on political appointees, partisanship, and the assumptions that will be made when it's time for the next decision to be made.

Finally, King and Baxter Magolda (2011) state that the "opportunities through which students learn to construct new frames of reference . . . make for powerful educational experiences" (209). They argue that rich learning environments include introducing students to places and people who are unfamiliar, providing hands-on experiences, and orienting students to the standards within their community. The experiences students have through involvement with student organizations provide the opportunity King and Baxter Magolda are pushing for. Advisers can transform the experience a student has because of involvement with an organization from simply enjoyable to one that triggers developmental change (while being no less enjoyable!). This can be done by having students share their reactions to experiences, reflecting on their interactions with others and applying what they experienced to other situations. Exhibit 4.3 shares an example of reflective questions in the context of a service-learning project, but the questions can be applicable to other settings.

EXHIBIT 4.3

How to Make Reflection Meaningful

The president of the student organization you advise asks you to help them reflect on the service-learning project they just participated in. You use the "What? So What? Now What?" framework that is based on Kolb's Experiential Learning Cycle (1984).

What? (happened . . . report the facts and events of an experience)

- What happened?
- What did you observe?
- What issue is being addressed?
- What were the results of the project?
- What events or critical incidents occurred?
- What was of particular notice?

So What? (does it mean to you . . . analyze the experience)

a) The Participant

- Did you learn a new skill?
- Did you hear, feel, or smell anything that surprised you?
- What feelings or thoughts seemed the most strong today?
- How was your experience different than what you expected?
- What do the critical incidents mean to you? How did you respond to them?
- What did you like or dislike about the experience?

b) The Recipient

- Did the "service" empower the recipient to become more self-sufficient?
- What did you learn about the people/community we served?
- What might impact the recipient's views or experiences of the project?

c) The Community

- What are some of the pressing needs and issues in this community?
- How does this project address those needs?
- How has the community benefited?
- What is the least impact you can imagine for the project?
- With unlimited resources, what is the most impact on the community you can imagine?

d) For Group Projects

- In what ways did the group work well together?
- What does that suggest to you about the group?

(*continued*)

EXHIBIT 4.3 (*continued*)

- How might the group have accomplished its task more effectively?
- In what ways did others help you today? How did you help others?
- How were decisions made? Were everybody's ideas heard?

Now What? (are you going to do . . . consider the future impact of the experience on you and the community)

- What seems to be the root cause(s) of the issue or problem addressed?
- What kinds of activities are currently taking place related to this project?
- What contributes to the success of projects like this? What hinders success?
- What learning occurred for you in this experience? How can you apply this learning?
- What would you like to learn more about, related to this project or issue?
- If you were in charge of the project, what would you do to improve it?

Adapted in part from the Service-Learning Center at the University of Minnesota http://www.servicelearning.umn.edu/info/reflection.html#Ideas.

Based on the University of Florida's Center for Leadership and Service Training Guide for Gator Plunge.

Group Dynamics

How a group or organization determines its rules and behaviors, the roles members play within the group, and how groups change over time is discussed as "group dynamics." Group dynamics, as defined by Saunders and Cooper (2001), "is the study of behavior in groups and includes research about the interrelationships between individuals and groups, how groups develop over time, the ways in which groups make decisions and the roles that individuals play within a group context" (318). Group dynamics is a field that includes theory, research, and practice. As an adviser to a student organization, you observe group dynamics and work with organizational leadership to solve problems, alleviate concerns, and remove obstacles to the organization or membership, which are all aspects of how the group functions. As Johnson and Johnson (2013) point out, "some groups are highly effective and achieve amazing goals, while others are highly ineffective and waste everyone's time. . . . [I]n those very roots of group development . . . lie many of the reasons why one group is productive and one is not" (18). They encourage that attention must be given to "the reasons for the group's existence, its structure, and its motivation" (Johnson and Johnson 2013, 18). In addition to this, as an adviser you may work with one function, or subgroup, of a larger organization. Therefore, understanding the dynamics within the larger group may help you be more successful advising the subgroup. For example, if you are the adviser to the Black History Month committee, a suborganization within the Black Student Union (BSU), being aware of the interaction of group dynamics between and within the committee and BSU may help student leaders be more effective and successful with their programming.

In this section we look at a number of theories and concepts of group dynamics, more specifically at group effectiveness, group norms, group development, and roles within a group. In order to provide practical information, we have applied these ideas to the various roles advisers play within student organizations. We have included activities, exercises, and case studies for you to use in determining an organization's or executive board's stage of development, to help you identify whether the organization is effective or ineffective, and to design programs to meet an organization's needs.

Group Effectiveness

Groups can function in either a productive or unproductive manner. Merely calling members together and expecting that the resulting group will be productive is unrealistic. Members must approach their group intentionally with a model of group effectiveness. The three core activities that an effective group performs are to "achieve its goals; maintain good working relationships among members; and adapt to changing conditions in the surrounding organization, society and the world" (Johnson and Johnson 2013, 23). Johnson and Johnson (2013) provide a seven-point model of group effectiveness.

1. Establish clear, operational, and relevant group goals that create positive interdependence and evoke a high level of commitment from every member.

2. Establish effective two-way communication by which group members communicate their ideas and feelings accurately and clearly.

3. Participation and leadership must be distributed among all group members.

4. Ensure that power is distributed among group members and that patterns of influence vary according to the needs of the group.

5. Match decision-making procedures with the needs of the situation.

6. Engage in constructive controversy by disagreeing and challenging one another's conclusions and reasoning.

7. Face your conflicts and resolve them in constructive ways. (25–26)

We feel it is valuable to take a quick look at conflict within organizations because, as an adviser, you may spend a significant amount of time as a mediator between individuals or factions within the group. According to Johnson and Johnson (2013), controversies promote high-quality decisions, creative problem solving, involvement in the group's work, and commitment to implementing the group's decisions. Managing conflict can be described as the art of balancing the engagement of students in the process who feel empowered to voice their opinions and concerns with the distraction of conflict and its potential for negative outcomes. Well-managed conflict usually involves ground rules within the organization that would include procedural elements, a culture of inclusivity and civility, and the confidence within the membership that some degree of conflict is inevitable when people are invested.

Group Norms

Group norms are the rules of behavior that have been developed and accepted by the group. "Group norms regulate the performance of the group as an organized unit" (Napier and Gershenfeld 1989, 114). When students join a group they may experience an initial period of anxiety. "The initial anxious feelings and thoughts are supplanted by firm, accepted ideas about personal security, safety, and membership status. Members come to feel comfortable in the group" (Napier and Gershenfeld 1989, 115). Tuckman (1965) has referred to this process of growing comfortable in the group as norming.

Group norms may range from explicit, formal, behavioral expectations of members to implicit feelings and behaviors. Johnson and Johnson (2013) define norms as "prescribed modes of conduct and belief that guide the behavior of group members" (232). Exhibit 4.4 provides an activity for the leadership or members of an organization to use in identifying the organization's norms.

EXHIBIT 4.4

Organizational Norms

Directions: Have each member of the executive board identify the organization's norms for each of the following categories. When they are finished, allow time for the members to compare and discuss their lists. Discussion questions are provided.

Process Questions

1. Are the norms you identified written or implicit?

2. Do the norms you identified apply differently among the executive officers than they do among the members?

3. Do any of the identified norms restrict or enhance members' ability to function?

4. Which of the norms were the clearest to understand?

5. Which of the identified norms are associated with organizational tradition or history?

Meeting structure (who leads, what pattern is followed, who reports, who makes decisions, who moves approval, who decides on seating, and so on):

Position requirements (academic, judicial, experience, length of service, and so on):

Dress (type of dress for occasions, conference travel, meetings, and so on):

(continued)

EXHIBIT 4.4 (*continued*)

Communication (frequency, type, formality, and so on):

Napier and Gershenfeld (1989) have identified three categories of norms that may regulate a group's performance:

- *Written rules.* Written rules may include a published set of standards or guidelines that is included in the organization's constitution. Student organizations may have judicial codes and written guidelines regarding membership, attendance, academic standards, committee involvement, appropriate dress, use of money, and access to offices.

- *Nonexplicit, informal norms.* These norms could be referred to as the silent norms. Blake and Mouton (1985) identify the silent norms as invisible group norms that can stifle the creativity of the organization. These unstated norms in a student organization can include, for example, who is exempt from having to attend meetings, who sits in a particular place during meetings, and who motions for approval of annual budget recommendations.

- *Norms beyond awareness.* Some norms operate without our conscious knowledge. These norms in a student organization might include "automatically raising the hand when one wants to be recognized; saying hello to those members who one is familiar with when entering the meeting; expecting a certain order at a meeting; an opening, the minutes, the treasurer's report, old business, then new business; expecting paid-up members to be notified of meetings" (Napier and Gershenfeld 1989, 127).

Group norms are especially important within student organizations since college-age students are developing their sense of self, finding independence, and determining their value system. Unlike roles, discussed later in this chapter, which differentiate members of a group, norms are what integrates the actions of all group members (Johnson and Johnson 2013). There have been many studies about the norming process and whether the group changes its norms to fit the values and beliefs of its members and leaders, or the members of the group change their values to fit those of the organization. As an adviser, you will see the interplay of norms within the organization regularly.

Group Development

Groups move through stages of growth over time. "In work groups, social or political groups, sports teams, and classroom groups, a predictable pattern of group evolution emerges in which each stage has certain definite characteristics" (Napier and Gershenfeld 1989, 470). In this section we summarize several theories about how groups are formed and the stages of their development. These theories are applicable to advisers and student organizations regardless of type, size, or tradition.

Tuckman's Model of Group Development Tuckman (1965) reviewed approximately fifty studies on group development that were conducted in a wide range of group settings within different time periods. Following this review he categorized group development into four stages: forming, storming, norming, and performing. Tuckman and Jensen (1977) conducted a later review and added a fifth group developmental stage, adjourning. In the forming stage, members determine their place in the organization, go through a testing or orientation process, and are more independent. The organization in the storming stage has members who react negatively to the demands of whatever tasks need to be accomplished; conflicts arise as members resist influence, and there is a high level of emotion. In the norming stage, in-group feelings and cohesiveness develop, and members accept the rules of behavior and discover new ways to work together. In the performing stage, the group becomes quite functional in dealing with tasks and responsibilities. Members have worked through issues of membership and roles; they focus their efforts and achieve their goals. In the adjourning stage, the group brings finality to the process, tasks are closed, and members anticipate a change in relationships.

You may assist the executive board and members in the involvement, participation, or planning of a number of activities for the organization during each of the five stages. The following lists outline activities for you to use at each stage.

Forming

- Develop icebreakers to help the members become acquainted.
- Coordinate a retreat or workshop for the executive officers or the organization members.
- Review the organization's mission and purpose with the membership.
- Identify the expectations of members and executive officers.

- Work with executive officers to share organizational history and tradition.

- Provide information to the executives and members on institutional policies and procedures.

- Have individual meetings with the organization president.

- Discuss effective meeting management, planning programs, and team building with the executive officers.

- Provide support to the executive officers.

- Provide an initial "to do" list for executives to assist them in beginning their duties.

Storming

- Provide mediation resources when conflicts become difficult for the group to manage.

- Teach confrontation and communication skills to the executive officers and members.

- Hold a roundtable discussion on issues with which the organization and membership are involved.

- Review the mission statement, purpose, and expectations in order to redefine the organization's action plans.

- Conduct a group decision-making activity.

- Discuss and review the executive officer roles.

- Develop a "rebuilding" team activity.

- Remind everyone that the storming stage is a natural part of the formation of a group.

Norming

- Schedule a more in-depth team-building activity that includes greater self-disclosure.

- Have the members design T-shirts, pins, or some other emblem with which to identify themselves and the group.

- Assist the group in starting a new program that will create a tradition.

- Review and possibly establish new goals for the organization.

- Maintain executive board and member relationships so as to avoid reverting back to the storming stage.

Performing

- Ensure that the organization and membership have a task.
- Support the members and executive officers by giving feedback about what is going well and what can be improved upon for the next year.
- Step back and allow the organization to perform.
- Provide opportunities for members to reflect on the meaning of their involvement with the organization, the skills they have developed, and how they hope to improve.

Adjourning

- Develop a closure activity to help members determine what they learned and benefited from during the year.
- Conduct an assessment or evaluation of the year.
- Develop transition reports for new executives.
- Ensure that a plan of recognition is in place for the close of the year.
- Coordinate a closing banquet with awards and other expressions of appreciation.
- Encourage the executive officers and members to assist the group for next year in training, orientation, or other responsibilities.
- Identify how the organization contributed to the history or tradition of the organization.
- Ensure that the minutes, reports, and correspondence are properly stored and maintained in an archive.
- Record the addresses and phone numbers of graduating and other departing members for future correspondence.
- Give the members gifts of appreciation for their involvement in the organization.

Napier and Gershenfeld's Stages of Group Development Napier and Gershenfeld (1989) analyzed more than twenty group development concepts and created a composite model of the stages of group development and the activities, events, and feelings associated with those stages. Napier and Gershenfeld acknowledge that a wide variety of groups exist and that those groups have individual differences; nonetheless, their composite, outlined in the following sections, identifies many of the common themes observed in groups.

The Beginning. During this stage, member expectations are established prior to a group meeting. Individuals bring their skills, experiences, and knowledge to the formative stage of group development. It is important for members to accept each other, after which they focus on the development of group goals. Studying the members of a group at this stage, we might observe the following feelings or behavior (Napier and Gershenfeld 1989, 471):

- Keeping feelings to oneself until the situation is known
- Being watchful
- Being pleasant, certainly not hostile
- Being confused as to what is expected of members
- Desiring structure and order to reduce personal pressure to perform
- Finding personal immediate needs to be of primary importance
- Waiting for the leader to establish goals . . . and responsibilities
- Looking more secure in the surroundings than people might feel

The beginning is a time for members to observe, determine their place in the group, and establish goals and parameters. Members may feel uncomfortable until they have found their place; they have little trust but are optimistic about the group's purpose.

Movement Toward Confrontation. The second stage begins when the initial discomfort passes and the searching for place is resolved. Leadership and power relationships begin to evolve among members during this stage. Members begin to feel comfortable voicing their opinions, resulting in subgroups taking sides. Arguments ensue as members attempt to test their power and influence. "Group members may feel dissatisfied, angry, frustrated, and sad because they perceive the discrepancy between the initial hopes and expectations and the reality of group life, between the task and the ability to accomplish the task" (Napier and Gershenfeld 1989, 473).

Compromise and Harmony. During this stage group members move to resolve differences, and their behaviors are more acceptable. The group is able to informally assess how the members have worked together and how they might enhance further work together; they allow each other time to express opinions, and they are open to those opinions. Group members have been observed to be less efficient during this time of harmony. Decisions are difficult to make because there is an increase in passive resistance.

Reassessment. During this stage, the group revisits and possibly revises its goals. Group member roles, "decision-making procedures, and leadership and communication patterns are likely to come under close scrutiny as are the personal behaviors that facilitated or inhibited the group" (Napier and Gershenfeld 1989, 474). Group members realize that efforts to achieve goals must be distributed to all members. With an understanding that all members must participate, communicate, and complete tasks, the group can better focus on determining its direction and on attaining goals. Group member trust and risk taking are increasing during this stage.

Resolution and Recycling. The group at this stage is very productive, highly efficient, and very positive. Members still may possess some feelings of conflict and distrust, but the productivity of the group has matured to a point that these are nonissues. A measure of the maturity of the group is not that tensions do not exist but how effectively the group deals with these issues through good lines of communication, openness to feedback, and secure positive relationships.

It is important to remember that not all groups move beyond subgroup influences, destructive communication, or high levels of tension and negative feelings. In many instances, however, the maturity of the group will prevail if the group's leadership provides direction. Exhibit 4.5 is a case study that an organization's student leadership can use to practice identifying potential problems and to discuss their observations. The group leaders will be able to draw on this practice and discussion throughout the year as their organization passes through its developmental stages.

EXHIBIT 4.5

Group Stage Case Study

Directions: You can use the following progressive case study with a student organization's executive board. Pass out the initial case to the participants and allow them time to answer the three questions. When they have completed the questions, take ten to fifteen minutes to discuss their answers. Following discussion, give the participants the first update and again allow time to complete the questions; continue with the second and third updates in the same way. To finish the activity, allow the participants time to complete the final questions prior to discussion.

(continued)

EXHIBIT 4.5 (*continued*)

Initial Case

You are members of the executive board to the Racquetball Club, a registered student organization. The club has been on campus for the past twenty years. You are all new members of the executive board. The club started meeting six weeks ago, with weekly meetings. Your adviser is a state champion racquetball player and has advised the club for the past ten years. At the last meeting, several new novice-level members of the club spoke up, stating that they feel the club does not have time for them because they are only beginners and the club stresses state and regional tournament play.

1. At what Napier and Gershenfeld stage is your organization, and why?

2. What Tuckman stage is the organization in and why?

3. What action do you take at this point in the situation?

Update One

The president of the executive board responds to the club members that she would like to form a committee to evaluate the club's emphasis on tournament play. The expert members of the club voice their displeasure, stating that the reason they joined the club was to participate in tournaments. They further state that if the emphasis on tournament play is decreased, they will leave the club and start a new club that meets their needs.

1. At what Napier and Gershenfeld stage is your organization now, and why?

2. What Tuckman stage is the organization in and why?

3. What action do you take at this point in the situation?

Update Two

The president is able to effectively close the meeting without any members quitting. The president contacts a member of the club who is seen as a leader by the tournament players. This member agrees with the president that the novice-level members should not be forgotten, considering that the expert members were once at that level themselves, and agrees to chair the review committee. By speaking individually with members, the president is able to recruit an equal number of novice- and tournament-level members to serve on the review committee.

1. At what Napier and Gershenfeld stage is your organization, and why?

(continued)

EXHIBIT 4.5 (*continued*)

2.   What Tuckman stage is the organization now in and why?

3.   What action do you take at this point in the situation?

Update Three

The review committee meets over the course of the next two months, providing updates every two to three weeks. There are still a few tournament members who feel that with a new purpose (to include the novice-level members), they will not receive the funding they have enjoyed in the past. The review committee makes its final recommendation; the club votes to accept the new purpose of equally emphasizing novice-level members and tournament members. The vote carries, with three of the thirty members voting against the recommendation.

1.   At what Napier and Gershenfeld stage is your organization, and why?

2.   What Tuckman stage is the organization in and why?

3. What action do you take at this point in the situation?

Final Questions

1. What was the role of the adviser throughout this situation?

2. How would this situation have been different if a different member of the club had chaired the review committee?

3. What future problems might the club face as a result of this situation?

(continued)

EXHIBIT 4.5 (*continued*)

4. What can the executive board and adviser do now to alleviate the potential future problems?

Intentionally Structured Groups An Intentionally Structured Group (ISG) is an "intervention designed to promote specific goals; it has a planned structure or framework and a specified duration—usually relatively short" (Winston, Bonney, Miller, and Dagley 1988, 6). Winston and his colleagues have found that as vehicles for enhancing student development, groups have a number of advantages over individuals:

1. Groups are economical.

2. Groups appear less threatening than an individual seeking an outcome.

3. Groups often have a synergic effect—that is, the members of the group gain more from the experience than they would have through individual interventions.

4. Groups often focus attention on developmental areas for which the stimulus for change is too diluted in the overall campus environment.

5. Students generally give positive evaluations of and report enjoying well-designed and implemented group experiences.

6. Groups are versatile; they can focus on a given population of students, an identified problem, or a developmental task.

7. Group settings can provide a "safe" place to try out new roles and to practice different ways of relating to others.

8. Well-designed, well-implemented groups make excellent use of the instructional strategies identified in several student development interventions.

An ISG will typically have five stages: (1) establishment, (2) exploration, (3) transition, (4) working, and (5) termination (Winston et al. 1988).

In the establishment stage, members begin to learn each other's name and background, establish ground rules, and identify group norms; members together form a group identity; and the leader identifies the goals. In the exploration stage, roles are assigned by the group, and a hierarchy is developed based on role assignment by the group; members test the ground rules, begin to develop trust, assess the leader's competence, and recognize the value of participating. In the transition stage, some members may violate group norms to determine consequences, noncommitted members may leave, and members recognize the importance of specific group members' influence, the power of the group, and the leader's limitations. In the working stage, achieving goals is a cooperative effort; members practice new behaviors, give and receive feedback, take more risks, express concern over group progress, and communicate among themselves; the leader acts as a consultant. In the termination stage, members achieve goal-related closure, evaluate the total experience, project into the future, and say goodbye to one another (Winston et al. 1988).

ISGs can be an effective tool for a student organization. You may recognize situations for which an ISG may be the best approach for resolving a problem; ISGs can be used when the organization seeks to identify student concerns, to conduct a needs assessment, to evaluate the organization's effectiveness, to train or orient leaders, to evaluate organizational structures, or to develop community responsibility.

Roles and Development of Members within Groups

Members of organizations are likely to adopt familiar patterns of interacting with others (Saunders and Cooper 2001). This is especially true in a new environment or meeting new people. It is important for the group, and its adviser, to be aware of the roles members can play, which roles are likely to emerge, and which roles have a positive influence on the group or work against the group's effectiveness.

Lifton's Group Member Roles Lifton (1967) identified three types of member roles in groups attempting to identify, select, and solve problems. The categories of roles are group task, group growing and vitalizing, and antigroup.

The group task roles for members attempting to identify, select, and solve problems are as follows:

Initiator contributor. Offers new ideas or a change of ways.

Information seeker. Seeks clarification of suggestions.

Opinion seeker. Seeks clarification of group values.

Information giver. Offers facts or generalizations.

Opinion giver. States beliefs or opinions pertinent to suggestions.

Elaborator. Gives examples or develops meanings.

Coordinator. Pulls ideas and suggestions together.

Orienter. Defines position of the group with respect to goals.

Evaluator. May evaluate or question the group's function.

Energizer. Prods the group to action or decision.

Procedural technician. Performs tasks and manipulates objects.

Recorder. Writes everything down and serves as the group memory.

The group growing and vitalizing roles for members are the following:

Encourager. Praises, agrees with, and accepts others' ideas.

Harmonizer. Mediates intergroup conflicts.

Compromiser. Operates from within the group to "come halfway."

Gatekeeper and expediter. Encourages and facilitates participation.

Standard setter or ego ideal. Expresses standards for the group.

Group observer and commentator. Keeps records of group processes.

Follower. Goes along somewhat passively.

The antigroup roles for members are the following:

Aggressor. Deflates status of others.

Blocker. Negativistic, stubborn, and unreasonably unrealistic.

Recognition seeker. Tries to call attention to self.

Self-confessor. Uses group to express non-group-oriented feelings.

Playboy. Displays lack of involvement in group's work.

Dominator. Tries to assert authority to manipulate members.

Help seeker. Tries to get a sympathy response from others.

Special-interest pleader. Attempts to grow a grassroots effort.

You can work with the organization's leadership to assist the students in identifying the members who might take on antigroup roles and list possible strategies should those roles become evident when the group is attempting to identify, diagnose, or solve problems. Exhibit 4.6 is a progressive case study illustrating several of the member roles described by Lifton (1967).

EXHIBIT 4.6

Group Member Role Case Study

Directions: You can use the following progressive case study with groups of students or the executive board. Pass out the initial case to the participants and allow them time to answer the two questions. When they have completed the questions, take ten to fifteen minutes to discuss their answers. Following discussion, give the participants the first update and again allow time to complete the questions; continue with the second and third updates in the same way. To finish the activity, allow the participants time to complete the final questions prior to discussion.

Initial Case

You are an adviser to a sorority. You have served as adviser for the past eight years. The sorority has developed a six-person committee to review and make recommendations regarding the sorority's organizational structure.

You attend the first meeting of the committee, and it appears to you that the committee is made up of two initiator contributors, one evaluator, one harmonizer, one aggressor, and one dominator.

  1.   What are your concerns as an adviser at this point in the situation?

  2.   What action do you take at this point in the situation?

Update One

Following the second meeting, the sorority executive board announces that the committee will be chaired by Cindy (the harmonizer). The committee has struggled for the past two meetings since no chairperson was identified.

(continued)

EXHIBIT 4.6 (*continued*)

1.   What are your concerns as an adviser at this point in the situation?

2.   What action do you take at this point in the situation?

Update Two

During the next meeting of the committee, all representatives are in character. The dominator is asserting herself, the aggressor is deflating the others' status, and so on. The committee chair, Cindy, is desperately trying to keep the group on track. Following the meeting (you were not in attendance), she calls you and wants to meet with you and the sorority president. During that meeting, she announces that she wants to step down as chair.

1.   What are your concerns as an adviser at this point in the situation?

2.   What action do you take at this point in the situation?

Update Three

Following a lengthy discussion, Cindy has decided to stay on as chair. Her plan is to start over with a team-building activity, a goal development activity, and a role identification activity.

1. What are your concerns as an adviser at this point in the situation?

2. What action do you take at this point in the situation?

Final Questions

1. Could the executive board have made a better decision about how it composed the committee?

2. How did the late announcement of the committee chair affect the committee's work?

(continued)

EXHIBIT 4.6 (*continued*)

3. How would this situation have been different if another member of the committee had been chair?

4. What other strategies could the chair have employed to keep the committee on task?

5. Have you experienced a similar situation?

Similar to the roles outlined by Lifton, as discussed by Saunders and Cooper (2001), Winston and colleagues (1988) based the description of common group roles on the descriptors used by Benne and Sheats (1948) and Blocker (1987). They outline two categories of roles, those that are productive and those that are unproductive.

Productive roles include the following:

Information seeker. Asks for clarification of suggestions.

Opinion seeker. Ask for clarification of values.

Initiator. Suggests a changed way of regarding group problems or goals.

Interpreter. Interprets feelings expressed by members or the significance of nonverbals.

Supporter. Agrees with and accepts the contribution of others.

Coordinator. Points out relationships among ideas and suggestions.

Energizer. Prods the group to action or decision.

Harmonizer. Attempts to mediate differences between members.

Examples of nonproductive roles include the following:

Aggressor. Attempts to deflate the status of other members.

Resister. Constantly reacts negatively to most ideas, opposes proposals for no reason.

Recognition Seeker. Calls attention to him- or herself by bragging or boasting.

Comedian. Attempts to make everything into a joke.

Dominator. Tries to assert authority by manipulating members or the entire group.

Victim. Attempts to elicit sympathy from others through self-deprecation and insecurity.

Expert. Treats members as an audience in order to demonstrate superior knowledge.

It is common for student leaders to catch themselves adopting the same role within the different groups of which they are members. However, depending on a number of factors including leadership position, level of engagement, value placed on the experience, commitment to others in the group, and the group's mission, students can find themselves using different roles. Having students reflect on the roles they adopt, why they adopt those roles, and whether they are healthy to the group can be beneficial to the student and the organization.

Cartwright's Group Dynamics Cartwright (1951) developed eight principles of group dynamics that can enhance behavior or change attitudes among group members:

1. If the group is to be used effectively as a medium of change, those people who are to be changed and those who are to exert influence for change must have a strong sense of belonging to the same group.

2. The more attractive the group is to its members, the greater the influence the group can exert on its members.

3. In an attempt to change attitudes, values, or behavior, the more relevant these are to the basis of attraction to the group, the greater will be the influence the group can exert upon them.

4. The greater the prestige of a group member in the eyes of other members, the greater the influence he or she can exert.

5. Efforts to change individuals or subparts of a group will encounter strong resistance if the outcome of those efforts would be the individuals' or subparts' deviating from the norms of the group.

6. Strong pressure for changes in the group may be established by the organization's leadership, creating a shared perception by members of the need for change, thus making the source of pressure for change the organization's membership.

7. For a change to be realized, information relating to the need for changes, the plans for change, and the consequences of change must be shared with all relevant people in the group.

8. Changes in one part of a group produce strain in other parts, which can be reduced only by eliminating the change or by bringing about readjustment in the related parts.

Astin (1993) conducted a number of empirical studies on the influences of the peer group. He concludes: "the student's peer group is the single most potent source of influence on growth and development during the undergraduate years" (398). He adds that "student's values, beliefs, and aspirations tend to change in the direction of the dominant values, beliefs, and aspirations of the peer groups" (398). This evidence supports Cartwright's assertions.

The effective student organization leader and adviser will recognize the power of group development, a process in which values, pressures, norms, and issues are at work. You and the leaders of your organization should observe the dynamics within the group early to identify subtle meanings, hints of potential problem areas, how the group exerts pressure on its members and relationships between members that could cause difficulty for the organization.

A final word about individual and group development—we cannot overstate the need for advisers to be as engaged in the process of the organization's development and of an individual's leadership development and learning. It is easy to get distracted with the output of a student organization. They want the biggest, most expensive, most popular programs and events. They want to double the money raised during a philanthropic activity or recruit the largest new member class. Although there is value in setting the bar high, educators know that it is through the process of trying to achieve these outputs that our students learn, grow, develop, and become contributors to the community.

Case Vignettes

Appropriate Norming?

You are the new adviser to a student organization that has been a significant part of the campus as it is responsible for performing all of the campus visits for potential students. You notice that the organization wants to discuss the announcement of the new member class and their annual new member retreat when you are not around. You notice that the organization spends the majority of meetings discussing their social events. You also become aware that recent alums are communicating on a listserv managed by the organization but one to which you do not have access.

- What have you learned about group norms which may help you explain how what the organization seems to value is not in line with performing a campuswide function?
- How could an ISG be used to help this organization?
- How could you apply Kouzes and Posner's five exemplary leadership practices with the new members in their retreat?

Looking in the Mirror

The campus programming board has been responsible for planning Homecoming events for the last ten years. Two months before Homecoming Week, the chair of the programming board learns that the Black Student Union and the National Pan-Hellenic Council are partnering to host Black Greek Homecoming the same week. The events for both weeks are in direct conflict with one another. As the adviser to the programming board, the student leadership shares their reactions. John's reaction: They can't do that. If they do we will cut them out of future leadership positions. Misty's reaction: What did we do wrong? How do we fix this? Demetri's reaction: We tried to include them. What gives?

- How can you apply the Social Change Model in discussions with the programming board's leadership?
- How would you describe the three students' stages of leadership development?
- Based on what you know about group dynamics, how can you help the programming board reflect on what may have contributed to this situation and how they may have made BSU and NPHC feel marginalized?

Chapter 5

Roles and Functions of Advisers

ADVISING STUDENTS IS one of the hallmarks of any university and has been an enduring function through the history of higher education. As Love and Maxam (2011) state, "advising may be the universal task in student affairs because it exists at the foundation of much of the work we do" (413). Whether you are advising one or many, no matter which department you work in, good advising takes practice, courage, and a whole lot of patience.

Throughout the chapter we discuss the qualities, skills, and knowledge you will find essential to be successful in your work with student organizations. We identify different roles you may adopt as an adviser: mentor, supervisor, and educator. We also discuss a few critical aspects of advising, including developing a mission, working with seasoned versus new organizations, differences between academic and campuswide organizations, motivating students, and implementing the organization's structure. We provide examples of forms, schedules, and case studies to use for training and maintaining the organization.

Adviser Roles

Those of us who have advised student organizations for several years will be quick to joke about all the roles you end up playing. From a quality control officer to a sounding board to the group's conscience, your role can change within a given day, maybe even during one conversation!

The reality is that you must play numerous roles while working with individual students and student organizations. An approach you take with one group may not work with another. How you advise an individual may look different in a group setting. Developing and practicing a number of roles will serve you well. Naturally, you will be most comfortable in the role with which you are most familiar; however, you must understand that although comfort in a specific role may diminish your sense of needing to know about other roles, student organizations will continually challenge you to assume and work with various roles depending on the situation. If you understand a variety of roles, take time to practice techniques associated with various roles, and work with student organizations to reach a collective agreement as to your limitations and expectations of the roles, you will be much more effective in your work.

We have included discussions about three of the roles we feel are adopted by advisers the most often: mentor, supervisor, and educator. Clearly, this is not an exhaustive list so do not be surprised if you are confronted with a situation that may require a different role.

Mentor

Perhaps there is nothing more rewarding than a random communication from an alumnus or alumna to tell you that, as an adviser, you had made a difference in his or her life. The one-on-one frank conversations afforded the student the unique opportunity to learn and develop and he or she is a better person because of it. Effective advisers take pride in cultivating this type of mentoring relationship with the members of student organizations. This type of relationship can last years beyond the student's involvement in the organization.

Mentoring can be defined as a one-to-one learning relationship between an older person and a younger person based on modeling behavior and on an extended, shared dialogue (DeCoster and Brown 1982). We cannot overstate the value of modeling appropriate behavior with the current generation of students (known as Net Generation) as these students have grown up in an environment where they were much less independent than previous generations and therefore need to see mentors follow through and hold themselves accountable (Junco and Mastrodicasa 2007).

The mentor can be characterized as a person having: (1) a knowledge of the profession; (2) enthusiasm for the profession and its importance; (3) a genuine interest in the professional and personal development of new professionals; (4) a warmth and understanding in relating to students and staff in all types of settings; (5) a high yet achievable standard of performance for self and others; (6) an active involvement in and support of professional associations; (7) an honest emotional rapport; (8) the available time and energy to give freely to others; (9) the time to stimulate others to extend themselves intellectually, emotionally, and professionally;

(10) the initiative to expose others to a select but broad-based network of professionals who can help with development of the new professional; and (11) the care to guard young professionals from taking on too much too soon in their career. At Guilford Technical Community College the majority of registered student organizations are academically focused. Therefore being a mentor is the most important adviser role. The goal is for students in organizations to forge valuable relationships with someone in the profession while still encouraging group development and positive outcomes (B. Cross, personal communication, February 10, 2014). Odiorne (1985, adapted from a citation in Schuh and Carlisle 1991, 505) identifies five qualities that characterize good mentors:

- Good mentors have been successful in their own professional endeavors.

- Good mentors behave in ways worthy of emulation.

- Good mentors are supportive in their work with subordinates. They are patient, slow to criticize, and willing to work with those who are less well developed in their careers.

- Good mentors are not afraid to delegate tasks to colleagues and are not threatened by others who exhibit talent and initiative. They provide support for protégés who have been unsuccessful and provide plenty of praise for those who have been successful.

- Good mentors provide periodic, detailed, and honest feedback to the protégé.

It is important to note that Odiorne does not mention giving advice as a characteristic of a good mentor. Occasionally advisers will fall into the habit of providing advice and justify such action by mistakenly assuming that is the responsibility of a mentor. As Love and Maxam (2011) state, "providing advice is a unidirectional relationship in which a person who 'knows better' tells another person what to do" (413). Advisers, when adopting a mentoring role, will serve student leaders much better if they are able to monitor their tendency to give advice.

We have seen a proliferation of peer mentoring programs within student organizations. Boatman (1986) suggests that student leaders can play an integral role in developing the environment in which an effective peer mentoring relationship can take place. This relationship allows students to direct the leadership development of their peers. Peer mentoring relationships can serve as a supplement to the more traditional adult-protégé relationships on campuses. Student leaders value the mentoring relationship they receive so they try to emulate it within the structure of their organization. As an adviser, be cautious that the organization is approaching any mentor-mentee relationship appropriately. You may need to clarify the goals of such a program and the limits that a peer mentoring relationship should have.

Exhibit 5.1 is a simple activity that you can use with students to assist them in identifying mentors. You can use the form with individuals or with several organization members including the executive board, when discussing the value a mentoring relationship has on their ability to improve their own leadership skills.

EXHIBIT 5.1

Mentor Activity

Directions: Give a copy of the sheet to each student, allowing him or her ample time to complete the questions prior to a facilitated discussion.

Facilitator Questions:

1. Are you still in contact with these individuals?

2. As you review the names, are there consistencies in their gender, race, or age?

3. What traits do these individuals have in common?

4. Who initiated each of these relationships?

5. What characteristics do these individuals possess that you have tried to emulate?

6. Can you identify other thoughts regarding these individuals?

Identify those individuals who have guided or assisted you with the following:

Your academics

Your career

Your spirituality

Your special interests and hobbies

Your family

Team building

Formal performance evaluation

Planning evaluation

(*continued*)

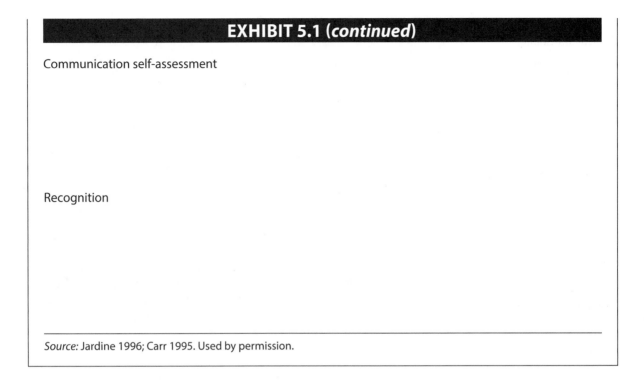

Source: Jardine 1996; Carr 1995. Used by permission.

Supervisor

Some writers argue that there are major differences between advising and supervising (for example, Kowalski and Conlogue 1996). One major difference has to do with who is ultimately responsible for the organization's outcomes. As a supervisor you would be responsible for the outcomes but as an adviser responsibility rests with the organization of which you are a part. A second major difference is that as a supervisor you can have unilateral decision-making authority whereas an adviser will share opinions and rely on influence to change a direction.

We believe that there are enough similarities that a discussion of a supervisor's role is warranted. Dunkel (1996) identifies the components of a supervisory cycle (see Figure 5.1); many of these components are transferable to effective advising. The six stages of the supervisory cycle are team building, performance planning, communication, recognition, self-assessment, and evaluation.

Team Building In team building, your role is to work with the president and executive board soon after their appointment or election. Team building establishes relationships that will enhance the ability of the organization's leadership, members, and adviser to work together. It is important for you to understand your strengths and weaknesses, work styles, and relationships with authority, and any intervening variables that affect your ability

FIGURE 5.1

The Supervisory Cycle

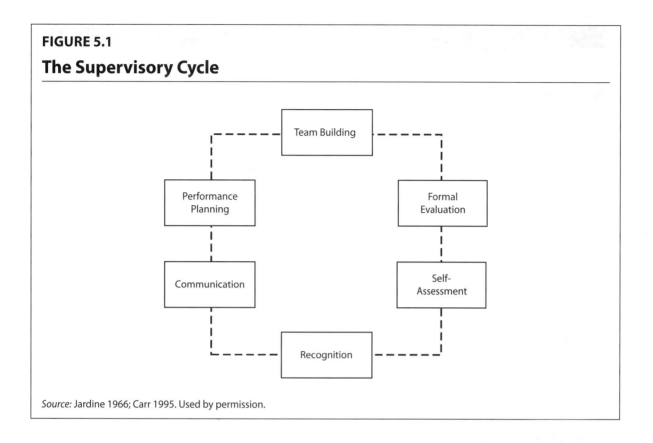

Source: Jardine 1966; Carr 1995. Used by permission.

to work. Student leaders need to understand their pressures, strengths and weaknesses, work styles, goals, ability to feel empowered, and any circumstances that affect their ability to work. A meeting between you and the student leaders to identify and discuss these factors will help establish a relationship of open communication and understanding. Exhibit 5.2 is a teamwork activity that executive board members can use to generate and discuss techniques to improve the symptoms listed.

EXHIBIT 5.2

Team Building Activity

Directions: Distribute a copy of the sheet to each participant. Allow them time to identify at least one technique to increase teamwork for each symptom listed. Following completion, discuss the techniques that participants have identified.

What do you do when you do not see evidence of cohesiveness and productivity or when cohesiveness and productivity begin to show signs of decline?

(continued)

EXHIBIT 5.2 (*continued*)

Symptoms	*Techniques to Improve*
Lack of participation in meeting	
Personal distance	
Putting effort in the wrong places	
Letting others do the work	
Putting off the start of new projects	
Slow progress	
Decreasing interpersonal contact	

"Same old stuff" attitude

Inaccurate, late work

Lack of direction

Whether you advise a new organization, inexperienced executive board, or group that has a long history, a team-building retreat or workshop is essential. Teamwork does not occur by accident. It is intentional, genuine, and active. Although we recognize that there are some inherent differences between the two, we will use the terms "retreat" and "workshop" interchangeably.

For any retreat involving a student organization to be productive it is important to involve its student leaders in the planning process. The first step in the planning process is to identify the desired outcomes of the activity: Are they to be focused on socializing, formulating a strategy or plan, discussing membership recruitment (Blank and Kershaw 1993), or something else? Second, planners should identify a location that provides a special environment, whether that be on or off campus. Third, planners need to build in a structure for the retreat. The environment will provide an informal, comfortable setting; a schedule that allows for time on task, breaks, meals, and casual free time will provide the needed structure. Fourth, you and the student leaders need to identify each person's roles and responsibilities. Identifying the facilitator of activities and the coordinators for meals is important in preparing for the retreat. Planners should also consider using a team-building activity early in the retreat schedule. The environment and atmosphere of working together away from campus will accomplish part of the team-building process, but intentional team-building activities will enhance the outcome. Finally, you and the student leaders need to consider what will need attention following the retreat. For example, how can the value of the workshop be extended for the next weeks and months?

A final note about selecting a facilitator: be strategic with the selection. Usually a facilitator comes from outside the organization because he or she can share a new perspective, offer an expert voice, and introduce new activities and processes. A person with strong facilitator skills, an understanding of the organization, and the ability to challenge the organization to develop plans consistent with the retreat's purpose is ideal. The student activities office will have ideas for a facilitator if the organization becomes stuck.

Performance Planning The second stage in the supervisory cycle is performance planning. Performance planning includes writing position descriptions, determining and listing expectations, and setting goals.

Each of the executive and key leadership positions in the organization should have a position description. Exhibits 5.3 through 5.7 are examples of position descriptions for the president, vice president, secretary, treasurer, and adviser which have been updated with help from information from Southeast Missouri State University's Campus Life and Event Services (2011). Some organizations will have additional officers like a parliamentarian, a historian, a vice president for programming or communications/public relations. You should participate in an open discussion of these position descriptions immediately following the appointment or election of students to these positions and remind the organization to share these descriptions with members prior to any election. This initial meeting should include a discussion of adding or deleting elements of the position descriptions for the time of appointment or election.

EXHIBIT 5.3

President Job Description

The following represent duties for which an organization president might be responsible:

- Preside at organization meetings
- Facilitate executive board meetings
- Represent the organization to the institution and (inter)national organizations
- Maintain contact with organization adviser, organization alumni, and campus and community partners

- Be aware of all money matters
- Appoint committee chair people
- Serve as spokesperson for the executive board and organization
- Provide motivation for the organization
- Prepare for all meetings
- Coordinate campuswide programs
- Serve on various committees or task forces
- Coordinate executive transitions
- Remain fair and impartial during all decision-making processes
- Provide follow-up to organizational tasks
- Inform the executive board of other meeting information
- Organize executive board retreats
- Prepare for the annual banquet
- Coordinate the executive board transition

EXHIBIT 5.4

Vice President Job Description

The following represent duties for which an organization vice president might be responsible:

- Assumes the duties of the president in his or her absence
- Serve as Parliamentarian
- Direct constitutional updating and revision
- Facilitate elections of officers
- Submit term reports
- Serve as liaison to committees
- Coordinate campus events and programs
- Organize end-of-year celebration
- Perform other duties as directed by the president

EXHIBIT 5.5

Treasurer Job Description

The following represent duties for which an organization treasurer might be responsible:

- Prepare the organizational annual budget
- Serves as the primary signatory on financial accounts

(*continued*)

EXHIBIT 5.5 (continued)

- Prepare all budget requests for funds, and pay bills
- Collect organization dues
- Audit books regularly with adviser
- Maintain a financial history of the organization
- Maintain a working relationship with institutional accounting
- Serve on various committees and task forces
- Coordinate solicitations and fundraising efforts
- Claim all stolen or lost equipment
- Maintain an inventory of all equipment and its condition
- Make quarterly reports of all receipts and disbursements to the members
- Perform other duties as directed by the president

EXHIBIT 5.6

Secretary Job Description

The following represent duties for which an organization secretary might be responsible:

- Record and maintain minutes of all organization meetings
- Send minutes to all appropriate members and institutional staff
- Prepare an agenda with the president for all meetings
- Keep the organization informed of both organizational and university business
- Maintain attendance (roll call) at all meetings
- Maintain a calendar of events
- Notify all members of meetings
- Prepare organization's calendar of events
- Serve as the organization's recognition coordinator
- Maintain contact information directory of all members
- Maintain organization website
- Handle official correspondence
- Reserve meeting rooms for the term and year
- Advise on public relations
- Maintain organizational records, storage, and office
- Perform other duties as assigned by the president

EXHIBIT 5.7
Adviser Job Description

The following represent duties for which an organization adviser might be responsible:

- Meet regularly with the organization's president
- Meet regularly with the executive board
- Attend organization meetings
- Give a report during the organization meeting
- Keep the executive board informed on institutional matters
- Maintain a relationship with institutional accounting
- Audit finances with the treasurer
- Attend and advise delegations during trips to conferences, business meetings, and competitions
- Serve as a liaison between the organization and the institution
- Assess risk management practices and assist with risk management decisions
- Provide developmental activities to the executive board to assist in developing group cohesiveness
- Assist the organization with election concerns
- Respect and encourage all organizational functions
- Provide a background history and insight to the organization
- Hold a goal-setting meeting for the executive board

Another aspect of performance planning is setting expectations. Expectations can be generated and agreed on by several different groups. The institution may have a list of expectations for the adviser, including attending organizational meetings, meeting regularly with the president of the organization or the executive officers, attending adviser training sessions, attending programs and events organized by the organization, learning the traditions and history of the organization, and in some cases traveling with the organization to conferences or competitions. Expectations of the adviser also can be generated by the organization's members. These expectations might include attending various meetings, being available, serving as a resource, or acting as a liaison to the administration. In addition, you can generate a list of expectations you have for the organization's members. This list might include informing you of decisions that are made, providing open and honest feedback, balancing their academic work with their activities, not expecting you to attend all events and activities, assisting with leadership development of the organization's members, or asking for help.

One other consideration in performance planning is goal setting. Goal setting can be completed for the organization by the president and executive board, with your assistance. Goal setting for the year is important for knowing what work will be required at various times of the year, what positions will need to be filled and the subsequent training involved, or what finances will be committed. Goal setting also can be accomplished for individual events, activities, and projects.

The process of setting goals involves some key ingredients. Goal statements must be measurable and realistic, and they must include a time period for attainment. Setting goals that the organization cannot attain can lead to frustration and a sense of underachievement by the students. Each goal statement should be followed by a set of objectives and an action plan for achieving each objective. An example of a goal statement, a set of objectives, and action plans is shown in Exhibit 5.8.

EXHIBIT 5.8

Sample Goal Statement

Goal: To increase fraternity chapter membership by 20 percent during next fall's recruitment week

  Objective: To create a publicity campaign informing students about the chapter

    Action plan: To send chapter representatives to summer orientation programs to talk about chapter activities

    Action plan: To have the membership chair meet with the student activities or Greek affairs office graphics staff to develop a membership recruitment brochure by March 1st which will be sent to incoming first-year students and transfer students

    Action plan: To have the chapter publicity director send weekly public service announcements to the campus newspapers between September 1st and December 1st highlighting the chapter's philanthropic efforts

  Objective: To ensure that the chapter's website and social media have accurate and positive information

    Action plan: Put together a team of current brothers to review the chapter's website to ensure accuracy of information and review other Web pages where the chapter would be mentioned

    Action plan: Develop a policy regarding the use of social media by the chapter and individual members

Objective: To develop an agreement with the on-campus housing office to release contracts of students wanting to live in the chapter house

Action plan: To have the chapter president secure copies of other campus agreements by September 1st

Action plan: To have the chapter president and membership chair meet with the director of housing by September 10th

As a final note on performance planning: one of the most often overlooked aspects of the organization's performance is officer transitions. Advisers can be instrumental in ensuring a smooth transition from one executive board to the next if they work with organizations to develop and use a transition plan. Transition plans can be as simple or complex as the organization needs to succeed. At minimum new officers should discuss with their predecessors any projects that are under way, the financial health of the organization, logistics on where to find important documents, passwords for websites, resources on campus the organization uses regularly, and challenges of the job.

Communication The third stage of supervision that includes transferable knowledge for an adviser is regular communication and feedback. Communication is both verbal and nonverbal.

The actual words in verbal communication carry only a portion of the intended message. "A psychologist devised this message: Of the total impact of a message, 7 percent is verbal (word choice), 38 percent is vocal (oral expression), and 55 percent is facial expression" (St. John 1985, 40). Students' posture, gestures, facial expression, hand and foot positions, and dress carry nonverbal messages. Based on St. John's conclusions (1985) an adviser should be aware of the following when helping student leaders communicate with others: (1) communication is perceived as negative if a person is kept waiting for a meeting; (2) the arrangement of furniture should not create obstacles to communication; (3) the surroundings should be attractive and well maintained; (4) the proximity of the speaker and listener should be relatively close to give a welcoming feeling; (5) a person's posture can convey several messages such as energy, interest, confidence, or approachability; (6) gestures convey attitudes (for example, open palms are welcoming, a clenched fist, threatening); (7) be aware of facial expressions (lack of eye contact expresses disinterest, nodding the head expresses approval, and shaking the head expresses disagreement); (8) the use of one's hands and feet convey messages (a foot tapping on the floor indicates impatience, and crossed arms are a barrier); (9) the use of silence can serve to emphasize a point or can be sensed as boredom; and (10) speakers' volume and voice characteristics convey emotions and attitudes. You can work with students to help them understand these aspects of nonverbal communication by giving them feedback about their actions in meetings. You also can use the communications activity found in Exhibit 5.9 to emphasize the importance of nonverbal communication.

EXHIBIT 5.9

Back-to-Back Communication

Directions: Everyone except the facilitator of this activity needs to find a partner and sit down back to back. One person, the speaker, will be given a small picture of a boat (the facilitator can draw and make copies of a picture of a sailboat on water, a fish in the water, a sun, and two or three birds flying) and the other person who will draw, the listener, will be given a blank piece of paper and a pen or pencil. (Make sure all the listeners are facing the same direction so that they cannot see another pair's boat picture.)

The speaker with the picture describes it to his or her partner using any descriptive wording except the following words: bird, sun, boat, sail, fish, and water. The listener cannot ask any clarifying questions. All the person can do is draw what he or she hears the partner describe. Once most people appear to have finished, take the new drawings and hang them on the wall.

The facilitator can repeat the activity with a different picture and have the partners reverse roles. This time the listener can ask clarifying questions, but again the person describing the picture may not use the key words. When the activity is completed, hang these pictures on the wall.

The facilitator can process this activity using the following questions:

1. For listener: What clues did your partner give you that were helpful?

2. For speaker: What frustrated you?

3. For listener: What did you want to do that might have made this easier?

4. Everyone had the same picture to describe, so what happened? What is responsible for the differences in the appearance of the final drawings?

5. Why is the ability to communicate effectively important, especially for students in an organization?

6. What did you do with your eyes during this activity?

7.   Did you use any nonverbal communication?

8.   What nonverbal actions would have made this activity easier?

   Have the group select the drawing that best represents the original picture. Have the partners describe how they approached the activity.

As an adviser it is important to be knowledgeable about how the students of this generation communicate. Many students struggle using formal communication methods, like memos, invitations, and thank-you cards, because they are used to communicating with each other through technology. Social networking, texting, instant messaging, and the like have perpetuated a habit of quick and informal communication using abbreviations and condensed sentences (Junco and Mastrodicasa 2004). This "chat" language does not necessarily lend itself to properly inviting the university president to speak at the organization's annual banquet. You cannot assume the students you advise understand how to appropriately communicate with other generations, especially when they are asking for a favor. Arthur Sandeen (2003) shared a few examples of how students invited him to different events.

> Dear Dr. Sandeen: Our annual parent's day banquet will be held in the union on Saturday night at 7:00 P.M. We would like you to be the keynote speaker. The charge for the banquet will be $27.00. If your wife comes it will be $54.00. Thank you.

• • •

> Hello? Is this Dean Sandeen? I am very honored to extend to you an invitation to be our keynote speaker at the annual Student Government banquet tonight at 6:30 in the union ballroom. We invited several distinguished leaders to speak, but they were not able to do it, so we thought we would select you.

If the second quote had come from a Net-Generation student it would have been e-mailed with the expectation of an immediate response! An example of a similar request written in a more professional manner is found in Exhibit 5.10.

EXHIBIT 5.10
Sample Memo

DATE: September 10, 2013

TO: Dr. Chris Smith

Vice President for Student Affairs

FROM: Mark Stone, President

Campus Debate Club

RE: Speaking at meeting

Dr. Smith, per our telephone conversation of September 8, 2013, I would like to formally invite you to speak at our October meeting. As we discussed, you would speak about your thoughts regarding leadership development and transferable skills.

Our meeting will be on Thursday, October 24, 2013, at 7:00 P.M. in the Student Union, room 282. We invite you to come at 6:30 P.M. to participate in a reception in the same location if you wish.

We look forward to your visit with us. Please contact me if there is anything I can do for you prior to the meeting.

Cc: Wayne Parks, Chair, Department of Communication

Mary Armstrong, Campus Debate Club Adviser

File

As the executive board plan for their general membership meetings they need to determine if a formal or informal structure should be employed. At a minimum, every meeting should have an agenda and this agenda may have few consistent topics from meeting to meeting. For example, the organization may have a financial update, open committee positions, and upcoming events listed on every agenda. The agenda guides the meeting, and if shared in advance, which we recommend, it allows members to prepare for the discussion. Exhibit 5.11 is a sample organizational agenda for a formal meeting. Informal meetings may use parts of this agenda. During the meeting, the secretary should take minutes of the general discussion and the decisions agreed on. These minutes should report any change in finances, any decisions made by the membership, dates of upcoming activities and deadlines and any other pertinent information that would benefit the organization. Minutes need not be a word-for-word transcription of the meeting; a summary will suffice. It is a best practice for the secretary to send the minutes to the executive board and membership within a reasonable time. An example of a set of organizational minutes is shown in Exhibit 5.12. Also, an organization with a more formal process, or with a complex issue to discuss, may use parliamentary procedure, an adaptation of it, or another approach to format meetings. Parliamentary procedure allows all members the opportunity to participate in discussion, debate, and decisions while assisting the president in keeping order. It would be helpful if you understood basic parliamentary procedure, particularly if the organization actively uses it. *Robert's Rules of Order: Newly Revised in Brief* (Robert 2011) provides information on all aspects of the rules of order. Exhibit 5.13 gives a basic summary of how different motions are handled in the student senate at the University of Florida.

EXHIBIT 5.11

Sample Formal Agenda
Community Involvement Club
Rolling Brook College

Date

Call to order—president

Roll call—secretary

Approval of the minutes—president

Officer and adviser reports

    President

    Vice president

    Treasurer

    Secretary

    Adviser

Decision and discussion

    Second readings

    First readings

Issue forum

Committee, event, and project reports

Announcements and comments

Adjournment—president

EXHIBIT 5.12

Sample Minutes
Community Involvement Club
Rolling Brook College

Date

Call to order: 5:15 P.M.

Roll call: 65 in attendance

    15 absent

Officer and adviser reports

    President: sign up for spring honor roll if eligible; accepting applications for fall dance director.

    Vice president: received and read a letter from the university president.

    Treasurer: we presently have $6,000.00 in the checking account and $352.00 in the housing account.

    Secretary: sign-up for Adopt-a-Highway was passed around.

    Adviser: passed out scholarship application materials.

Decision and discussion

    Second readings: none

    First readings: the treasurer presented the fall budget of $6,352.00. John S. moved and Nancy D. seconded to approve the budget. Following minimal discussion, the budget passed 60–4–1.

Issue forum: There were questions raised as to why the garbage trucks pick up trash so early in the morning. The adviser responded and explained the garbage pickup schedule.

Committee, event, and project reports

    Adopt-a-Highway: a sign-up sheet was passed around, and training has been scheduled for October 5, 1996, at 7:00 P.M. in the workshop.

    Fall dance: applications are available for the director position.

Announcements and comments

    Bill B.: thanked the body for all their good input

    Amanda P.: announced a birthday party

Adjournment: 6:25 P.M.

EXHIBIT 5.13

Basic Motions

LIST OF COMMON PARLIAMENTARY MOTIONS

(Listed in Order of Precedence)

Motion	Debatable	Amendable	Vote Required
To adjourn	No	No	Majority
To recess	No	Yes	Majority
Question of privilege	No	No	May be raised any time
Call for the orders of the day	No	No	May be raised any time
To lay on the table	No	No	Majority
Previous question	No	No	Two-thirds
To limit, extend, or close debate	No	Yes	Two-thirds
To postpone definitely	Yes	Yes	Majority
To commit/refer	Yes	Yes	Majority
To amend	Yes	Yes	Majority
To postpone indefinitely	Yes	No	Majority

OTHER PARLIAMENTARY MOTIONS

(No Order of Precedence)

Motion	Debatable	Amendable	Vote Required
To suspend the rules	No	No	Two-thirds
To adopt special rules of order	Yes	Yes	Two-thirds
Use vote records for final roll call	No	No	Two-thirds
To order a roll call vote	No	No	One-fifth
To take up from the table	No	No	Majority
To divide a question	No	Yes	Majority
Object to considering a question	No	No	Two-thirds
Call for division	No	No	Raised following a vote
To open the floor to nominations	No	No	One-fifth
To close nominations	No	Yes	Two-thirds
Adopt a committee report	Yes	Yes	Majority
Discharge a committee	Yes	Yes	Two-thirds
Point of order	No	No	May be raised any time
Appeal the decision of the chair	Yes	No	Majority
Point of information	No	No	May be raised any time
Point of parliamentary inquiry	No	No	May be raised any time

There may also be a time when the organization you advise wants to take a position on a specific issue and desires to communicate that position to the public. The organization has a few options: an interview with the local media, a memo to the institution (usually addressed to the president with copies to vice presidents), or even a Twitter feed or Facebook post. A more formal document for expressing the organization's position is a resolution, a sample of which appears in Exhibit 5.14.

EXHIBIT 5.14

Sample Resolution
STUDENT SENATE RESOLUTION 2013–107

Title: A Resolution Supporting the Collegiate Housing and Infrastructure Act

Authors: Student Body President Elect Christina Bonarrigo

Sponsors: Senate President Lauren Verno, Senate President Pro-Tempore Cory Yeffet, Chief of Staff Abby Whiddon, External Affairs Director Collin Thompson

WHEREAS, the Collegiate Housing and Infrastructure Act eliminates a distinction in existing tax law that would result in allowing tax-exempt charitable and educational organizations to make grants to non-University-owned not-for-profit student housing entities that provide collegiate student housing; and

WHEREAS, the Collegiate Housing and Infrastructure Act would make college more affordable at no cost to taxpayers by offering a housing alternative less expensive than University housing; and

WHEREAS, the Collegiate Housing and Infrastructure Act results in safer student housing by encouraging charitable contributions to collegiate housing for installation of life-saving equipment such as fire sprinklers, smoke detectors, and alarm systems; and

WHEREAS, 1,613 of 31,280 students currently live in non-University-owned not-for-profit student housing and 5.2% of students at University of Florida live in non-University-owned not-for-profit housing during their collegiate years;

THEREFORE LET IT BE RESOLVED that the University of Florida Student Government supports Congressional passage of the Collegiate Housing and Infrastructure Act;

BE IT FURTHER RESOLVED that the University of Florida Student Government asks the Florida Congressional Delegation to sponsor the Collegiate Housing and Infrastructure Act.

Organizations increasingly are relying on technology to communicate. Many organizations have Facebook pages to make announcements, the vast majority have a website, and they e-mail their listserv reminders and updates. Some organizations have moved to online voting and even hold general body meetings virtually. Many institutions have implemented online organization management software. There are definite positives to this. Organizations can be more transparent and more inclusive; however, the organization needs to clearly identify who is responsible for maintaining accurate information on all Internet platforms as the quality of the information is only as good as its accuracy. What is the point of having a Facebook page announcing an event when the time and location are incorrect? There have been many times when the student managing the website graduates without passing on login information, leaving the current organization in the lurch. Therefore, organizations should have a communications plan that allows for the most effective use of available technology and incorporates a transition in leadership.

Recognition Recognition is the fourth stage of the supervision flowchart that you can use in your work with students. As a faculty or staff member advising an organization, you will participate in many conversations with individual students. During some of these interactions students may express a myriad of emotions, disclose information of a serious nature, or act in a way that makes you suspicious that something is just not right. Sometimes a student's reaction is easily explained. For example, a student beginning to cry when you express your disappointment in his or her behavior could be considered a normal reaction to the conversation. But if in the same situation the student gets extremely angry and threatening, then there may be something of a more serious nature going on. It is important for you to think about how you will react when students express different emotions and know where, when, and how to refer students to another office for support. The dean of students office or counseling center will be glad to discuss a situation with a student that has escalated beyond normal behavior. Always trust your instincts when it comes to student behavior. As the adviser you very well may be the first "adult" to recognize concerning behavior and taking appropriate action could very well save a life.

Some situations require documenting the incident for your protection and the protection of the institution and can be in the best interest of the student. Written documentation should include the specific nature of the exchange and situation, the date and time, the individuals involved, and the outcome of the exchange. Other situations may result in violations of the student code or institutional rules. These circumstances generally necessitate documentation and referral to the student conduct office.

Self-Assessment The fifth stage of the supervision cycle is self-assessment. If you meet frequently with students, you should ask them to complete a verbal or written self-assessment of how they are progressing in their position and their academics. This opportunity allows students to reflect on programs, their skills, their involvement in the organization, and their responsibilities. Students can break down their duties, academic progress, or goal achievement into reflective thoughts. This self-assessment can be formal, in which the student completes a form, or the student can simply take time to reflect. This process is important for student leaders to use with their executive boards, committee chairpersons, or project managers; in addition, it serves as a checks-and-balances system for a process or project, slowing down the timeline for a moment to ensure that all aspects of the project are being covered.

Evaluation The sixth and final stage of the supervision flowchart that can be valuable for you is formal evaluation. Some institutions require students to complete various evaluations, including the following: program evaluations such as the one found in Exhibit 5.15 that can be used by the organization to determine the need for similar programs; performance appraisals of paid students in organizations; audits of records and accounts; and progress reports for various institutional office staff. Evaluations may come with rating scales, checklists, rankings, or open-ended responses, or may use a management-by-objectives approach. You should know what evaluations the students need to complete as part of the duties of their office or in order to fulfill institutional requirements.

EXHIBIT 5.15

Sample Program Report

_____

Student responsible for organizing the program

_____

Program title or topic

_____   _____   _____

Program date   Time   Location

_____

Program presenter(s)

Type of program (circle all that apply):

Educational   Community development/service

Entertainment   Leadership

Please give a brief description of the program and what you hoped the participants learned/experienced:

Rate the effectiveness of the program in achieving your desired outcomes:

Ineffective   Effective

1   2   3   4   5

What types of publicity and resources did you use?

What funding was used?

Did this program meet your expectations? Why or why not?

What would you do to improve on this program?

A formal evaluation is an opportunity for you to provide feedback to the organization or to individual members. Your participation in the evaluation process should be understood early in your relationship with the organization so as not to come as a surprise to students. You may receive the evaluative audits of records or accounts as the institution representative, you may be required to sign off on performance appraisals of paid students, and you may receive copies of progress reports to be ensured that money is spent within institutional guidelines or that institutional liability concerns are being attended to. Again, it is important for you to understand the role and implications of your involvement in the evaluation process. The first step in any evaluation is for participants to understand that evaluation is beneficial to the organization and to the individuals involved.

Educator

Often advisers to student organizations are called "faculty advisers" because of the relationship faculty had with students throughout the history of higher education. However, with the proliferation of student organizations and the broad range of their interests and purposes, faculty are not the only employees of an institution who serve in this role. Many institutions permit any employee to serve. Therefore faculty, staff, and sometimes graduate assistants and affiliate members (for example, campus ministry) are all eligible.

For the context of this discussion, we will use the term "student organization adviser" to describe anyone in that role. It is important to note that all institutions also have full-time positions responsible for ensuring the opportunity for organizations to exist and thrive. This role is usually the responsibility of the student activities office, which could be known on your campus as an involvement, engagement, student union, or student life office. The professional staff of these offices have studied students and made a career out of supporting their endeavors. They often have learning outcomes associated with involvement in student organizations and are committed to contributing to the institution's mission (Magolda and Quaye 2011). Learning outcomes are discussed in chapters 4 and 12; however, following is an example from the Student Leader Learning Outcome Project at Texas A&M (2013a) related to membership selection outcomes:

Students will be able to:

- Evaluate membership criteria for consistency with the organization's vision, mission, and values

- Recruit potential members and effectively communicate necessary information to them

- Create application or interview questions that are purposeful and helpful in the selection process

- Prepare themselves for the search process

- Evaluate candidates based upon membership criteria

- Provide a professional environment during the interview process

- Justify reasons behind who is and is not selected for membership and incorporate those reasons into the notification process

- Welcome new members to the organization

Advisers who also serve as full-time student affairs professionals have developed and participated in numerous training sessions. These advisers are capable of facilitating training sessions, because for many of them, training is one of their job responsibilities. For advisers to student organizations who primarily serve as faculty from any discipline, their preparation has been to teach. In drawing the distinction between training and teaching, Fried (1989) states that the "purpose of training is to help people learn skills to solve problems. . . . [T]raining imposes a certain uniformity on the practice of a skill, and this uniformity is the basis on which skill development can be evaluated" (355). About teaching, Fried states: "the purpose of teaching is quite the opposite—to broaden a person's understanding, to help the person examine a problem from several different points of view, and to place the problem in a cultural and historical context" (355). Regardless of what type of position you have as your "day job," the common thread between all advisers should be the educative role you must play for the organizations and the individual students in those organizations to succeed.

Creamer, Winston, and Miller (2001) describe a number of behavioral characteristics of educators. Two of these are particularly meaningful to this discussion. They describe the characteristic of advising as "listening to interests and concerns; aiding in identification of available resources; explaining institutional rules and procedures; initiating cooperative problem solving; challenging unexamined assumptions, beliefs and prejudices; providing emotional support" (14) and the characteristic of facilitating as "assisting an individual or group to make meaning of experiences; encouraging expression of feelings and examination of effects on others; encouraging discussion of ideas and exploration of implications, enabling democrat decision making" (14). These two characteristics of educators give a clear description of how advisers spend the majority of their time. It further ties the adviser role to the purpose of higher education. As Creamer et al. state, "the raison d'être of higher education is to enable individual development in a context of creating and maintaining community" (6).

All advisers want students to succeed academically and socially and to be satisfied with their campus experiences in and out of the classroom. Astin (1993) maintains that it is not the number of hours teaching in class or advising students but the quality of the contact that is most critical. Love and Maxam cite Hunter and White (2004) who state that "advising is perhaps the only structured campus endeavor that can guarantee students sustained interaction with a caring and concerned adult who can help them shape such an experience" (Love and Maxam 2011, 413). You should review your level of involvement with the student organization and its members in this context. You should examine the quality of your involvement in terms of meeting the needs and expectations of the students in the organization. You can perform this review shortly after the election of officers as expectations are identified for officers, through informal review sessions during the course of the year, or as part of a formal evaluation of the organization. Regardless of when the review is scheduled, discussions between you and the organization's president should cover the quality of the relationship between you, the executive board, and the members.

Assisting in the Organization's Success

A major component of your function as an adviser will be to help the organization stay healthy and succeed. Success will look very different depending on the organization's structure and purpose, whether it is departmentally affiliated, how many years it has operated, or even how experienced and motivated the student leaders are.

Organizational Purpose, Mission, and Values

Any seasoned student activities professional can share stories about the numerous times students would walk into the office stating that they have the greatest idea for a new organization and if it could just get the appropriate funding it would change the world. When that professional asked the students the mission of this new organization the bewildered look would enter their eyes. Mission? Why do I need a mission?

As the adviser, you have the ability and perhaps the responsibility of ensuring that the student organization can clearly articulate its purpose and values and that there is consistency with the passage of time. There are a few methods to help with this. The first is to ask. During the organization's first meetings of the year, have the executive board ask the general members why they joined, what they believe the organization values, and why the organization exists. Comparing this feedback to the goals set by the organization will give you a good idea if the purpose is aligned with its values (demonstrated by how the students want to spend their time and resources).

Reviewing and revising a constitution is another excellent way to determine if both mission and values are still relevant and purposeful for the campus community. The constitution is the most important organizational document. It gives the organization and membership purpose, direction, and guidance. The document is not intended to be static; rather it should be reviewed periodically so that it fits the needs of the contemporary student group. The language should be clear and concise, leaving little to interpretation. Depending on the complexity of the student organization, the constitution may be only one page in length. More complex organizations have fifteen- to twenty-page constitutions. Whether an organization is new and in the process of creating a constitution, established and undertaking a periodic review of its constitution, or established and reviewing the constitution for the first time in twenty years, the organization's constitution must include enough components to serve as a "rulebook."

It is standard practice for institutions, usually through their student activities offices, to maintain the most recent constitution for each organization registered with the campus. Most likely there are constitution guidelines which will outline all the elements required by the campus. The parts of the guidelines used at the University of Florida are shown in Exhibit 5.16. This could include nondiscrimination language and an agreement to adhere to campus policies. If the organization is the custodian of a foundation account, scholarship, or fellowship funds, there should be information about how funds will be distributed if the organization is dissolved. Also, the constitution should indicate what positions compose the executive board, how those officers are elected or appointed, and what authority the organization grants to the adviser.

EXHIBIT 5.16

Elements of a Constitution

ARTICLE I. NAME OF ORGANIZATION

The name of the organization should be unique from any other currently registered student organization and should reflect the nature and activities of the organization. In addition, any organization abbreviations or acronyms must be formally referenced in this article. Use of "University of Florida" or "UF" as part of the organization name is prohibited. At no time should the organization refer to itself as a part of UF. If the organization is affiliated with a local or national organization, that information must be stated in this article of the constitution.

Example: The name of this organization is Blue Leaders. This organization will utilize the acronym BLDS in all publicity materials and correspondence. Blue Leaders is affiliated with [affiliate organization (if applicable)] operating in [city, state]. The website of [affiliate organization] is [www.affiliate organization].

(continued)

EXHIBIT 5.16 (*continued*)

ARTICLE II. PURPOSE STATEMENT

The purpose of the organization must be clearly stated and must be unique from all other currently registered student organizations.

> *Example 1: Blue Leaders is established for the purpose of developing leadership skills and to encourage UF students to participate in community service projects such as voter registration.*

ARTICLE III. COMPLIANCE STATEMENT

Upon approval by the Department of Student Activities and Involvement, [*name of organization*] shall be a registered student organization at the University of Florida. [*Name of organization*] shall comply with all local, state, and federal laws, as well as all University of Florida regulations, policies, and procedures. Such compliance includes but is not limited to the University's regulations related to Nondiscrimination, Sexual Harassment (including sexual misconduct, dating violence, domestic violence, and stalking), Hazing, Commercial Activity, and Student Leader Eligibility.

ARTICLE IV. UNIVERSITY REGULATIONS

Section A. Nondiscrimination: [*Name of organization*] agrees that it will not discriminate on the basis of race, creed, color, religion, age, disability, sex, sexual orientation, gender identity and expression, marital status, national origin, political opinions or affiliations, genetic information, and veteran status as protected under the Vietnam Era Veterans' Readjustment Assistance Act.

Section B. Sexual Harassment: [*Name of organization*] agrees that it will not engage in any activity that is unwelcome conduct of sexual nature that creates a hostile environment.

Section C. Hazing: [*Name of organization*] agrees that it will not initiate, support, or encourage any events or situations that recklessly, by design, or intentionally endanger the mental or physical health or safety of a student for any purpose including but not limited to initiation or admission into or affiliation with any student group or organization.

Section D. Responsibility to Report: If this organization becomes aware of any such conduct described in this article, [*Name of organization*] will report it immediately to Student Activities and Involvement, the Director of Student Conduct and Conflict Resolution, or the University's Title IX Coordinator.

ARTICLE V. MEMBERSHIP

Additional stipulations regarding active membership (e.g., GPA requirements, attendance requirements, etc.) may be added.

Membership in this organization is open to all enrolled students at the University of Florida. Nonenrolled students, spouses, faculty, and staff may be associate members; however, they may not vote or hold office. All members and associate members are free to leave and disassociate without fear of retribution, retaliation, or harassment.

ARTICLE VI. OFFICERS

Registered student organizations are required to have a minimum of a President and Treasurer as elected officers. This article must contain the following information: titles of elected organization officers; titles of appointed organization officers (including appointment process—e.g., appointed by whom?); term of office; the general duties of each officer; and the procedures for handling vacancies (e.g., resignations, officer ineligibility, impeachments, or similar occurrences).

Example:

Section A: The elected officers of Blue Leaders shall be President, Vice President, and Treasurer.

Part 1: The President shall preside at all meetings of the organization and shall coordinate the work of the officers and committees.

Part 2: The Vice President shall serve as an aide to the President and shall perform the duties of the President in her or his absence or inability to serve.

Part 3: The Treasurer shall receive all monies of Blue Leaders; shall keep an accurate record of receipts and expenditures; shall pay out local funds in accordance with the approved budget as authorized by the organization.

Section B: The appointed officer of Blue Leaders shall be Secretary.

Part 1: The Secretary shall be appointed by the Vice President.

Part 2: The Secretary shall record the minutes of all meetings of Blue Leaders and shall perform other duties as may be delegated.

Section C: Officers shall assume their official duties at the close of the last general meeting of the academic year and shall serve for a term of one academic year and/or until their successors are elected/appointed.

Section D: Any officer of Blue Leaders may be removed from office through the following process:

Part 1: A written request by at least three voting members of the organization shall be submitted to either the President, Vice President, or Treasurer. Written notification shall be sent to the officer in question asking that officer to be present at the next meeting and prepared to respond to the removal request.

Part 2: A two-thirds majority vote of members present is necessary to remove the officer.

Part 3: In the event of the removal of an officer, a special provision may be granted to the remaining officers to appoint an interim replacement until an election may be held.

(continued)

◦ **EXHIBIT 5.16 (*continued*)**

ARTICLE VII. ELECTIONS

This article must contain the following information: the month of elections; officer eligibility; the nomination process; balloting procedures; election rules and procedures (including required margin of victory); and runoff procedures in the event of a tie.

> *Example: Nominations for all officers will take place annually from the members starting in January. Any member may nominate any other voting member, including himself or herself. Nominations may also be made during the election meeting prior to closing of nominations. Voting will occur by secret ballot and a simple majority vote is required to elect an officer. If there are more than two candidates running and no candidate receives a majority vote, there shall be a runoff vote between the top two vote recipients at the next general meeting. No person shall be eligible to serve more than two consecutive terms in the same office. Elections should take place in late March to early April.*

ARTICLE VIII. STUDENT ORGANIZATION ADVISER

Each registered student organization must have an adviser. The adviser shall serve as a resource person and provide advisory support for the officers and members of the organization. The adviser must be a faculty member or full-time salaried employee at UF. This article must include: the selection method; term; duties and responsibilities; and process of replacement for faculty advisers.

> *Example: The adviser shall serve as a resource person and provide advisory support for the officers and members of the organization. The adviser should attend executive and general meetings; however, the faculty adviser may not vote in any Blue Leaders matters. The adviser shall be nominated by the officers and confirmed by a majority vote of the members. The adviser will serve a term of one (1) academic year. In the event that the adviser is unable to continue in the position, officers may nominate a replacement at any time, to be confirmed by a majority vote of the members.*

ARTICLE IX. FINANCE

This article must include information about how the organization will be funded. If an organization requires membership dues, the maximum dollar amount and/or other financial obligations of members, as well as when payment is due, must be clearly stated in this article. If an organization does not require membership fees or other financial obligations, a statement to that effect should be included in this article.

> *Example 1: Blue Leaders will be funded through the collection of annual membership dues in the amount of $100 to be paid during the month of September. This fee covers the cost of T-shirts, travel to leadership conferences, and other operational expenses of the organization.*

ARTICLE X. DISSOLUTION OF ORGANIZATION

Requirements and procedures for the dissolution of the student organization must be stated in this article. Should any organization assets and/or debts exist, appropriate means for disposing of these assets and/or debts must be specified clearly and unequivocally. A specific charity must be designated as the recipient of any remaining assets at the dissolution of the organization.

Example: In the event this organization dissolves, all monies left in the treasury, after outstanding debts and claims have been paid, shall be donated to [Name of charitable organization].

ARTICLE XI: AMENDMENTS TO CONSTITUTION

All constitutions must conclude with this article. The article must include: the process for amending the organization's constitution; and the necessary vote to approve the change(s). All amended constitutions must immediately be submitted directly to the Department of Student Activities and Involvement for review and approval.

Example: Amendments to this constitution may be made at any regular meeting of Blue Leaders provided notice of the proposed amendment was given one week prior to a vote. Amendments require a two-thirds vote of the voting members in attendance at the meeting.

It is in the organization's best interest to periodically review the constitution. We recommend a constitutional committee, charged by the president, which should make any appropriate revisions and present those revisions to the general membership for approval and adoption. Each time the constitution is updated a copy should be sent to the student activities office as part of the organization's file. As adviser, you should have a copy of the constitution and review it at least annually to stay informed as to its contents.

Organizational Structure

Similar to how a student organization should periodically review its purpose, mission, and values, it should also review its structure. Occasionally the student leaders of the organization are too involved in its day-to-day responsibilities and operations to step back to determine whether the structure is still relevant. Therefore, the adviser can function as the organizational development specialist who periodically facilitates a review of the executive board positions, significance of standing committees, reporting structure, and gaps in assignments. It may be pertinent for the organization to do this every few years. Here are a few questions to ask:

1. Does the organization's mission align with how it allocates resources?

2. What are the responsibilities of the officers?

3. What are the trends on campus of which the organization needs to be aware?

4. Does it seem like there are goals that conflict with one another?

5. Are there expectations from the community that the organization is not prepared to meet but would like to?

6. Is the organization being efficient in delegating responsibility or does one officer carry an unfair burden?

7. How does the organization maintain its health in the future?

We discussed position descriptions previously in this chapter and offered a few examples of the most common student leader positions. Position descriptions can help evaluate whether responsibilities are being assigned appropriately. There are times when some positions become obsolete and others need to be added. For example, twenty years ago few organizations had webmaster as a leadership position. Now this is common practice.

Organizations in Different Stages of Development

Those who have served as an adviser for a number of years, whether with one organization or multiple, would have been cognizant of stages of their development. Using Tuckman's popular model (1965) of forming, storming, norming, performing, and adjourning to describe stages that organizations will progress through, you can see that, as an adviser, you may need to adopt different roles and attend to different functions throughout the continuum. Student organizations will progress through these stages at their own pace and can occasionally move backwards. For example, even if an organization has been in the performing stage for a while, a major crisis within its leadership could place it in the storming phase again.

If you overlap the length of time an organization has been in existence then you can better plan for what it will need from you. New organizations, in the forming and norming stages, will need an adviser to serve as more of a supervisor. As discussed earlier in the chapter, using the knowledge and skills we discussed in the supervisory role, an adviser would be able to work with the organization on team building, goal setting, and performance planning. Organizations with a few years of experience on campus under their belt, those in the norming stage, may be in more in need of an adviser who is an educator. This is the time when an adviser can challenge students to make a difference and to make meaning of the organization's purpose and values. Advisers can encourage student leaders to perform at an even higher level while also infusing time for students to reflect on their experiences, thus more intentionally tying learning to the involvement experience. Those organizations which have become institutionalized in many ways, either through longevity or by having evolved into highly functioning groups with a purpose that uniquely benefits the institution, will often need an adviser to serve as a mentor. These organizations will probably have student leaders in the performing and adjourning stages who are looking for opportunities to make greater meaning of their involvement and to share with others what they have learned. As an adviser, you can guide these seasoned student leaders through the process of giving back and leaving their mark in a tangible way.

Motivating Students

Understanding what motivates students may be your single most desirable skill. If it isn't evident to you already, you will soon find in your work with students that some of them have what appears to be an innate desire to become involved, work hard, and make a difference in the organization. Conversely, some students do not seem to be ambitious at all or are incapable of completing any assignments. Understanding the range of motivating factors will enable you to help individual students take on responsibilities and become involved.

"Motives are sometimes defined as needs, wants, drives, or impulses within the individual. Motives are directed toward goals, which may be conscious or subconscious. . . . Goals are often called incentives by psychologists" (Hersey and Blanchard 1988, 19). As you would expect, different individuals will possess different motives for participating in an organization. Exhibit 5.17 describes an activity that you can work on with students to help them identify what motivates them; you can then begin to assist the students in preparing a plan to achieve these goals (or to acquire the motivating items).

EXHIBIT 5.17

Identifying Motives

Directions: Tape three sheets of newsprint to the wall with sufficient space between the sheets that a group of five or six participants can stand in front of each sheet. The sheets should be labeled with one of the following as a heading.

1. List the things that motivate you

2. List ways that you would like to be recognized

3. List items that de-motivate you

Allow the participants ten to fifteen minutes to create a list on their sheet. Rotate the groups of participants from one sheet to the next, allowing them time to add to each list. Discuss the following questions:

1. Which items involve money?

2. Which items can our organization control?

3. Which items can we individually control?

4. Does our organization practice any unmotivational actions? Do our members?

5. Which items should our organization or membership spend time on?

Student motivation can be divided into two major categories: extrinsic (recognition, money, and achievement) and intrinsic (desire, value, the experience, and approval). In the following sections, we look at the subcategories of motives.

Extrinsic Motives As just mentioned, three types of extrinsic motives for students are recognition, money, and achievement.

Recognition. In our experience, recognition is the subcategory advisers use most frequently to motivate students. There are many ways to recognize the good work of students. Recognition can be systematically implemented by the organization through providing time for members to thank people who stood out that week or giving out an award for going above and beyond at general body meetings. Organizations have used a variety of things to recognize a job well done, from certificates to T-shirts, an article in a newspaper, or a spotlight award on the website. When using recognition as a way to motivate students it is important to understand that no one item will be warmly received by all members. You must be sensitive to each student's desires to be recognized and their comfort level with being in the spotlight.

Money. To pay or not to pay students is a question advisers, administrators, and students have struggled with for years. The vast majority of student organizations do not have to consider money as a reward for student leadership. Honor clubs, departmental organizations, special-interest clubs, and the like generally have positions of leadership for which the duties and responsibilities are limited in scope when compared to campus student governments, residence hall associations, or fraternity and sorority chapters.

The issue of paying student leaders is divisive; many institutions take the philosophical position that students who serve in leadership positions do so as volunteers and should not be compensated. This line of thinking assumes that students can manage their responsibilities and duties, and that paying them removes the volunteer nature of their job. Other institutions recognize that because of the heavy responsibilities, time commitments, and pressures of these positions, student leaders do not have the time to hold a part-time job to augment their finances. In addition, the key leadership positions which are paid become more inclusive of students who cannot afford school without a part-time job. Paying the student is absolutely necessary for them to fulfill their duties. Magee (1994) states that "some schools have found it necessary and valuable to compensate student leaders for their time and efforts, whether that compensation is offered through academic credit or through a monetary stipend. However, when a volunteer receives a stipend, the rules of the game take on a new dimension. Justification for that stipend becomes necessary because most stipends are generated from student activities fees. Accountability and supervision of students receiving stipends become additional responsibilities for staff members" (30–31). Some of the leadership positions that are more likely to receive compensation are: student government officials, programming board presidents, resident assistants, and orientation leaders.

Mitchell (1993) surveyed advisers of residence hall associations and developed a list of perceived advantages and disadvantages of paying students for leadership positions within residence hall associations. The perceived advantages were as follows: (1) possible higher motivation and commitment to the position, (2) appropriate recognition of the time and energy students devote to the positions, (3) encouragement of students to participate who might not have because of financial constraints, (4) greater accountability of the student in a particular position, and (5) stability in leadership if competing compensated positions are readily available for talented students. The perceived disadvantages were the following: (1) the opinion that remuneration is contrary to the spirit of volunteerism,

(2) a narrowing of the roles between the student and adviser, (3) concerns about whether pay is a primary motivator for students instead of altruistic reasons, (4) problems in identifying resources to fund positions, and (5) issues about which roles would be compensated and possible inequities with unpaid roles.

If the association decides to compensate, it can take several possible forms:

- Reimburse the costs to attend and travel to conferences and professional development opportunities.

- Offer room and board stipends which can include covering all or part of the costs.

- Defer the costs of tuition during the time a student leader is in office or provide class credit for the leadership experience gained from the position.

- Provide a stipend to executive board members. In residence hall associations, the stipend can range from $100 to $1,500 per term. For student government officers the range can be from $100 per term to over $20,000 per year. Some campus programming boards provide executive officers $200 to $3,000 per year.

- Miscellaneous; campuses can provide special parking privileges or waive parking costs, cell phone reimbursement, and travel per diems.

The salary and stipend rewards given to students can be viewed as reinforcers that "strengthen behavior in the sense that rewarded behaviors are likely to recur" (Beck 1983, 171). Salary and stipend rewards can also be seen as incentives that lead to the anticipation of rewards. Whether the salary or stipend is considered a reinforcer or an incentive, you, the administrator, and the students must work together to understand the nature of the student leader's motive and subsequently, the need to provide a salary or stipend.

Achievement The need for achievement may be defined as a tendency "to overcome obstacles, to exercise power, to strive to do something difficult as well and as quickly as possible" (Murray 1938, 80–81). Students motivated by achievement are driven to take on increasing levels of responsibility and authority; they may be looking for additional power to be gained from a position; they exercise control and seek tasks that other students may not assume because of the difficulty of the tasks. When you recognize the achievement motivation in a student, you should work with the student leadership to assist in identifying positions of increasing responsibility, sense of autonomy, or authority. You must work closely with students motivated by achievement in order to avoid their advancing too quickly, losing motivation because of the attitudes of less driven students, becoming frustrated at the pace of a project, or failing to involve other students to achieve a task or project.

Career Advancement. One of the greatest assets of the existence of student organizations on college campuses is the plethora of skills and competencies students can develop and apply in a practical setting. Administrators have referred to student organizations as "learning laboratories" for good reason. Student organizations provide the training ground for students to link their organization experience and leadership to highly sought-after job skills like communication skills, working in teams, motivating others, managing conflict, and values-based decision making. And this training ground has a safety net because institutions are interested in seeing these students and their organizations succeed. Effective advisers can call on the campus career center staff to provide a workshop about how to appropriately represent on their résumés the skills students have developed through their organization experiences.

It is important to note that some students are only motivated by career advancement. These are the students who look for involvement opportunities in organizations so that they can have another line on their résumé. Advisers can challenge these students to think about depth of experience versus breadth of experience. Most employers want to hire students who have demonstrated a commitment and can articulate examples of the critical thinking that comes with complex situations. Students who look to pad their résumés only have surface experiences to draw on.

Intrinsic Motives Four types of intrinsic motives for students are desire, value, the experience, and approval.

Desire. As we would expect, students are interested in becoming involved in organizations and activities that will provide a desirable outcome; they do not look for organizations or activities that will lead to an aversive outcome. Students will consider a leadership position, a project, travel to a conference, or a presentation desirable if they understand it to be an outcome already known to be desirable. For example, students who had previously held the position might state that the position led to greater things or that travel to a conference helped them to grow and to develop their leadership skills. Similarly, if an outcome is already known to be aversive, students will be less likely to desire to attend or participate.

Value. The student who perceives a value in participating in an organization, chairing a committee, or attending a conference will be motivated to become involved. You and student leaders can determine the value of various involvements by surveying the membership. Members may, for example, determine that the values received from chairing a committee are visibility on campus, increased communication and organizational skills, a better understanding of the organization, and a leadership role in the organization.

The Experience. There are many students who are motivated simply by the experience. For example, student leaders in an outdoor recreation organization will vocalize that they want to share the outdoor experience with others so much that they are willing to put time and energy into providing that opportunity. For others, students perceive value in the experience in terms of skill development, which can be shared with others through their résumé.

Approval. Approval is a feeling that a student may perceive. Students may be motivated by earning a sense of approval from friends, family, or advisers. Approval may come in the form of a note, a pat on the back, public recognition, or a kind word on a job well done; you need to identify which students are motivated by approval and provide the appropriate recognition.

Case Vignettes

We provide the following vignettes to allow you to think about the different roles and functions you may have as an adviser.

What's in a Standard?

You advise a multicultural Greek letter organization whose president has just shared with you the results of their community standards review. It seems that the organization fell short on both scholarship and service. The organization's GPA has fallen from a 3.25 to a 2.9 over the last three semesters and the time spent on service projects has decreased by 25 percent. You know that the organization has planned socials with other organizations each week for the next six weeks to meet their goal of developing relationships with other chapters in their community. How do you approach the president about whether or not the chapter is living its values and the those of the Greek community? How do you help the organization get on track? What role(s) do you play in this situation?

To Restructure or Not to Restructure

You have served as the adviser to the Lesbian, Gay, Bisexual, Transgender Student Organization for fifteen years. Over the course of the last three years you have seen increasingly more debate among the students over the purpose of the organization. Historically the organization has worked diligently to educate students about the LGBT community and serve as a safe place. Strategically it did not involve itself in politics nor did it do much to "rock the boat." There is a vocal group within the organization that is calling for more advocacy, greater involvement in social justice issues, and partnering with political action centers. The president is frustrated as she believes this demonstrates a conflict with the organization's mission. As the adviser, how can you help the organization determine the appropriate course of action? Do they wait out the vocal minority? Do they adjust their mission? Do they restructure the organization to incorporate a more diverse purpose? Do they split into two organizations?

We Can All Be Mentors, Can't We?

You have been asked by one of your students to advise the Hispanic Pre-Law Society, a newly formed organization with its first ten founding members. You are excited about the mission the organization has developed, however when you attend their first goal-setting meeting the members are committed to developing a mentoring program for other Hispanic/Latinos interested in pursuing the law profession. What role should you play as this organization begins to define itself? Will you choose to share your concerns about starting a mentoring program too early? Why or why not?

Chapter 6

Providing Academic and Career Assistance

YOU WILL FIND that many students begin their college education confused and indecisive about choosing their major; they may be concerned about how their peers will view them and about finding their way around campus. Becoming involved in campus life is one of the best ways for students to deal with their concerns, and it is also the most important variable in determining student academic success (Astin 1993). The first step in providing academic and career guidance is to understand the crucial role that involvement plays in a student's success.

As an adviser, you become students' confidant, informal academic counselor, career counselor, and reference. Understanding the basic functions of career and educational guidance will prepare you to work more effectively with the organization's members. You do not need to become an expert at career services or academic counseling, nor should you attempt to replace the services of other campus offices. In many cases, however, you are the first institutional representative a student will approach with regard to career issues. Through your involvement with the student organization, you will develop relationships with students in which they feel comfortable seeking your advice about career and academic matters. You should develop a relationship with a colleague in the career services office. The career services staff will work with your organization's students as a group or individually and this connection is important for the students throughout their academic preparation.

In this chapter we provide information on career development that you can use in your work with students. The student's career development process includes developing an involvement log; completing an occupational analysis; understanding how values, ethics, and moral development influence the decisions made in their career development process; completing a transferable skills exercise; writing cover letters and a résumé; networking;

identifying job and non-job factors in choosing a career; interviewing; and completing a time management analysis. Our discussion of educational guidance includes selected academic issues and information on making proper referrals.

Career Development

Career development is a process. A student's career identity and the role that work will play in his or her life emerge gradually (Super 1980). Students will explore their values to clarify such career-related decisions as their choice of major, choice of career, work experience, and so on.

Students also must work within specific guidelines and requirements imposed by the institution as part of its registration process or placement services, and you need to be aware of these broad institutional policies. An institution may, for example, require that students declare majors upon matriculation or that students will be admitted to an academic department only on the condition that they have completed a certain number of credit hours. The aspects of career development that we discuss here can help you assist students as they encounter challenges during these turning points in their academic careers. (If you are an adviser who is not directly involved in academic advising, teaching classes, or another academic aspect of the institution, a student's selection of a college and subsequent major are issues that you should refer to the responsible campus agency.)

Involvement Log/Profile

Students benefit from beginning an involvement log/profile upon enrollment and maintaining it throughout their time on campus, as they become involved in numerous leadership positions and work opportunities, or receive honors and awards. By keeping track of these experiences as they occur, students will later be able to identify the key activities from the involvement log to use in the development of their résumé or for interviews. The involvement log/profile should be as complete as possible. Students also should begin to identify the supervisors, faculty, or student organization advisers they would want to have serve as references for job searches, internships, or scholarship applications. You can promote the use of an involvement log/profile and pass out copies to organization members. Exhibit 6.1 provides an example of an involvement log/profile. Also, some campuses have moved to managing organizations through databases, many of which have a feature that tracks the involvement of a student. The student has the ability to generate a personal involvement profile.

EXHIBIT 6.1

Involvement Log/Profile

Directions: Create an involvement log/profile by filling in the items that follow.

Full Name _____

Education: Include degree-major-minor, GPA, date, location.

Honor Societies (for example, Golden Key): Include activity, dates, leadership positions.

Residence Hall Involvement (for example, hall government): Include activity, dates, leadership positions.

Campuswide Groups (for example, summer orientation staff): Include activity, dates, leadership positions.

Greek Life (for example, Delta Delta Delta): Include activity, dates, leadership positions.

(continued)

EXHIBIT 6.1 (*continued*)

Spiritual Organizations (for example, Jewish Student Organization): Include activity, dates, leadership positions.

Service Organizations (for example, Habitat for Humanity): Include activity, dates, leadership positions.

Recreational Sports (for example, intramural football): Include activity, dates, leadership positions.

Departmental and Professional Organizations (for example, Geology Club): Include activity, dates, leadership positions.

Conferences and Workshops Attended (for example, Graduate Student and Faculty Forum): Include activity, dates, leadership positions.

Presentations and Publications: Include activity, dates, locations, publishers.

Other Activities: Include activity, dates, leadership positions.

On-Campus, Off-Campus Employment: Include position or organization, description, any promotions, dates.

Awards, Scholarships, Special Recognition: Include name and basis for award.

References: Include name, position, address, phone, e-mail address.

Occupational Analysis

For students to confirm their choice of academic major, work experience, or career, it is crucial that they find out enough information about the career or occupation to know whether it matches their skills, aspirations, and interests. Performing an occupational analysis is a simple approach to identifying the information and skills necessary for that specific career or occupation. You should encourage students to use the campus placement office and that office's various online resources to access information on various companies and occupations. Exhibit 6.2 illustrates an occupational analysis form.

EXHIBIT 6.2

Occupational Analysis

You will find much of the information necessary to complete this occupational analysis in the campus placement center's on-line resources or library. Please make comments on as many of these items as possible.

Position, title, occupation, or career field:

Types of companies and organizations that would employ such occupations:

Opportunities for advancement in such a company:

Advantages in the position or occupation:

Disadvantages in the position or occupation:

Training programs available:

Salary range:

Geographical mobility—any restrictions:

Sources of challenge and support for this position or occupation:

Status of influence or position:

Scope of responsibilities in the position or occupation:

Problem-solving responsibility in the position or occupation:

Competition for positions:

Stress of work environment:

Educational background or experience needed:

(*continued*)

EXHIBIT 6.2 (continued)

Physical abilities needed:

Merit rewards for results:

Source: Adapted with permission from Dunkel, Bray, and Wofford 1989.

Values, Ethics, and Moral Development

You can provide information that augments students' ability to make academic and career decisions by helping them develop an understanding of values, ethics, and moral development. In the following sections, we provide relatively simple definitions of these concepts as well as several models that can be applied to situations you might encounter with student organizations. The literature on values, ethics, and moral development is extensive; we encourage you to explore these writings for more complex approaches to these vitally important topics.

Values According to the *Merriam-Webster Dictionary* (2013) a value is "something (as a principle or ideal) intrinsically valuable or desirable." One's values determine the worth that is placed on things. "Our values even influence the selection and formulation of the facts. There are no totally value-free observations. People often agree on the facts and still disagree about the facts' meaning, because people use different values to evaluate them" (Brown 1990, 36).

Following are two examples illustrating how differences in values among members can be quite dramatic even when there is agreement on a basic concept. The situations described would provide excellent opportunities for organization members to discuss differences in values.

A group of student organization members who will be driving to a conference agree that they will need to rent two vans. Some students want fifteen-passenger vans with a monitor to play movies because they believe there should be additional space for comfort and the opportunity to watch movies for entertainment. Other students disagree: they want to settle on two seven-passenger vans with standard interiors because they believe that spending money on larger vans with enhanced entertainment systems is a waste of money.

• • •

All the organization's members agree that an end-of-the-year banquet is a good idea. Some members want to have the meal on campus, using the institution's dining service. Others would like to go to a local restaurant buffet and use a private room, and still other members would like to go to the local conference center and hotel, rent a dining room, and have a sit-down catered meal.

"Whether the values are taught formally in the curriculum or not, the attitude, conduct, and belief of students have always been influenced by their colleges. The specific organization of knowledge, . . . the manner in which faculty relate to the students, the role accorded to out-of-class experiences, . . . all reveal certain values of the college, and their expectations for values development in students" (Sandeen 1985, 2). As an adviser, you have an opportunity to assist students as they make difficult, value-laden decisions for themselves and their organizations.

Ethics Ethics is "the discipline dealing with good and evil and with moral duty and obligation" (*Merriam-Webster Dictionary* 2013). Brown (1990) asserts that "ethics assumes that people have the freedom and power to respond—that is, the freedom and power to consider different options, to analyze the options' strengths and weaknesses, and to choose one option over the others based on its merits" (16). Guiding students' decisions are the right and wrong or good and bad actions that are the consequences of those decisions.

Karen Kitchener (1985) provides an excellent model for ethical decision making. She has adapted five principles that are relevant in dealing with the behavior of students. The first principle, respecting autonomy, includes the right of individuals to decide how to live their lives as long as their actions do not interfere with the welfare of others. The second principle is doing no harm. (Harm is further defined as either psychological or physical.) This principle encourages organizations to examine their policies and practices to ensure there is no long-term potential for doing harm. The third principle, benefiting others, includes the assertion that one should make decisions that have the potential for a positive effect on others. The fourth principle is being just, which incorporates the need for people to be fair and to treat others as they would like to be treated. The final principle is being faithful, which involves issues of loyalty, truthfulness, promise keeping, and respect.

These five principles can serve as a basis for student discussion in dealing with individual or organizational decisions. Similarly, using the following "ethics check" questions can sharpen the decision-making process and ensure that the organization is adhering to the five ethical principles.

Blanchard and Peale (1988) provide questions to help examine ethical decisions. The first question an individual or organization must ask is, Is the proposed action or decision legal? This includes the issue of whether or not the decision will violate civil law, the university code of conduct, or university policies. The second question is, Is the decision balanced? Balance means that the decision must be fair to all concerned in the short and long term and should promote a winning relationship. The third question is, How will the decision make me feel about myself? The decision should make one feel proud; one would feel good if it were released to the media and good if one's family knew about it.

These three straightforward questions allow students to understand the ramifications of their individual and organizational decisions more clearly. Exhibit 6.3 provides a progressive case study on ethical decision making.

EXHIBIT 6.3

Ethics Case Study

Directions: You can use this progressive case study yourself or with students. Pass out the initial case to the participants and allow them time to answer the question at the end. When they have completed the question, take ten to fifteen minutes to discuss their answers. Pass out the first update and discuss; continue with the second, third, and fourth updates in the same way.

Initial Case

You are a senior and sorority president at Southern Gulf University. The football team beat one of its major rivals last night and there were numerous parties following the game. A nineteen-year-old member of your sorority attended one of the parties. On Saturday afternoon, the day following the game, the nineteen-year-old files a report with the University Police Department claiming she was raped at the previous night's party.

The student stated that she drank a great deal and went looking for a bathroom. A young man took her to a bathroom, where she was grabbed by a second man and subsequently sexually assaulted by both. Because the light was out she could not recognize the men.

The next morning, her roommate convinced her to go to the police. The investigators found evidence of the party in a residence hall, and the hall director gave full support. The police identified one suspect, Wayne, who was discovered unconscious in the bathroom. Wayne has a reputation for being a ladies' man and enjoying parties.

Because the lights were out at the time of the assault, the student could not identify Wayne, and no arrests were made.

Three years before this case, you lived in a coeducational residence hall with Wayne. Wayne came back to you after the recent incident and told you that he could not remember anything from the evening. He stated that he didn't think he assaulted the woman, but he was so drunk he was not sure. He was certainly not going to share that information with the police.

What do you do with the information Wayne has provided to you?

Update One

It is one year later. Wayne is applying to law school and has asked you to be a character reference for him. What do you tell him?

(continued)

EXHIBIT 6.3 (*continued*)

Update Two

It is ten years later. Wayne is interviewing for a faculty position at the university where you work. You personally know the selection committee chair. Do you contact the chair? If so, what do you say?

Update Three

It is five years later. You are now the dean of students. Wayne is up for tenure, yet there is a rumor that he dates students. An assistant dean has made you aware of the rumors. What do you do at this point?

Update Four

It is three years later. Your daughter now attends the university; one day she comes home and tells you that she has met a wonderful man named Wayne who is an assistant professor at the university. Now what do you do?

Morals Morals are "of or relating to principles of right or wrong in behavior" (*Merriam-Webster Dictionary* 2013). We have found three models of moral development to be particularly useful to advisers; we will briefly describe each.

The first is Rest's Model (1983), which identifies four distinct activities that an individual must perform in order to engage in moral behavior. They may be summarized as (1) interpreting the situation, (2) deciding what is morally right, (3) choosing between moral values and other values, and (4) implementing a plan of action. This model provides a simple, understandable approach that students can apply to their individual and organizational decisions. Differences of opinion may emerge among the students as to what is morally right or even regarding their interpretation of a given situation. Facilitated discussion of these differences will benefit everyone.

The second model is Carol Gilligan's Theory of Moral Judgment (1982). According to Beabout and Wenneman (1994), Gilligan believes that Kohlberg's approach places "too much emphasis on moral rules, and not enough accent on relationships. . . . She claimed that Kohlberg's method of evaluating moral development emphasized rules and was therefore biased against females" (39–40). Gilligan believes that the moral development of women is different from that of men. In her view, women focus on relationships, which includes caring and sensitivity, whereas men focus on judging, which includes rules, confrontation, and conflict resolution.

The third model is Kohlberg's Six Stages of Moral Development (1984). In this model, stages of moral development describe what motivates individuals to make decisions about right and wrong action.

1. *Fear of punishment.* The person is motivated to obey not because he or she agrees with the rules but simply to avoid punishment.

2. *Seeking rewards.* The person is motivated to act if there is something to gain.

3. *Seeking approval.* Friendship and mutual understanding of one another's feelings, needs, and wants lead to cooperation.

4. *Obeying rules of societal order.* People follow the law and do their jobs knowing that others are doing the same.

5. *Concern with individual rights and social contracts.* Laws are in place and ensure basic rights; each person has a say in the decision-making process.

6. *Concern with consistent, comprehensive, and ethical principles.* No person deviates from cooperation because doing so would give some members an advantage at the expense of others.

Exhibit 6.4 is a brief case study to assist students and advisers with questions of moral development.

EXHIBIT 6.4
Moral Development Case Study

Directions: You can work on this case study yourself or with students. Pass out the case study and allow participants time to read and individually answer the questions. Facilitate a group discussion of the responses.

Case Study

You are the adviser to the rugby club at Maple College. You have served as adviser for the past three years. The rugby club has been at Maple College for over twenty-five years and has a winning reputation.

Mark is the rugby club president. He is a sophomore majoring in journalism. At the beginning of the fall term, Mark is aggressive in his recruiting of new members, and once he recruits them, he wants to initiate them with the traditional night of heavy drinking and activities.

Paul is a senior and has been a member for the past three years. At the beginning of his fourth year, he has the idea that new members ought to participate in building a home for Habitat for Humanity.

Mike is a graduate student and has been a member for two years. As an undergraduate he had been a member of the rugby club at a large university. Mike states that when he was at the other institution, his rugby club was on probation for two years because of hazing and serving minors at alcohol functions. He does not want that to happen to the Maple College rugby club and presses the membership to become involved as security escorts at night as part of a program offered by the college police.

1. At what Kohlberg stages are Mark, Paul, and Mike? Why?

2. What will likely occur with the club if Mark has his way? If Paul has his way?

3. What is the role of the rugby club adviser in this situation?

4. Who can the rugby club adviser go to for assistance with this situation?

5. How could Rest's Model be applied to this situation?

Transferable Skills

You have an opportunity to assist students in identifying the skills they have acquired and refined through their involvement in organizational meetings, writing reports, traveling to conferences, participating in competitions, presenting programs, coordinating events, facilitating speakers, and so forth. These skills and traits should be reflected in résumés and interviews, and they may be transferable to the students' daily practice or in their career position following graduation (Dunkel, Bray, and Wofford 1989). As an adviser, an excellent discussion with your students is how to word transferable skills on their résumé or in response to the interview questions. It is also an opportunity to bring in a career services office staff member to present to the students.

Sidney Fine (1985) developed a widely accepted definition and taxonomy of career skills. His first category includes adaptive skills, or self-management skills. We acquire these skills in our early years from family, peers, and school; they relate to environments, and particularly to the requirements or demands for social conformity and continuity. An example of this might be managing oneself in one's relation to authority or punctuality.

The second category is functional skills, which are instrumental or transferable skills. We acquire these skills either as natural-born talents, through experience or education, or through specific educational, vocational, or avocational training. Transferable or instrumental skills are related to people, data, and things in a generalizable or transferable fashion (for example, from one field, profession, occupation, or job to another). Examples of this type of skill are operating machinery and compiling or analyzing data.

The third category is specific or work-content skills, which relate to particular job conditions or vocabulary skills. These skills are acquired through reading, apprenticeship, technical training, institutes, or school, and are often acquired on the job. These skills relate to performing a job in a particular field, profession, or occupation, according to the specifications and conditions of a particular employer.

Exhibit 6.5 is an exercise to help students identify their transferable skills.

EXHIBIT 6.5

Transferable Skills Exercise

Directions: This exercise can be completed by one student or a group of students working individually. Students should be given ample time to review the following list of skills and traits. The list represents adaptive, functional, and work-content skills. Remind students to check only those skills they have used in their position. At the end of the exercise is a discussion on how to apply the findings.

Communication

_____ negotiating   _____ foreign language

_____ mediating   _____ reading

_____ public speaking   _____ writing minutes

_____ debating   _____ sign language

_____ interviewing   _____ braille

_____ arbitrating   _____ active listening

_____ creative writing   _____ briefing

_____ business writing   _____ technical writing

_____ editing   _____ telephoning

_____ speech writing   _____ translating

_____ proofreading   _____ summarizing

_____ persuading

_____ spelling

_____ lecturing

_____ influencing

_____ informing

Physical

_____ motor coordination

_____ strength

_____ speed

_____ endurance

_____ agility

_____ competitiveness

Self-Management

_____ self-directing

_____ patient

_____ time management

_____ prioritizing tasks

_____ dependable

_____ calm

_____ mature

_____ assertive

_____ risk taking

_____ vision

_____ goal setting

_____ ambitious

_____ realistic

_____ follow-through

_____ stress management

_____ self-disciplined

_____ handle variety of tasks

_____ traveling

_____ modeling

Researching and Data Collection

_____ record keeping

_____ memory for detail

_____ organizing data

_____ retrieving data

_____ testing

_____ investigation

_____ scientific writing

_____ technical reading

_____ observing

_____ note taking

_____ analyzing quantitative data

_____ developing a budget

_____ information processing

_____ researching data

(continued)

EXHIBIT 6.5 (*continued*)

Mathematical and Scientific

_____ lab techniques	_____ use of lab equipment
_____ inventing	_____ accuracy
_____ accounting	_____ finance
_____ administer a budget	_____ advanced math abilities
_____ detailed instructions	_____ field work abilities
_____ memorization	_____ conceptual thinking
_____ pragmatic	_____ systematic

Creative

_____ imaginative	_____ composing
_____ illustrating	_____ musical ability
_____ interior decorating	_____ singing
_____ drawing	_____ performing
_____ painting	_____ dance
_____ sketching	_____ showmanship
_____ landscaping	_____ creative visual displays
_____ photography	_____ culinary talent
_____ pantomime	_____ computer freehand

Leadership

_____ directing	_____ team building
_____ group facilitating	_____ motivating
_____ supervising	_____ teaching
_____ coaching	_____ mentoring
_____ policymaking	_____ chairing committees
_____ parliamentary procedure	_____ organizing
_____ delegating	_____ promoting
_____ planning	_____ self-confidence

_____ decision making   _____ programming

_____ business approach   _____ developing procedures

Logic

_____ troubleshooting   _____ problem solving

_____ rational thinking   _____ diagnosing

_____ forecasting   _____ problem identification

_____ quick thinking   _____ cause-effect relationships

_____ legal concepts   _____ decision making

Programming

_____ hosting conferences   _____ energetic

_____ productive   _____ educational

_____ social   _____ resourceful

_____ enterprising   _____ solicitations

_____ publicity   _____ designing projects

_____ financial planning   _____ assessment

_____ evaluation   _____ reports

_____ foresight   _____ referrals

Interpersonal Relationships

_____ advising   _____ patience

_____ understanding   _____ liaison

_____ sensitivity   _____ warmth

_____ goal clarification   _____ empathetic

_____ training   _____ serving others

_____ positive attitude   _____ crisis intervention

_____ counseling   _____ recruiting talent

_____ rapport   _____ trust

_____ personable   _____ poised

_____ networking   _____ enthusiasm

_____ personal growth   _____ helpful

(continued)

EXHIBIT 6.5 (*continued*)

Review the skills and traits you have checked. Identify the twenty most applicable to your current position and record them below:

1.   11.

2.   12.

3.   13.

4.   14.

5.   15.

6.   16.

7.   17.

8.   18.

9.   19.

10.   20.

Review Sidney Fine's definition of skills. Identify which of your twenty are adaptive, functional, or work-content skills. List each of your twenty skills or traits under the appropriate column below:

Adaptive   **Functional**   **Specific or Work Content**

These twenty skills or traits will be most valuable to you in composing your résumé (mention the skills or traits in the description of your experiences), preparing for interviews (identify key skills or traits that were gained or enhanced through involvement in a specific position or organization), and in recruiting students to leadership positions (when seeking applications, identify the skills and traits gained or enhanced by involvement in the leadership position). You should review this list on an annual basis; make changes and revisions as you remain in your position or when you change positions.

Source: Adapted from Dunkel, Bray, and Wofford 1989.

Cover Letters and Résumés

In the next two sections we discuss the cover letter and the résumé, and provide tips for students to help them in preparing each of these documents. Hiring agents are increasingly moving to online applications and materials submission. Your files should be saved in PDF format as "Last Name—Résumé" or something similar as it will be reviewed by company personnel.

Cover Letter The cover letter is a student's response to a notice about a particular job or position, and it serves to introduce the student to the employer. The letter should highlight aspects of the student's work, education, or experience but not duplicate his or her résumé. The following tips will assist students in the preparation of a cover letter, and Exhibit 6.6 provides a sample.

- Always include a cover letter when sending a résumé.

- Each cover letter should be written for a particular position. Never send a form letter to replace a cover letter. Take the time to tailor an individual letter to each employer.

- Do not begin each line or paragraph with "I."

- Address the cover letter to an individual, preferably the individual who will make the hiring decisions. Students may have to do some research to identify that person.

- Start the cover letter with information on how you learned of the vacancy and the title of the vacant position.

- Highlight information from your résumé that is relevant to the qualifications of the position.

- Highlight one or two achievements that indicate how you can meet the needs of the company to which the application is directed.

- Include any information that is not provided on the résumé, such as a change in telephone number during spring break.

- Keep the length of the cover letter to one page. Allow the résumé to provide the specific information on education, work experience, awards, and so forth.

- Sign the letter with black ink. If an employer wants to make additional copies, black ink reproduces much better than other colored inks.

- Print the cover letter on paper that is white, ivory, eggshell, gray, or some other conservative color. The paper should be of the same weight as the résumé (usually greater than twenty pounds) and should be of the same color.

EXHIBIT 6.6
Sample Cover Letter

Street Address

City, State, Zip

Date

Name of Contact Person, Title

Organization

Street address

City, State, Zip

Dear (Contact Person)

Opening Paragraph: Who and Why?

- Use a strong opening to attract the reader's interest.
- Name the job for which you are applying and how you learned about it.
- Mention the name of a person (if any) who referred you to the organization.
- Highlight your skills and experience, including education and graduation date.

Second Paragraph: Your Skills and Qualifications

- Acknowledge the skills required by the open position.
- Discuss the skills and strengths you bring to the job, being sure to connect them to needs of the employer.
- Consider briefly describing a related achievement or success story and discussing how it transfer to the job.

Third Paragraph: You and Company

- Comment on your knowledge of the company (their products, services, or special projects) and why you are interested in working for them.
- Briefly state how you think you would be a good fit for the company, emphasizing how you can help the company reach its goals.
- Show that you've researched the company, incorporating information such as their mission statement, training, and job description.

Closing Paragraph: Action Step

- Restate any important themes, creatively tying them together into a cohesive sales pitch.
- Refer to enclosed résumé.

- Assert yourself by telling the contact person that you will call on a designated date. Alternatively, state that you are available for a personal interview at your reader's convenience.

- Make it easy for the person to contact you: list your e-mail address, as well as your phone number and times you can be reached. Even if this information is on the résumé, list it here again, as you do not want make the employer search for a way to contact you.

Sincerely,

(sign your name)

Your Name Typed

Encl: Résumé of [your name]

Source: Adapted from Career Resource Center, University of Florida, 2013.

Résumé   Munschauer (1986, 26) states that the "uses of a résumé are many. It might be used to convince an employer to interview you, perhaps as part of a prescreening program. Sometimes it is used as a follow-up to an interview to summarize and highlight your qualifications. It might be tailored to complement a letter of application for a particular job, or it might be designed to appeal to employers in a broad field—sales, for example—and used as an attachment for a letter to sales managers." A résumé can provide information to an employer that will reveal the following four qualities (Munschauer 1986): "(1) Industriousness and ambition through activities, employment, and achievements, (2) Cooperative attitude through participation in activities, clubs, and sports, (3) Interest in the work and enthusiasm for the employer's product or service through a positive job objective or statement of career interest . . . , and (4) An orderly and businesslike mind through a crisp, neat format which reflects a businesslike mind. A poorly typed and sloppily reproduced résumé triggers a dislike" (26).

You should refer students to the campus placement center for consultation on the process of preparing a résumé. The following suggestions will also be of help; in addition, Exhibit 6.7 provides a sample résumé and Exhibit 6.8 provides a résumé checklist.

- Provide your formal name, address, telephone number, and e-mail address. You must be available at all times. If there is a point during the term when your availability is different, include that information in your cover letter.

- Identify a clear, job-specific professional objective.

EXHIBIT 6.7

Sample Résumé
John B. Smith

johnsmith@ufl.edu

123 Rock Road   246 Hurricane Street

Gainesville, FL 32608   Miami, FL 34567

352-345-9786   305-876-6754

OBJECTIVE

Seeking a full-time professional management position utilizing my managerial experience, organizational abilities, and interpersonal skills.

EDUCATION

Bachelor of Science in Business Administration Management   May 2013

University of Florida,   Gainesville, FL

Minor: Psychology

GPA: 3.57/4.00

EXPERIENCE

Assistant Manager, Pop's Deli   September 2012 to Present

Gainesville, FL

- Supervised serving staff of 10 and trained 3 new employees by creating new training handbook
- Increased sales by 10% by training staff in suggestive selling
- Coordinated budgets and the purchase of food, beverages, and supplies to insure proper inventory levels

Human Resources Intern,   June 2010 to August 2012

All-State Insurance Agency   Gainesville, FL

- Revised industry standard job descriptions to support extensive recruitment effort
- Assisted in the training of supervisory staff in the areas of disciplinary action, sexual harassment, and discrimination
- Developed a new employee relations program that included attendance awards and post-hire evaluations

LEADERSHIP

President, Kappa Sigma Fraternity, Inc.   April 2009 to May 2010
University of Florida

- Cooperated with 10 other executive board members to ensure proper procedures
- Allocated an annual budget of $25,000 to five committees for alumni and philanthropic events
- Increased membership by 10% by reaching out to incoming freshmen students

Senator, Student Government   June 2008 to May 2009
University of Florida

- Allotted funds for more than 100 student organizations and governed major issues and concerns of student body

AWARDS/AFFILIATIONS

Boys & Girls Club August 2010–Present

American Marketing Association August 2008–Present

Psi Chi, Psychology Association August 2009–Present

Presidential Scholarship Award May 2010

Florida Merit Scholarship Recipient June 2008

SKILLS

Computer: Microsoft Office, Adobe Photoshop, HTML, FTP

Language: Fluent in German

Source: Adapted from Career Resource Center, University of Florida, 2013.

EXHIBIT 6.8

Résumé Checklist

Use this before asking someone to critique your résumé for you.

- **Most Important Info First:** Everything on your résumé should be written with the most important information first. This is true with decisions such as which section should go first after the Objective and what information should come first within each entry.
- **Consistency:** Everything from dates to abbreviations to formatting should remain consistent throughout your résumé.

(continued)

EXHIBIT 6.8 (*continued*)

- **Relevant to Objective:** When you're trying to decide what to leave in and what to leave out, make certain that everything relates back to your Objective. Also, make sure that your descriptions highlight and accentuate the connection to your Objective.
- **No Pronouns**
- **Sentence Fragments:** Employers look for short, direct pieces of information. If it is too long or overly descriptive, people may just skip it.
- **Reverse Chronological Order:** Most recent first.
- **Past Tense:** Use action words to demonstrate the transferrable skills you can offer the employer.
- **Include Skills, Memberships, and the like.**
- **Meet the Employer's Needs** (academic, experience, leadership): Everything on your résumé should communicate to the reader that you know what the employer's needs are and that you have the experience, skills, leadership, and education to meet those needs.
- **Professional:** When people seek an entry-level position, they are generally trying to bridge that gap between student and professional. You can accomplish this by keeping out or changing the items which remind people you are a student (high school education/activities, listing dates by semester rather than month, listing many "interests").
- **PROOFREAD!**

Source: Adapted from Career Resource Center, University of Florida, 2013.

- Design your résumé to show the most important qualification first. Typically, this will be the education category. Include your grade point average in the education category if it has received recognition.

- Develop a leadership category to include student leadership positions and active memberships. Employers are interested in these experiences, because they indicate leadership, communication skills, organizational skills, and so on.

- Pay attention to how you highlight the headings. Boldface, underlining, capitalization, italics, and colons highlight words or headings. Do not combine several of these in the same heading, as that will overaccentuate that heading and look unprofessional.

- Try to keep the length of the résumé to one page if you have a bachelor's degree. Understand the standards of the field to which you are applying. Some career fields allow for a lengthier résumé, whereas others dictate clearly that the résumé should be one page, with black ink on white paper.

- Provide a list of at least three references when requested. The references should be individuals who have served as supervisors from your work experience, advisers from your organizational experience, and faculty from your major course work. Include the complete address, telephone numbers, fax numbers, and e-mail addresses of the references.

- Print the résumé on paper that is white, ivory, eggshell, gray, or some other conservative color. The weight of the paper should be at least twenty pounds and be the same color as the cover letter.

Networking

Networking is the process of making personal and professional contacts for the primary purpose of advancing one's career. These personal contacts can provide a student information about what it is like to work in a particular job. Professional contacts can assist the student in opening doors to discuss job opportunities with an appropriate person or can provide information on the best way to apply, interview, or possibly negotiate for a job. Through networking, students also can gain firsthand knowledge of potential job opportunities that might not be made public (George Mason University 2013).

Networking can also utilize social media and online resources. Using these resources is one of the best ways to identify jobs and internships. "Social media allows employers to target job candidates with a very specific set of skills, recruit passive job candidates who might not otherwise apply for positions, and is less expensive than other methods of recruiting job candidates" (George Mason University 2013, 31). There exist three commonly used online resources for employers and candidates.

LinkedIn (www.linkedin.com). "Invite friends, coworkers, and supervisors to join the student's network, receive recommendations from people students have worked with, and search the more than 100 million professionals already on the LinkedIn network. Find jobs using the jobs and employer directories" (George Mason University 2013, 31).

Facebook (www.facebook.com). "Use Facebook to build a network with classmates, alumni, friends, family, and coworkers. Highlight students' work experience and education on their profile. Be sure to keep the students' profile professional and tasteful. Facebook has networking applications like BeKnown, Branchout, and Glassdoor" (George Mason University 2013, 32).

Twitter (www.twitter.com). "Using Twitter, students can follow and have real-time communications with hiring managers and working professionals in their industry area. A few tips for using Twitter include: maintaining a professional profile, using Twitter add-on applications for job hunting, following career coaches, résumé writers, job industry experts, and government employment agencies to keep up with hiring trends, follow hashtags which tag individual tweets or conversations on specific subjects, and participate in chats sponsored by professional groups, career experts, or agencies" (George Mason University 2013, 32).

Exhibit 6.9 provides a list of possible personal and professional contacts for networking and Exhibit 6.10 provides a list of sample networking questions to ask a contact.

EXHIBIT 6.9

Networking List

It is important to begin developing a networking list early in your student career. Your list can include many people you have known even though you did not realize they had networking potential.

First, contact people you know well to discuss your résumé and experiences. As you become comfortable discussing these experiences, broaden your network by making an appointment to meet with an individual in a company, or by talking on the telephone with a person you met at a conference.

Friends:

Family	Relatives
Doctors	Neighbors
Dentists	Faculty
Adviser	Classmates
Organization members	Spiritual
Sports	Alumni

Business:

Political	Recruiters
Former employers	Owners
Colleagues	Trainers
Personnel directors	Contributors
Sales	Administrators
Insurance	Attorneys

EXHIBIT 6.10

Sample Networking Questions

Whether a planned or chance meeting, you should always have questions prepared to ask a potential contact. These are some examples:

- What led to your interest in your career field?
- What preparation did you have (i.e., classes, activities, experience, etc.) to begin your work?
- What skills, abilities, and personal qualities do you find most important in your work?
- How would you advise me to get started in building experience in this field?
- What's your perspective for the next few years in terms of job prospects in this field?
- What are typical career paths in this field?
- What academic major would you recommend as preparation for your field?
- I have built a target list of organizations in this field. Would you be willing to look at my list and give me any suggestions you might have?
- What kinds of projects do you work on?
- What kinds of backgrounds do people in this field have?
- Which academic courses best prepared you for your work?
- What types of experience, paid or unpaid, would you recommend as preparation for this type of work?
- What do you like most about your job?
- What do you see as disadvantages to working in your type of job?
- What are the most pressing needs and issues for your field?
- Would you change anything that you did to better prepare you for your work?

Source: Adapted from George Mason University, University Career Services, 2013.

Job and Non-Job Factors

Students inevitably will ask you questions about the location of a job, how much money they will make, or what kind of weather exists in a certain part of the country. All these questions pertain to what we can call job and non-job factors. It is important that students determine which values in their lives are of higher priority than others and which they might compromise in order to secure a specific job. For instance, if a student practices a specific religion and a job is offered in a part of the country where the closest house of worship is fifty miles away, is the student willing to compromise in order to work for that company? Exhibit 6.11 is an exercise to help students identify the job and non-job factors they will want to take into account when considering a specific company or job.

EXHIBIT 6.11

Job and Non-Job Factors

The job factors listed below are examples of what you might want to consider prior to selecting a job. Read through the list and then rank your five most important job factors.

Hours worked per week	Salary
Vacation time	Sick time
Travel	Type of supervisor
Work environment	Frequency of moves
Type of product	Training available
Opportunity for advancement	Type of coworkers
Opportunity for education	Flexibility of hours
Size of company	Technology availability and support
Supplies provided	Break facilities
Clientele served	ADA compliant
Dress policies	

Select your five most important:

1. _____

2. _____

3. _____

4. _____

5. _____

The non-job factors listed below are examples of what you might want to consider prior to selecting a job. Read through the list and then rank your five most important non-job factors.

Recreational opportunities	Climate
Schools and universities in area	Cost of living
Cultural events	Opportunities for partner
Local taxes and fees	Spiritual opportunities
Volunteer opportunities	Size of community
Proximity to family	Proximity to friends
Distance to work	Crime
Condition of roads	Shopping opportunities
Data, phone, and cable service	State taxes
Parking/costs	

Select your five most important:

1. _____

2. _____

3. _____

4. _____

5. _____

Interviewing

The student and the hiring authority get to know one another during an interview, which is far more than the typical informal conversation. The student needs to complete certain activities prior to, during, and following the interview; Exhibit 6.12 summarizes some of these activities. Becoming familiar with them will be valuable to you in your work with students; you may also want to arrange a program in which students conduct mock interviews.

EXHIBIT 6.12

Interviewing

The following are tips to help students have successful interviews.

Pre-Interview

- Start a file on the company that has the vacancy (include any correspondence, salary information, locations, and so on).
- Know your top two or three skills so that you can openly discuss them.
- Role-play the interview with friends, colleagues, or staff for practice.
- Know the interviewer's full name and write it down for quick reference.
- Avoid extremes in dress (check with the campus placement office for published material on what to wear during interviews).
- Bring paperwork to the interview (including extra copies of your résumé, application, portfolio, and so on)—in addition, have an electronic copy with you.
- Be prepared to ask one or two standard questions (for example, What are the opportunities for professional development?).
- Use a good-quality portfolio to bring materials to the interview, and have a nice pen.

(*continued*)

EXHIBIT 6.12 (*continued*)

- Arrive about ten minutes prior to the interview; stop by the restroom and look in the mirror to ensure that your hair, clothes, accessories, and so forth are in order.

Interview

- Follow the interviewer's lead as to where to sit.
- Offer your hand and use a firm grip.
- Walk with good, upright posture.
- Smile and practice good eye contact with the interviewer.
- Use a nice balance of nonverbal communication when answering questions.
- Use a good, upright sitting posture to appear businesslike but not too rigid.
- Sit with your legs uncrossed, if possible.
- Be concise in your answers but not too brief.
- Give the interviewer an opportunity to ask several questions.
- Use some levity, if appropriate.
- Be enthusiastic about the company, the position, and the interview.
- Don't be afraid of a few moments of silence when you are collecting your thoughts.
- Do not fill silences with "ah" and "um."
- Take care not to overtly drop names—of employees working for the company, former employees, or other individuals.
- Concentrate on your strong points when answering questions.
- Be prepared to answer skill-set questions about goals that you set this past year, what skills you developed through your involvement in a specific leadership position, or situations in which you have had to solve a problem and follow up on it in writing.
- Prepare for the conclusion of the interview.
- Let the interviewer take the lead in the closing.
- Be prepared for the interviewer's asking you if there are any other or points that should be shared.
- Exit as gracefully as you entered.

Post-Interview

- Send thank-you notes (handwritten or electronic as appropriate) immediately to the interviewer, support staff, and anyone else who assisted in the interview process.
- Call the appropriate person if other questions come up as a result of the interview.
- Send any additional information that might have been requested at the time of the interview.
- Follow up with any travel information or receipts that need to be submitted to the company.
- Analyze the interview to determine your strengths, areas that need improvement, and so forth.

Educational Assistance

We stated in the Preface that this book does not provide information directly related to academic advising. We have also pointed out, however, that students will be asking you any number of questions related to academic concerns. You may be well prepared to respond to academically related questions if you are a member of the faculty, perform academic advising functions as a responsibility, or work in a campus department that provides related services such as registration or admissions. If you are not in one of these departments, you will want to refer students with academic questions to the appropriate campus resource. Regardless of your position, knowledge of some academic issues will help you respond to basic student questions. Advisers who are prepared to respond with information or a proper referral will enhance their relationship with the members of the student organization. Making a commitment to understand the details of this aspect of the campus will be a small investment that leads to great benefits both personally and professionally. The following list itemizes some of these academic issues. Some advisers will have access to student grades. You will need to fully understand your role to student records as it applies to the Family Educational Rights and Protection Act (FERPA) of 1974 (Van Dusen 2004). FERPA is a federal law that protects the privacy of student education records. FERPA does allow an institution to disclose these records, among others, to school officials with legitimate educational interest. It is always a good practice to visit with your institution's attorney with questions regarding a student's educational record and your use of that record.

- Know critical academic dates: when students register for classes, the last day to add or drop, the last day to withdraw, when classes begin, when classes end, deadline to apply for graduation, last day to pay fees, and when midterms and finals are scheduled.

- For community college students, you needs to know the deadline to apply for admission to local universities.

- Understand the process for withdrawing from a course or term for medical, psychological, or other reasons.

- Identify the location of academic advisers or counselors on campus.

- Know when a student must declare a major and what minimum grade point average is required to enter a department, college, or degree program.

- Know the cost of tuition.

- Know where to refer students when they are having difficulty taking tests, taking notes, or studying for exams.

- Know key exam dates including the GRE, MCAT, and LSAT.

- Understand the application process and qualifications for admission to the graduate school.

- Know where to send students if they have a grievance or want to petition for a grade change.

- Understand the academic requirements for students to maintain an elected position in a student organization, such as carrying a full load of classes, maintaining a certain grade point average, being accepted into a degree-granting program, and so forth. Also, know where a student can petition for an exemption from the requirements.

- Know where to refer a student if he or she is having difficulty selecting a major (typically the campus academic advising center, the counseling center, or the career planning center) or wants to change a major.

A student's ability to manage an academic load and cocurricular involvement is determined by his or her time management skills. Inevitably, you will spend considerable time working individually with students as they struggle to manage their time. In some cases an adjustment to the student's daily routine is all that is necessary, whereas in other cases, dropping activities, reducing his or her workload, or limiting other involvements may be the only answer to alleviating scheduling problems. Exhibit 6.13 provides a time management analysis that you can use to assist students in identifying their activities and the amount of time involved.

EXHIBIT 6.13

Time Management Analysis

Directions: Have the student log all his or her activities for the course of one typical week on an Activity Log. The log should include time spent sleeping, getting ready in the morning, being in classes, going to and from classes, eating, time on their computer, watching television, and so on. All twenty-four hours of each day should be accounted for.

Following the student's completion of the log, meet with him or her to analyze the information in order to plan accordingly.

1. Analyze the present situation by asking the student to respond to the following questions:

    How are you presently using your time?

    What are your time-wasting activities?

    For which activities do you have control of the amount of time you spend?

2. Have the student establish priorities for a given week.

3. Have the student set goals for the amount of time for each activity.

4. Have the student schedule the week according to the priorities set.

(continued)

EXHIBIT 6.13 (*continued*)

5. Have the student experience the week and record any modification to the schedule.

6. Meet with the student to analyze the modification and develop another week's schedule.

Chapter 7

Representing Group and Institutional Interests

BY DEFINITION, STUDENT organizations function within institutions of higher education. These organizations exist within a framework designed for them by the policies and procedures adopted by the college or university. Some organizations are affiliated with national organizations. The framework for these groups will be informed by national standards. Policies are established by administrators or faculty, national organizations, or by the students themselves, either through their governmental organizations or their constitution and by-laws.

The leadership of student organizations changes almost every year: there is a new president, a new treasurer; new members join, former members and leaders drop out for various reasons. As a consequence, the new leaders and members may have a very limited sense of the history of the organization, and they may not know how to accomplish their objectives within the framework of the institution. In these situations, you play a key role, because as an adviser you are likely to have a better sense of the history of the organization and how the institution operates than any of the student leaders. Although there are always exceptions, it is possible that you will serve in your role for several years, especially those who are advisers as a result of their assignment in the university. Included in this group is the Greek adviser, the student union board adviser, the residence hall association adviser, and so on. You will thus provide a framework to your student leaders and organization members for such matters as how to accomplish administrative tasks on campus and what activities the organization can expect to participate in during the course of the academic year. In short, you serve as a bridge from one year to the next for the organization, providing organizational memory, reminding leaders about administrative procedures, keeping members apprised of campus policies, connecting students to campus resources, and serving as a point of contact for faculty and administrators in special situations.

In this chapter, we first briefly describe many of the common activities that student organizations will participate in as full members of the university community. Not all organizations will participate in all of these activities, but many organizations will participate in most of them. Second, we discuss a wide variety of policies and practices that influence how organizations function on campus. We provide suggestions about how you can work with the organization to navigate its way through administrative requirements. To be sure, every college is organized in a different way, but most colleges will have many of these policies and practices, and we think it is important that the adviser know about them and how to deal with them. (You would also be well served to visit with staff in the office of student activities for additional advice on policies unique to your campus.) At the end of the chapter you will find several case vignettes that deal with topics introduced in this chapter. We think it may be useful for you to read the cases and develop answers to the issues described in them.

Community Participation

Much has been written about college campuses as communities (Boyer 1987; Kuh 1991). This literature emphasizes how important it is for all members of an institution to share common goals and values, a sense of history, symbols, and so on (Kuh, Schuh, and Whitt 1991), and the lack of student community has been shown to have a negative effect on students (Astin 1993). Student organizations contribute significantly to the sense of community that is shared on campus, often directly shaping the environment for students, faculty, staff, and visitors. As members of the campus community, organizations will often be called on to fulfill certain obligations and to uphold a communal set of expectations.

Although student organizations can have a direct impact on the campus community, many organizations look outside the campus footprint in search of ways to make a positive impact on the local, regional, national, and international community. Usually pertaining to organizations with service as their mission, this focus will bring a unique set of challenges to an adviser, including legal issues discussed in chapter 9, but will also offer thought-provoking and potentially life-changing experiences.

New Student Recruitment and Orientation

Student organizations can play an important role in recruiting new students to the college. Members and leaders can be available on "prospective student days" to visit with prospective students and their parents. Student organizations can be a part of the recruitment process by developing displays, giving presentations to parents and students, handing out brochures, and providing general information about the campus. In some cases they will host breakfasts or luncheons, organize receptions, and provide valuable support to the office of student recruitment. Prospects want to know about the life of the campus and what is available for them outside the classroom. Extracurricular involvement has a salutary effect on students (Pascarella and Terenzini 1991), and new students can be encouraged to join various student organizations.

Student organizations can be essential for the institution's recruitment process for a number of reasons. The presence of student organizations demonstrates the institution's commitment to cocurricular activities. Also, student organizations reflect the breadth of the current interests and diversity of the student body.

Just as colleges and universities spend considerable resources and effort on the recruitment process, a student's orientation to campus is just as important. The old adage that you only have one chance to make a first impression represents the philosophy many institutions have about orientation. Student organizations are often engaged in orientation activities. They can be involved in anything from new student tabling fairs, to new student move-in, to organization welcome events. We know that student organizations help new students transition successfully into the life of college students because they serve as a niche and a safe, comfortable place to be themselves.

It would be helpful to be aware of the calendar of the university and to know when recruitment and orientation days are scheduled. The organization you advise may have specific recruitment or orientation responsibilities. For example, the Law Association for Women may have an active role in the law school's orientation program. You can ensure that the organization's leaders are part of broad-based efforts to recruit and orient new students and that the organization's representatives know how to present themselves and their organization effectively and persuasively to prospects and new students.

Advisory Boards and Committees

Many student leaders are asked to serve on various institutional advisory boards and committees. For some of these positions, students will serve on an ex officio basis, meaning that the office they hold automatically entitles them to serve on a specific board. For example, the president of the residence hall association may have a seat on the campus food advisory committee. In other cases they are appointed to the assignments by an officer of the student body or an administrator. The president of the student government association may have the responsibility to recommend students to faculty senate or a transportation fee committee. Let us look at some of these positions.

Departmental Assignments Among the departmental assignments that may be available to students are promotion committees, search committees, and curriculum committees. Not all colleges will include students on these committees, but some of these assignments can be found on most campuses.

How is a student appointed to these committees? One of the most likely ways is for a student leader of a departmental club to be asked by the departmental chair to serve, perhaps as a result of a recommendation by the club's adviser. Another possibility is for the student to be appointed by the organization's president in consultation with the adviser. Occasionally volunteers simply are sought for committee service. The point is that the student organization will likely play a key role in this process, and you are likely to play a complementary role as well.

College Assignments College in this case means a degree-granting unit within a university. As is the case with departmental assignments, students may serve on college search committees (including the search committee that fills the dean's position), promotion committees, and curriculum committees, again depending on traditions, campus policies, and the culture of the specific college.

Hosting special guests of the college, organizing interdisciplinary symposia, and planning special events for the summer are some of the special activities that take place in the life of a college. Regardless of the activity, students often are sought for their perspective as well as their help in accomplishing various tasks associated with hosting the event.

The students appointed to these committees are likely to be leaders in the college, and obviously, departmental clubs or other organizations in the college, such as the Model United Nations, and organizations that cut across several academic disciplines provide an excellent "leadership pool" from which to select student appointees. For example, the president of an advertising society would make an excellent choice as a host when the Journalism School has private corporations visit.

Institutional Assignments Students also serve on institutional boards and committees. These bodies tend to be much more wide ranging than those at the departmental or college level. Besides the boards and committees that may be found on the academic side of the institution, students may also be members of the alumni association board, the athletic committee, the traffic ticket appeals board, or the conduct committee. Many student affairs units will have an advisory board, and students can play important roles on these boards, perhaps even serving as chair.

Appointments to these boards may come from the president of the student body, who often has a major role in the life of the institution simply because he or she makes appointments to these campus boards and committees. Other appointments result from an office that a student holds or another role that a student plays on campus. For example, the president of the student programming board is a likely candidate to serve on the college student union advisory board.

Your role in these campus appointments is consultative only. The student body president or other experienced student leader is very likely to have ideas about whom to appoint to these various committees, many of which will evolve from the campus political process. You should be available to the student making the appointment, but it is unlikely that the student will seek much advice unless problems with confirmation arise. The role you can take is to be knowledgeable about committee opportunities, encourage the students you advise to seek out those opportunities that align with the interests of the organization, and deliver on the expectations that come with these appointments.

Service Learning and Civic Engagement

In this section we use "service learning" as a term to encompass both community service activities and civic engagement. There are differences between all three terms but we chose to use service learning because of the value we place on the action of service as the catalyst for students becoming productive members of the community's civic life and their responsibility to engage in issues of social concern. Though linked to civic engagement, as demonstrated by the number of offices of service learning and civic engagement on college campuses, service learning has the purpose of connecting the action of service and the outcomes of that service to academics. For our purposes we will discuss all three as service learning.

Also, we will use the term "volunteer" as a shorthand synonym for participating in civic engagement and service learning, although participating in service learning experiences and volunteering are not the same (see Jacoby 1996).

"Higher education is being called on to renew its historic commitment to service" (Jacoby 1996, 3). Students give of their time in all kinds of ways to advance their institution—for example, by tutoring each other, escorting each other across campus at night, and helping clean up after disasters.

In addition, there has been a growing interest from students to be of service to their community, which has spawned numerous service projects by student organizations. According to www.compact.org, "service-learning programs involve students in organized community service that addresses local needs, while developing their academic and life skills, sense of civic responsibility and commitment to the community." These projects range from an organization doing a service project together as a team builder to organizations with the purpose of supporting medical relief in third-world countries. Regardless of its mission, service learning can be an invaluable component of the organization's overall health as it can unite students for a common cause through a shared experience of giving back.

Institutions benefit from the public's perception that the college students in their midst are engaged in service to their immediate community. As Jacoby (2003) states, "in many instances, service learning partnerships have served as a catalyst for broader and deeper engagement and civic responsibility by colleges and universities" (2). Increasingly institutions are becoming active members of their local communities and, when done well, service learning projects strengthen the relationship between the institution and the surrounding community.

Frequently nonprofit agencies will seek college students to serve as volunteers, publicize the cause the agency supports, and promote fundraising efforts. Student organizations have a ready network that can be supportive of the interests of a nonprofit. Whether members are volunteering for ongoing activities (Scheuermann 1996) or participating in one-time or short-term activities (McCarthy 1996), organizations can play a crucial role in the success of a service learning project by encouraging their members to participate. Some organizations, such as Volunteers in Action (VIA) at the University of Vermont, provide a direct connection between students and the surrounding community with the primary purpose of providing service and connecting service to learning. Another approach to community service is that taken by Michigan State's residence halls orientation week program, which incorporates volunteer service (Scheuermann 1996).

When the organization you advise shows interest in performing service, it would be helpful for you to ask some clarifying questions. What is the purpose of the service project? Can the organization commit to the project? What are the intended outcomes for the students involved? The answers to these questions will help the organizers better understand that service is not an activity to take lightly and that the benefits of participating can be far-reaching. Many institutions have offices of civic engagement which can provide valuable resources to student organizations looking to become engaged in service and which are interesting in tracking the number of hours students contribute to volunteering.

As an adviser you can also encourage service learning by emphasizing its value to students: what students learn from volunteering can be applied directly to some aspects of their coursework, and volunteering experiences help students become well-rounded, contributing citizens of their communities. Also, you can be instrumental in ensuring that students learn from the experience by taking the time to lead them through a reflection exercise. Reflecting on the experience is essential as "we know that service learning can enhance students' critical thinking skills and the combination of community service, academic knowledge and reflection can help students develop an understanding of the root causes of social problems" (Jacoby 2003, 3). However, most advisers will tell you they never have enough time to do reflection justice. The University of Minnesota's Community Service Learning Center (2014) offers examples of reflection exercises that will keep students engaged. Example exercises include journals, video of photo documentaries, analyzing the agency, blogging, and letters to the editor. Reflecting does not need to take a significant amount of time and can be done immediately following the project, or at the organization's next meeting. Here are reflection questions from Eastfield College Service Learning (2014) that you could use during a general body meeting:

- What is the impact of your service in your community?
- What did it mean to you personally?
- What skills and knowledge from your coursework did you apply during your service?
- What skills and knowledge did you lack?
- What impact might your service have on your lifelong learning process?
- How did your service experience affect your daily life?
- What insights did you gain concerning your career goals?
- What did you learn about civic engagement and community service?
- How will you use what you've learned through your service experience?

Policies and Procedures

In this section we describe a number of policies and procedures that are essential to understand to conduct business on campus, and your role in each.

Probably one of your primary questions as an adviser is why there are so many policies and regulations related to student organizations. These regulations exist so that all student organizations are treated equally and have a reasonable opportunity to conduct their business and accomplish their objectives. In addition, health and safety need to be ensured. Colleges and universities are complex enterprises, and for this reason, many university organizations are not aware of what the other organizations are doing, or they all want to do the same thing at the same time. Thus, for example, if many organizations want to reserve the most desirable meeting rooms on Tuesday night, some mechanism needs to be in place to ensure that rooms are not double booked.

Developing the Constitution

Most campuses require that student organizations have a constitution. You need to know whether the campus requires the organization to provide a copy of its constitution; if filing is required, you also need to know where and how often the organization should do so. Your group will also need to review its operating by-laws at least annually and bring them up to date as needed. Help on technical questions related to constitution development is usually available at the student activities office, and we discuss the development of organizational constitutions in chapter 4.

Many institutions require a clause in the constitution stating that the organization will not discriminate in its membership policies and practices. This clause may be controversial in some instances; you can play a helpful role in explaining the purpose of such a clause and why it makes solid educational sense to have the statement included in your organization's constitution.

Registering the Organization and Officer Eligibility

An organization frequently, or perhaps annually, has to file certain documents with the student activities office so that it can be registered on campus. Registration documents normally include a constitution, a list of officers including their contact information, and the name of the adviser. Other material may need to be filed depending on the requirements of your campus. An organization must also choose a name, which may pose a challenge. For example, an organization may want to call itself the XYZ University Mentoring Group. Some institutions will not allow a student organization to use its name for legal reasons. This policy may also extend to the athletics moniker as well.

In return for being registered, an organization is eligible for certain institutional benefits. Among these may be the use of space on campus for free or for a reduced charge, eligibility for funding from the student government association, and certain privileges related to fundraising on campus.

Although registering may not be required, you need to make sure that students understand the value of having their organization registered on campus and to gently remind them of the deadlines they must meet to be registered.

There may also be regulations regarding the eligibility of student officers. Some campuses have minimum standards which may include a minimum grade point average, minimum credit hours, and a clean conduct record. As an adviser it is important to know whether the organization's leaders are eligible to serve.

Student Organization Review Boards A current trend within the management of student organizations is the development of review boards. The reason for this is the growing commitment to the community holding itself accountable and involving students in decision-making processes that had historically been managed university administrators.

There are two types of review boards. The first is a board of students who review a student organization's application materials to determine whether everything is in order for the organization to register. An example of this type of board is found at the College of Charleston. According to their website, the Student Organizational Review Board is "the body that reviews all potential student organizations and clubs. The committee is there to review organizational by-laws to ensure a benefit to the College of Charleston community with the registration of the new organization" (2014).

The second type of review board is best described by Florida A&M University's Clubs and Organization Review Board's website which states "the CORB was developed by the Office of Student Activities in order to champion in an era of accountability for registered clubs" (2014). In most cases, an accountability review board is supported by a student activities office and its scope is to review complaints or policy violations of student organizations. Types of violations could include a complaint that the organization damaged a classroom during a meeting, or an organization that is a habitual no-show for their reserved space, or even an organization that misused funds. With these types of boards there needs to be a clear delineation from the university's student conduct office. Student conduct deals with violations of the institution's code of conduct. An organization review board looks at student organization policy violations. The purpose of the Student Organization Review Board at Grand Valley State University is an excellent example. Their purpose is to (a) review student organization registration requests and determine classification status; (b) review complaints regarding student organizations and conduct the Student Organization Misconduct Review Process; and (c) coordinate and oversee the annual student organization recognition and awards process (2014).

Advertising

Student organizations commonly have to comply with specific regulations dealing with where advertising may be posted or flyers distributed. For example, the campus may not allow the use of banners for publicizing events, or it may not permit the posting of signs or flyers on the sides of buildings, or the taping of such flyers to the sidewalks on campus. The campus may require that organizations receive permission to set up tables or booths on campus malls. Special permission may be needed for a non–residence hall organization to distribute flyers in a residence hall lobby, and it is highly unlikely that nonresidents can go door to door to notify residents of an event. Similarly, Greek houses are considered private on most campuses, and nonmembers may not enter a house without having specific permission to do so.

You should be aware of these various campus policies related to advertising and to publicizing events, including the highly debated issue of whether or not a registered student organization may use the institution's logo and any associated trademark restrictions; information about them is usually available in the student activities office. When students get together to discuss how to publicize events, you can point out that the campus has a policy governing such activity and let the students know where they can find a copy of the policy if it is not already in the organization's files.

Reserving Space

As already mentioned, registered student organizations are allowed to use campus space for meetings, lectures, and social events. To prevent rooms from being double booked, to provide for adequate security, and to ensure that buildings are unlocked, organizations normally are required to reserve their space through a scheduling office. Clubs and special-interest organizations may not have a home, unlike residence hall groups or Greek letter organizations. The student union is consequently the likely place for their events to be held on campus.

As is the case with other policies, you should have a working knowledge of the campus space reservation policy. A copy of this policy should be in the organization's files. If the student leaders appear to be unaware of the policy, you can provide them with this information.

Registering Events

It is common for campuses to have policies that require student organizations to register events they are sponsoring with the organization's governing body. For Greek letter organizations and residence hall groups, registering events may be part of the by-laws of the governing organization. For other organizations, events must be registered with the office of student activities.

You should be knowledgeable about the campus's event registration policy and should notify your students if the policy applies to the events they are planning. For example, such a policy might not apply if the event is held off campus. The last thing an organization needs is the threat of cancellation hovering over an event that the organization has failed to register.

Event registration is usually the gatekeeping mechanism the institution uses to ensure that the student organization is adequately prepared for their event, that they have reserved an appropriate space, and that any associated risks have been discussed and planned for.

Event management is a key skill that student leaders need to develop as this is one of the main activities of organizations. As advisers, we have some responsibility to help students understand the risks of an activity and any potential liability they may open themselves up to given the nature of their event. It serves advisers well to have a basic understanding of the institution's insurance practices and when a student organization would benefit from having an insurance policy. The general public often views the actions, events, and competitions of student organizations to be those of the university. Although case law may not support this, the perception is real. Therefore it is important for both the adviser and the executive board to understand the nuances of the relationship between registered student organizations and the institution.

Working with Food Service

Institutions often have an agreement with a food service vendor (either a private company or a campus food service operated by institutional employees) that provides the vendor exclusive rights to sell food on campus. This is done for two reasons. First, such an agreement helps to ensure the health and safety of those who consume the food. Food service purveyors need to work in clean kitchens, and those who are involved in food preparation normally are required to have a food handlers' permit or other certification. From a risk management perspective, having a professional responsible for preparing food is a means by which the institution can protect itself from various problems resulting from improper food handling. Second, the institution may receive as a commission a percentage of the receipts from food sales. The institution will not collect the commission if the students provide the food themselves.

Consequently, you will need to remind students who are planning an on-campus event with food that the campus policy will need to be checked, and if an exclusive arrangement to provide food has been granted to an operator, the students may not be able to provide the food unless the food is purchased or ordered through the on-campus vendor. The students can confer with the food service operator to determine whether any relief from the regulation can be provided.

Contracts For many of the events student organizations plan, both on and off campus, there could be a need for a contract with either a venue or a performer, or both. Although frequently asked for signatures by students, it is rare for a student organization adviser to have signatory authority. Be cognizant of the policies on your campus and the expectations for your involvement with contracts. Your student activities office or the institution's legal office will be able to answer questions.

Collecting and Disbursing Funds

Many campuses require student organizations to use a campus banking system for collecting and disbursing funds. Although it is not the same as a federally chartered financial institution, the campus bank allows student organizations to deposit funds and write checks (or request that checks against its account be drawn) to pay bills as instructed by the organization. In some cases, student organizations may not be able to receive funds from the student government association or funds collected by the institution (such as activity fees appropriated for residence hall units as part of room and board fees) unless the campus banking system is used.

You should be knowledgeable about the campus banking system, if one exists, and the institution's policy towards student organizations holding off-campus bank accounts. Aside from the issue of campus policy, the transition in student leaders from one year to the next makes it very difficult to maintain the continuity of off-campus accounts. In addition, it is very likely that off-campus financial institutions have no knowledge about campus spending policies and will thus routinely process checks for the purchase of alcoholic beverages or for other purposes that are not in keeping with campus policies. Further information is available from the campus controller, the bursar, or from the campus office that works with accounts receivable and payable. We discuss fiscal issues further in chapter 8.

Receiving Activity Fee Funding

Registered student organizations may be eligible for financial support from activity fees collected by the institution. The campus student government association is usually responsible for the allocation of these resources to student organizations. This money often is available through the activity fees that students pay as part of their tuition and fee bill. Exactly what kinds of funding are available to student groups will depend on the statutes of the campus student government, but among the expenses that may be covered are such items as printing, advertising, travel expenses related to conference attendance, and fees associated with inviting speakers to the campus.

The process that groups must follow to apply for such support will vary from campus to campus. Generally, however, they will need to make a case that the funds are being spent wisely and in line with student government statutes. Student governments likely will ask the group to demonstrate how the student body will benefit from the expenditure, and the organization will need to present a plan detailing how members of the student body will become aware of the event. Some campuses will not fund expenditures for food or travel.

You can be very helpful in this kind of activity by reminding students that such funding is available and by helping the leaders develop a funding proposal. Many organizations, particularly those that have modest membership rolls and no direct funding (such as room and board fees for residence hall groups), will find this kind of funding to be extremely helpful in underwriting their costs for the academic year. Some campus student governments will accept requests for this kind of funding on a routine basis throughout the year, whereas in other cases, organizations need to submit proposals by a specific deadline. A call to the activities office will be helpful in identifying the deadlines, if any, for the academic year.

Raising Funds

Most campuses will want all fundraising activities, especially those related to seeking gifts from institutional benefactors, to be coordinated with its fundraising arm, commonly known as the college foundation or endowment association. This activity typically falls under the supervision of the advancement office. (We further discuss this topic in chapter 8.) Institutions want to ensure that donors are not asked for multiple gifts in a given time, and if a college is cultivating a donor for a large gift, it will want to make sure that a small gift to a student organization does not short-circuit the process.

Once again, you need to be aware of the institution's approach to fundraising. In some cases the students can proceed and ask for a gift, but you or the student leaders can make a call to the fundraising office to head off potential problems.

Traveling

In chapter 9 we discuss several issues related to the legal aspects of travel, but from a procedural point of view, student groups will need to take certain steps to be able to travel. Travel, especially those involving overnight trips out of state, requires planning and administrative work so that the trip can be funded and the costs of the trip provided for appropriately. Clearly, if students want to travel to another campus, pay for it on their own, and not go as institutional representatives, there is little the institution can do to stop them (even if it makes a tremendous effort to do so). But if the students want some campus support (for example, funding for the trip), they will need to work their way through the administrative processes. In addition, if the students want to attend a conference as the representatives of the college, they will need to do some planning before the trip.

Students will need to file forms, signed by the staff on campus required to do so, well in advance of the trip. Estimated costs may be part of the information included in the forms. Some colleges require that individuals stay in lodging arranged by a travel agent under contract to the institution; other lodging may not be approved. If the trip involves using a common carrier, an institutional travel agent may need to make the reservations. Reservations made by the students may not be reimbursed.

If institutional vehicles are to be used for transportation, students will need to reserve them well in advance of the trip. In chapter 9 are some suggestions related to how to handle the safe assignment of drivers. Simply reserving the vehicles does not mean that the trip will go smoothly.

Be aware of the post-travel process. Most institutions will fund student organization travel by reimbursing certain expenses. This will require documenting expenses and maintaining receipts.

Websites and Social Media

Whether or not an institution will host a student organization's website or link it to a college's site is still under debate because problems can arise when students put material on their page that the institution does not want. An organization's website may include material the institution finds undesirable. What if students sell advertising on their site to businesses that the institution will not allow to advertise on campus, such as a liquor distributor? Because of these concerns, and given that most student organizations have a website, many institutions have a web platform operated by the student activities office with links to the sites of the organizations hosted by noninstitution servers.

Student organizations are finding social media to be instrumental in recruiting new members, advertising events, and communicating with members. Institutions have developed policies regarding the use of social media that may affect student organizations.

Facebook, Twitter, mobile applications, and other platforms provide an easy, affordable, instant vehicle for mass communication. There are numerous benefits for an organization to be active on social media and to utilize the tools available through mobile applications; however, there are some challenges. You can be helpful to the organization by discussing how they intend to incorporate social media into their communication plan and remind them that their posts represent a group and not an individual. Messages must be crafted with care as they can often be misinterpreted because they are condensed. The nature of social media often results in immediate feedback and the organization must be prepared to respond appropriately.

Case Vignettes

We provide the following vignettes to provide you an idea of the variety of situations involving policies and procedures that you may encounter as an adviser.

End-of-Year Party

You are the adviser to a major organization on your campus. This organization has a large number of members and a strong alumni group. Funds are ample, and whenever the group has a financial problem, it can call up an alum who will gladly write a check. The group is planning a large end-of-year party off campus.

What policies would you need to review with the leaders before they hold the party?

(continued)

(*continued*)

Starting a Club

Early in the academic year, a group of students in your department approach you in your office. They share a common interest in your discipline and would like to start a club. They are all underclass students and really are not active campus leaders. They would like to have you serve as their organization's adviser.

What steps might you take in advising the students about how to start an organization on campus? What policies would they need to review before they can start the club? What suggestions can you make about recruiting members?

International Service

You advise the Mechanical Engineering Society on campus. They have developed a strong reputation for being supportive to first-year students interested in the field. The newly elected president shares with you her plans to organize a service trip to Central America over winter break for the members. She believes she can find financial support from either the student government association or a private corporation.

What questions might you ask? What resources on campus exist for the president to become more aware of risk management issues? What resources exist for you to ensure you are advising her properly?

Community Partnership

The sorority you advise has teamed up with a local nonprofit agency to perform "Sunday Day of Service" all football season long. During every home game the sorority wants to promise 100 percent of their membership on Sundays from 8 A.M. to 12 P.M. to mentor elementary at-risk students.

As the adviser, what are your concerns? What options or compromises can you suggest to make this a more manageable venture?

Retreat!

The organization you advise has done an excellent job of recruiting new members and would now like to focus on its orientation program. The executive board is planning a fall retreat to an off-campus retreat center located three hours away. Their team-building plans include tailgating games and a scavenger hunt. This organization is well funded so they have made an offer for a popular motivational speaker to speak on Saturday night. The retreat center is insisting that an "adult" sign the facility rental agreement and the speaker's agent is now asking you for a contract.

How can you help this organization with their event? What institutional policies do you need to be aware of? What risk management concerns may you have?

Chapter 8

Financial Management and Budgeting

ONE OF YOUR most important responsibilities as an adviser is to assist the organization in managing its financial matters. This activity can be quite simple, or it can involve handling hundreds of thousands of dollars each year in revenue and expenditures. Although you will not serve as the organization's treasurer, it is likely that you will work closely with the treasurer on financial matters. You may, depending on institutional policy, be asked to cosign check requests, review purchase orders, and advise the organization's executive officers on financial matters.

The importance of impeccable fiscal management cannot be overstated in higher education. In the case of many student groups, the organization is funded, completely or in part, by a "tax" that students have decided to levy on themselves. These organizations typically include organizations related to governance, such as the campuswide student government association, the residence hall association, or governance organizations related to Greek letter organizations. The organizations often receive a certain amount of money on a per capita basis, meaning that for every student who lives in the residence halls, the residence hall association (RHA) receives X dollars. In effect, then, this money represents a tax that each resident pays to the RHA. So, the fee is not voluntary and students cannot opt out of paying the fee.

Fiscal management also can fall under the scrutiny of groups external to the institution. Although people inside higher education understand the difference between money that is considered part of the state's appropriation and fees paid by students, those external to higher education may not understand the difference or may not care. The consequence is that if an external audit is conducted that is unfavorable, the result can be embarrassing. An example might be that officers of a student governance group use organizational funds to attend a national conference and travel "first class." Normally first-class travel is not allowed by institutions of higher education without special permission and extenuating circumstances. The publicity generated by first-class travel can be particularly embarrassing for the institution and does not represent wise use of student funds.

One other reason that expenditures need be carefully reviewed is that although the expenditures might appear to be legal in a general sense, they might not be legal because of special state statutes. For example, purchasing liquor by citizens might be legal if the purchasers are over 21, but it might not be legal to purchase liquor using "state" funds, which the student organization's funds may be considered to be, even if the linkage is something of a stretch. That is, in some circumstances all institutional funds, unless otherwise so designated, are considered to the resources of the state, even though in practical terms the state legislature is unlikely to take the funds of a student organization and use them to repair a state highway. So in this case, even if the purchase of liquor is generally legal by adults in a given state, it might not be legal to use state funds to do so and the result could be that by doing so the law has been broken and the consequences will be unpleasant for all involved.

This chapter is designed to provide you with basic information about financial management. We discuss various approaches to budgeting, introduce two common methods of accounting, describe how a typical budgeting process works, provide information about balance sheets, identify several fiscal controls that are available to you, and provide information about fundraising. We again provide case vignettes at the end of the chapter. Clearly, much more could be written about financial management and budgeting than could ever be contained in this chapter. Excellent resources are your institution's principal financial manager, often called a bursar or controller, or the student government finance office director. You should get to know these people if your organization's funds are deposited with the institution (more about this later on) and contact these people as additional questions arise.

Budgets

Most organization budgets are straightforward from a conceptual point of view. This part of the chapter describes several common ways that budgets are configured, but it does not discuss more complex budgeting approaches such as Program Planning Budgeting Systems (PPBS), responsibility-centered budgeting, performance budgeting, or formula budgeting, all of which have extremely limited applications to student organizations.

Incremental Budgets

Many forms of budgets are based on the concept of incremental budgeting. An incremental budget is one that essentially uses the budget from one year to serve as the basis for the budget for next year and assumes that "both needs and costs vary only a small amount from year to year" (Barr 2009, 497). Thus, if in year one the organization spends $100.00 on postage, and postal rates are projected to increase by 3 percent in year two, then the postage budget for year two will be $103. Of course this approach also assumes that expenditures in year one will be duplicated in year two plus or minus whatever adjustments are necessary for inflation or deflation.

Typically, although not always, this approach develops its expenditures first and then leaders figure out how to generate sufficient income to cover the expenses. Let us assume that the overall increase in year two will be 4 percent. Using this approach, income would have to increase by 4 percent to provide a balanced budget. So, dues might increase by 2 percent and initiation fees by 5 percent to provide for a balanced budget.

In some respects, making assumptions that all expenditures in year one will be replicated in year two can be a product of faulty reasoning. Year one might include support for travel for two leaders to attend a biennial regional convention but because the convention is not held in year two, there is no reason to budget for two leaders to attend the conference. Other costs similar to the travel example might not recur and, as a consequence, the budgeting approach is more nuanced than simply applying a percentage increase (or decrease) across the board and calling the budget process completed.

Although this form of budgeting is simple and easy to understand, it does not require hard thinking by organization leaders or the adviser. Simply plugging in adjustments from one year to the next is formulaic and assumes that everything done in one year should be repeated in the next. An exception to this critique, however, is an organization that has only one program or event in a given year, such as the initiation of new members by an honorary society. In this case the financial elements of the event may be replicated from one year to the next with adjustments to costs as necessary.

Zero-Based Budgeting

Zero-based budgeting (ZBB) takes quite a different approach from incremental budgeting. Instead of assuming that everything done in year one will be repeated in year two, this form of budgeting assumes that nothing will be repeated. Consequently, the budgets for expenses and revenues start at zero and are built to accomplish the tasks and conduct the programs that the leadership envisions. It can start either by forecasting revenues and apportioning the funds to pay for the programs that the revenue will allow, or it can start by determining what programs the groups wishes to offer and then determining how to finance them. In reality, most organizations will have some initiatives of both types, that is, some programming that is repeated year after year, such as a long-standing philanthropic activity, and other programs that are offered on an occasional basis, such as bringing in a speaker to address a topic of interest to the members.

After taking revenues and expenses to zero, organizational leaders build a budget based on the programs offered and revenue available as mentioned earlier. This approach is time consuming and labor intensive (Barr 2009) but it does require leaders to think hard about the programming the organization wishes to offer in the budget year under consideration. It does make it possible to eliminate programs that have grown "tired" and are of little interest to the members. On the other hand, the process of ZBB is an excellent way of making sure that the leaders of the organization are well informed of the fiscal plans for the year in which they are in office, and also provides an excellent basis for members to understand the financial picture of the organization. Most student government allocation processes use ZBB as the approach—meaning they expect new budget requests starting from zero funding from one year to the next.

Budgeting for Cost Centers

Though student organizations typically will not use responsibility-centered budgeting, which can be quite complex and really not appropriate for the typical student organization, there may be times when identifying specific events or programs as "cost centers" is appropriate. For example, if the organization has an awards dinner each year, and all members may not be able to attend, it may make sense to have the cost of the event set aside from normal organizational operations and funded by revenues, such as tickets to the dinner. In effect, then, all the members are not subsidizing the cost of the event for just those who can attend. Whether or not to establish cost centers that essentially are designed to be freestanding operations without organizational support reflects the philosophy of the membership and absolute answers may be elusive. But such discussions are healthy in that the desires of the membership will prevail and it is entirely possible that what is done in one year may not be repeated in the next. It is also possible that a blended approach might be taken. In the case of the awards dinner, the cost of meals consumed are charged back to the members in the form of dinner tickets that they purchase, but the honorarium or gift provided to the after-dinner speaker might be paid out of organizational funds.

Line Items

Our previous volume (Dunkel and Schuh 1998) included a section on line item budgeting. In this volume we want to recognize that the line item, in our opinion, is akin to a cornerstone in budgeting. That is, virtually all forms of budgets will have line items. Put simply, a line on a budget represents a source of revenue, let's say dues, or an expenditure source, such as office supplies. The lines may be aggregated to form larger categories, such as operations that could include office supplies, telecommunications, and rental of office space. The point to remember is that line items generally are determined no matter what budgeting strategy one uses from those enumerated above (incremental, zero-based, and so on).

Revenues and Expenses

The following is a brief discussion of the sources of revenue and the common expenses of student organizations. We provide Exhibit 8.1 that illustrates many of the categories included in this section.

Revenue

Student organizations are fairly limited in terms of the sources they use to generate revenues. Among the most common methods of raising revenue are assessing membership dues or activity fees, charging individuals a fee to participate in a specific program, and holding fundraisers.

Dues and activity fees are self-explanatory. In the case of a club, for example, the organization may elect to assess each member an annual or periodic fee (such as by academic term) to remain in good standing and receive the benefits of membership. Setting the amount can be difficult: on the one hand, the organization needs to generate sufficient revenue to operate; on the other, if the fee is too high, people may choose not to join. Normally, the executive officers propose the amount to be charged, and the membership votes to accept or reject it.

Activity fees also may be charged by such organizations as residence hall units or Greek letter organizations. These fees may be included in a room and board charge or may be assessed separately. The elected officers decide on the fee, and students must pay the fee to remain in the housing unit. The amount may range from just a few dollars per term to a more substantial amount in the case of a fraternity or sorority.

EXHIBIT 8.1
Sample Operating Statement

	Previous Year	Current Year
Revenue		
Dues	_____	_____
Activity fees	_____	_____
Services rendered	_____	_____
Commissions from machines	_____	_____
Sales of items	_____	_____
Fundraisers	_____	_____
Program receipts	_____	_____
Prior year carry forward	_____	_____
Gifts/donations	_____	_____
TOTAL REVENUE	_____	_____
Expenses		
Personnel services	_____	_____
Salaries	_____	_____
Hourly wages	_____	_____
Fringe benefits	_____	_____
Worker's compensation	_____	_____
Social security	_____	_____
Insurance	_____	_____
Operating expenses	_____	_____
Telephone service	_____	_____
Other communications/Internet	_____	_____
Office supplies	_____	_____
Printing	_____	_____
Postage	_____	_____
Equipment rental	_____	_____
Equipment repair	_____	_____
Program expenses (Develop a separate budget for each program)		
Newsletters	_____	_____
Travel	_____	_____
Outstanding debt payments	_____	_____
Miscellaneous	_____	_____

Capital Items
(List each item individually)
_____   _____

Contingency expense
TOTAL EXPENSES
NET (REVENUE MINUS EXPENSES)

At times organizations will charge students a specific fee to support a social event, such as a dance or dinner, or to take a trip. In this case the organizers of the event determine the cost of the event, project the number of participants, and arrive at a per-person fee. These kinds of events might be budgeted as cost centers (as described in the section on cost center budgeting).

Fundraisers are those activities, such as a car wash or bake sale, which are designed expressly to supplement the organization's revenue. We discuss fundraising in greater detail later in this chapter.

As we touched on elsewhere, one other likely source of revenue, particularly for clubs, is funding from the student government allocation process. On many campuses, the student government receives funds from activity fees that all students pay; the government in turn allocates some of the money to student organizations through a defined process: it accepts applications on certain dates and holds formal hearings. At times student government has a committee that consists of several of its officers, faculty, and members of the student body who are not part of student government.

Often the extent to which organizations receive funding from the student government rests on the opportunity that all members of the student body have to attend the event or events funded by this allocation process. For example, if the organization wants support to invite a speaker to campus, the potential for funding is enhanced if it is convenient for all members of the student body to attend the speech. That, of course, does not mean that all will attend. The emphasis here is on the potential for all students to attend. This process of fee allocation overseen by student government should not be overlooked as a source of funding for student organizations. The old adage that you won't be funded unless you ask applies here.

Some organizations may be able to generate other funding through such campus work projects as directing traffic or supervising parking at major events, receiving commissions from vending machines, cleaning the stadium after an athletic event, or renting equipment such as refrigerators and microwave ovens for the residence halls. These sources will vary from campus to campus, but they have the potential to provide substantial sources of funds.

Expenses

Expenses vary dramatically from organization to organization. In the case of a club, expenses might not be much more than printing and mailing, in addition to those incurred by perhaps one major event per semester. Other, more complex organizations can have very complicated budgets.

If a student organization has any employees, it may incur expenses that can be characterized as "personnel services." An example of employees could be workers who are paid to provide clerical services for a student organization. The costs could include salaries, wages, and fringe benefits. The institution very well may determine fringe benefits, and they could include Social Security contributions, disability insurance, and worker's compensation. The student organization treasurer should check with the institution's human resources office to determine exactly what fringe benefits must be paid. Fringe benefits can represent substantial expenses, so it is important to know what percentage of payments to individuals need to be set aside for fringe benefits.

Most organizations may have some operating expenses: data line charges, telephone line and long-distance charges, and office supplies, printing, and postage costs. The range of operating expenses again will depend on the organization's complexity.

Program costs might be budgeted separately. By program costs we mean special events or activities that are not part of the routine expenses of the organization. Social events, speakers, and convocations are examples of programs. In some cases these events might be funded entirely out of fees charged to participants, without support from the organization. How to fund special events is as much a political decision as a financial decision, and it should be made by the officers in consultation with the membership.

If the organization's members take trips, they will incur travel expenses, including transportation costs, lodging and meal charges, and perhaps registration fees for a conference. Travel, which can be quite expensive, can perhaps be budgeted as a separate item. Travel also can be highly regulated by institutional policy and in the case of state-assisted institutions, state laws and regulations. Just because travel expenses are legitimate does not mean that they are reimbursable. For example, some institutions strongly discourage travelers from renting cars. Instead they prefer that travelers use common carriers regardless of the cost and renting a car requires permission in advance of the commencement of the trip. It is strongly advised that applicable policies be reviewed before anyone travels on behalf of the organization.

Two other items also may be identified as expense categories, namely, capital items and prior year debt. The definition of what constitutes a capital item will vary from college to college but, generally, items with a value over a certain amount (perhaps anywhere from $100 to $500 or $1,000) that are not consumable (unlike paper or staples) are considered to be capital items. Organizations without offices generally will not be purchasing capital items, which could include computer equipment or copy machines. But a Greek letter organization, a student government association, or a residence hall association very easily could buy substantial numbers of capital items.

In order to buy capital items, student organizations may at times borrow money. The lender could be the institution itself or perhaps the student government association or the residence hall association. To pay back the lender, the organization will have to budget funds, thus creating the prior-year debt category in the budget. This category is not all that common, as most organizations do not purchase substantial numbers of capital items, nor do they incur long-term debt. But if the government of a specific residence hall needs to purchase new office furniture, it might borrow the funds to do so from the central RHA.

Finally, there is a budget category for expenses that cannot be anticipated, which is referred to as contingency. A modest amount can be budgeted for contingencies, perhaps not more than 5 percent of projected expenses. The contingency allows for flexibility in funding an activity or project that could not be planned when the budget was developed.

The Budgeting Process

Institutions and organizations have budgets for several reasons (Schuh 2011). One reason is to provide a means by which leaders can track their revenues and expenditures over the course of a fiscal year. A second is that budgets provide a plan for how the entity will use its resources. Both of these reasons apply to student organizations.

The budgeting process will vary substantially from one organization to another, mostly as a consequence of the level of sophistication and complexity of the organization's financial structure. An organization that collects modest dues and charges small fees for social events will have a very simple budget planning process. A residence hall association or Greek letter organization that has many members and is managing substantial ancillary operations will have a more complex budgeting process. In this section we discuss a budget planning process that applies to most organizations; please remember that the budget details and complexity can vary widely from organization to organization. An excellent description of the budget process for a complex entity is provided by Barr (2009).

The place to start in budget preparation is determining the extent of the programs that the organization intends to develop for the budgeting year. Program, in this case, refers to what the organization plans to do—take a trip, have a dinner, publish a newsletter, hire a part-time secretary, show three movies, and so on.

Committee chairs, executive officers, and even group members will make proposals for the activities that might be considered during the organization's fiscal year. These proposals are presented to the budget committee, which might be a separate group chaired by the treasurer or other organization member in the case of a large organization, or the executive committee in the case of a smaller group. Small organizations might have the budget committee consist of the executive officers.

Programs require money, and to a great extent they drive the budget. Once the program is sketched out, the organization needs to estimate the amount of money it will require to underwrite the program and to determine the necessary sources of revenue. As mentioned earlier, revenues can include dues, fees for participation in certain events, special fundraisers, and gifts.

The budget, including projected revenues and expenditures, is then presented to the executive group for initial review. Changes to the budget may be made based on the recommendations of the officers. Revisions could include changes in the amount of dues charged, the number of special events held, or the amount of money that can be raised through special events. Assuming that the revised budget is approved, it is then presented to the organization's members for adoption. In the case of large, complex organizations, this step might be taken for informational purposes only. For smaller groups, such as a special-interest club, a vote of the members to adopt the budget is in order.

The adopted budget then becomes the organization's financial road map for the year. It can be changed if circumstances dictate, but that would require a vote according to the process prescribed in the organization's constitution or by-laws. It is common for organizations to make adjustments to their budget during the fiscal year. For example, the membership may be greater than anticipated, and consequently the dues revenue realized would be a larger amount than was planned. Another example is when a piece of equipment breaks and has to be repaired or replaced.

The treasurer prepares periodic reports related to the budget and presents them to the executive officers and members. We discuss this process later in the chapter.

Accounting Methods

You are likely to encounter one of two accounting methods, cash accounting and accrual accounting (Schuh 2011). Cash accounting is the approach that most people take when balancing their checkbooks. That is, every check they write is entered as an expense. Each time they make a deposit into the account, that amount is entered as well. On a periodic basis (at least monthly) they balance their checkbook and with proper planning some money is left in their account. Every transaction for the account needs to be entered at the time of the transaction so that an accurate financial picture can be provided at any given time. Most financial institutions have online banking so the checkbook can be reconciled with the bank's records with just a few keystrokes. In short, every transaction is recorded as the activity takes place.

Accrual accounting is different from cash accounting in that income and expenses are recorded when the commitment to receive or expend funds is made. Using this approach, for example, when a student is billed for books, the bookstore records the income. When a purchase order for food items is processed, the food service commits its resources to paying for the items, even though the supplies have not been received and a check has not been sent to pay for them. Accrual accounting operates under the assumption that all billed funds will be received and that all obligations of the organization will be met. (Unfortunately, at times debts are not paid, requiring an expense category for bad debts.)

Auxiliary units such as housing or food service, which can have a cash flow in the millions of dollars each year, often use an accrual accounting approach. Cash accounting will serve most student organizations well as their finances are not very complicated; however, it is important to remember that the person authorized to keep the organization's books must know when commitments are made. One of the most common problems that can occur is when members of the organization make financial commitments for the organization that cannot be met. For example, a committee orders hundreds of dollars worth of fresh flowers as centerpieces for banquet tables when only $75 was budgeted for decorations. After delivering the flowers, the vendor expects to be paid. This example illustrates what can happen when too many people get involved in making financial commitments beyond the amount that was authorized.

Some colleges and universities have an arm of the bursar's office or student government finance office dedicated to student organization accounts. These units keep accounts for student groups, receive funds, and disburse funds for legitimate expenses. In these cases the organization authorizes certain students to charge items against their student organization account. The adviser and the treasurer ought to review the periodic statements from the student organization accounts office so that what the organization's leaders believe is its financial situation squares with reality.

Operating Statements and Balance Sheets

Operating statements and balance sheets are fiscal tools that help the organization's officers and adviser develop a picture of the fiscal health of the organization.

Operating Statements

Operating statements are produced on a periodic basis (preferably monthly but possibly quarterly) by the organization's treasurer. Assuming that such statements are developed monthly, the report would include all transactions that have occurred since the previous statement was prepared one month before, income and expenses are recorded, and a balance is reported at the end of the statement. The monthly statement also is reconciled with the year-to-date activity of the organization so that a clear picture of the organization's financial position can be established. A review of the statement will indicate the income of the organization, its expenses, and the organization's cash balance. Refer to Exhibit 8.1 for a sample operating statement.

Sophisticated operating statements will report the amount of money the organization has projected it will receive for the fiscal year and the percentage of income that has been received to date; similarly, they report expenses. This level of detail may be a bit too much to expect of a student organization, but the more complicated the organization's finances, the more important it is to take advantage of fiscal tools such as well-conceived operating statements. It is important to note that not all organizations will expend the same amount of money each month. For example, an honorary society may not spend much money until it holds the annual, or semester, initiation banquet. Similarly, revenues may not be equal each month. The residence hall association very well may receive credits from room fees at the beginning of each semester and then only experience adjustments as students either move in or out of the residence halls during the semester.

Balance Sheets

For the purposes of this explanation, the balance sheet is viewed much like an individual's statement of net worth. This sheet, which is produced quarterly at most, provides a complete representation of the assets and liabilities of the organization. It reports the cash position of the organization along with any other assets that the organization might have, minus its liabilities.

Examples of assets other than cash include certificates of deposit or other investments the organization might hold (or that the institution might hold on behalf of the organization as sometimes assets of several organizations are pooled), as well as any other physical assets such as equipment or inventory. Most organizations have limited assets other than a checking account or the equivalent, and perhaps some money on deposit.

Liabilities include any long-term debts owed to other student organizations or the institution, and funds owed to outside sources. Let us look at an example of a long-term liability. Suppose that the residence hall association decided to rent refrigerators to residence hall students and needed to purchase an inventory of mini-refrigerators. If a $50,000 loan, to be paid back in five $10,000 annual installments, had been underwritten to purchase the original inventory, a liability is recorded on the balance sheet. The $10,000 is an annual expense that is listed on the monthly operating statement. The overall debt of $50,000 appears on the balance sheet of the organization and is reduced each time a payment is made. The value of the refrigerators appears as a physical asset on the balance sheet of the organization, less any depreciation or other reduction in the value of the items (such as theft of or damage to the items).

Most student organizations have almost no assets or liabilities. An honorary society, for example, may have some funds in a checking account and nothing more in the way of assets and no liabilities after initiation fees are paid to the organization's national office and the cost of the initiation activity has been paid. Consequently, the balance sheet looks very much like an operating statement. Regardless of the complexity of the operating statement or balance sheet, it is very useful for the adviser to pay careful attention to each month's activities. Any apparent irregularities should be discussed immediately so that problems do not go unresolved. A sample balance sheet is shown in Exhibit 8.2.

EXHIBIT 8.2
Sample Balance Sheet

Date: _____

	Amount/Value

ASSETS

Cash on hand (in checking account or institutional account)   _____

Accounts receivable   _____

Savings accounts (by savings institution, account number and amount)

_____   _____

_____   _____

Equipment (fair market value by item name)

_____   _____

_____   _____

Other property (fair market value by item)

_____   _____

_____   _____

_____   _____

TOTAL ASSETS   _____

LIABILITIES

Accounts payable   _____

Long-term debts (list by name and amount)

_____   _____

_____   _____

TOTAL LIABILITIES   _____

NET VALUE OF THE ORGANIZATION   _____

Fiscal Controls

Now that we have gone through the process of developing balance sheets and operating statements, one of the issues that need some attention is that of fiscal controls. How do you ensure that the organization's money is received and spent without irregularities? Several techniques help avoid problems.

Program Budgets

We believe that one of the classic mistakes organizations can make is to plan events or activities that require an expenditure of funds without having first developed a budget. A budget in this case is nothing more than a plan for how funds will be spent and how revenues will be generated to pay for the expenses. Any program or activity that expects to generate revenue and pay expenses should have a budget that is published for the officers and members to review, and that is approved through the appropriate process in a regular business meeting. The person or persons who are charged with managing the budget should provide periodic reports as to the progress that has been made on program planning and how expenses are being managed. Are revenues in line with the budgeted projections? What about expenses? Have any anomalies been encountered? The leadership should review these questions and others regularly, and if adjustments need to be made, the membership should have a chance to react. We believe that variances of more than 5 percent should be approved by the organization's appropriate authority, for example, the executive board or membership, as defined by the organization's by-laws.

Some program budgets are very simple. If a reception is held for a speaker in a residence hall lounge, the expenses might consist of nothing more than purchasing refreshments, say punch and cookies. Another example might be the purchase of a book that is given to a presenter as a gift for conducting a workshop for sorority leaders. Other activities, which involve income in addition to expenditures, can be more complex. We have provided a sample budget for an initiation luncheon that includes substantial income and expenses (Exhibit 8.3). An organization that badly manages its program expenses can face early bankruptcy. We therefore recommend that you pay close attention when members propose programs and that you work closely with the leadership to make sure that budgets are executed in the spirit with which they are conceived. Sometimes members propose programs, for example, that are of keen interest to them but may not have much appeal to the broad membership.

Banking

One of the questions you will encounter is whether or not to use the campus banking service, if one exists, as opposed to a commercial banking facility. Campus banks are not banks in the traditional sense; they are an arm of the institution's business office and are not chartered financial institutions. Campus banking services generally will provide limited services to customers: receiving deposits, preparing periodic statements, and making

EXHIBIT 8.3

Sample Program Budget

Budgeted Event: Initiation Luncheon

	2013 Budgeted	2013 Actual	2013 (Over/Under)	2014 Budgeted
Expense Items				
Food	1400.00	1345.18	54.82	1430.00
Decorations	180.00	184.02	(4.02)	100.00
Table favors	280.00	262.40	17.96	300.00
Publicity	100.00	35.18	64.82	50.00
Entertainment	150.00	150.00	0.00	250.00
Printing	50.00	40.25	9.75	50.00
Transportation	75.00	87.10	(12.10)	90.00
Contingency	150.00	75.00	75.00	75.00
Total	2385.00	1178.77	206.23	2345.00
Income Items				
Program ads	100.00	125.00	25.00	125.00
Luncheon tickets	2100.00	1995.00	(105.00)	2050.00
Donations/gifts	50.00	105.00	65.00	100.00
Transfer from operating account	135.00	0.00	0.00	70.00
Total	2385.00	2225.00	15.00	2345.00
Net Surplus (Loss)	0.00	46.23	191.23	0.00

payments upon receiving an appropriate form and documentation requesting such. These services are often provided without charge to the student organization. Vendors in college towns often are quite familiar with the process by which their bills are paid while in larger, metropolitan areas, such may not be case. The extent to which the community is familiar with the process by which the campus pays the bills of student organizations may tip the scales in terms of which form of banking your organization will use.

Commercial banks can provide a checking account for a student organization as well as deposit funds. They are open for longer hours and, if one has an ATM card, can provide twenty-four-hour service. Frequently, banks assess a monthly service charge. The charge may not be appropriate for a student organization and it may need to work with a credit or other financial organization that does not levy periodic fees.

Each form of banking service has certain advantages and disadvantages. Commercial banks can act faster and provide more services than campus banks, and are more flexible. These advantages, however, do not come without cost. Campus "banks" are more used to dealing with the special situations that arise with student organizations; however, they may take more time to process checks and will not write checks counter to institutional policy (such as for the purchase of alcoholic beverages).

Our general recommendation is that student organizations should use the campus "bank." As mentioned elsewhere in this volume, in some cases the campus banking facility must be used in order for an organization to be registered or recognized on campus. Check with your student activities office about the requirements of "banking" on or off campus and expectations related to advisers having signatory authority on organization accounts.

Cash

To put it simply: avoid using cash. The organization's revenues should be collected in the form of checks made out to the organization rather than in cash. Dues, fees, and other receivables should be collected by check. Using this method provides a record for the issuer of the check in the form of the canceled check, thereby eliminating the need for receipts. More important, the check is negotiable only to the extent that it can be deposited in the organization's account. It is much more difficult to keep track of cash, and, unfortunately, cash has a way of disappearing.

The organization's obligations should also be paid by check, not in cash. Cash payments by officers, for example, will require reimbursement, which can be a bit messy. The person paying with cash on behalf of the organization will have to produce a receipt in order to be reimbursed. People lose receipts, and at times commingle personal purchases with organizational purchases, which is a nightmare. The best process is to produce a payment request with appropriate documentation from a vendor and let the campus "bank" handle payment.

Cosigning Checks

If the organization has a checking account off campus, then checks ought to be cosigned. Checks over a certain amount, say $50, should require a second signature, but our preference is that all checks require a second signature. Institutional policy may govern the amount of the check that is the floor for obtaining a second signature. Our view is that this amount should be discussed and reviewed periodically. A number of $25 checks can add up quickly if they are used counter to the institution's policy. This approach will ensure, first, that significant expenditures are reviewed to make sure they are appropriate, and second, that the checks are being drawn to the right person or organization. Little could be worse for an organization in a financial sense than a misunderstanding that arises over a large expenditure that was for the wrong item or that was drafted to the wrong payee. Failing to follow this procedure could be devastating for the organization and its members.

Periodic Reports

Periodic reports, as mentioned earlier in this chapter, should be produced by the treasurer, reviewed by the leadership of the organization and the adviser, and presented to the members. In the case of a large organization, such as the campus student government, the report can be posted on the organization's website.

At a minimum, operating statements should be produced every quarter, although every month would be far more desirable. Balance sheets should be produced at least once each quarter, preferably at the end of the quarter. These materials are very useful to the leadership in determining whether the budget for the organization is being managed as it was proposed. If there are substantial variances from the budgeted plan, they should be pointed out by the treasurer to the executive committee as soon as the problems are identified. You should spend extra time with the treasurer if problems arise that could potentially affect the organization's financial health. Financial problems rarely solve themselves; they should be addressed as early as possible in the fiscal year.

Audits

Most organizations will undergo a change in leadership at least once a year, sometimes every semester. Consequently, student organizations frequently are in a state of transition, and the dilemma of who exactly is responsible for which tasks can lead to real problems. Even though student leaders come and go, the fiscal records of the organization must be maintained from one year to the next. Accordingly, we recommend that an audit of the organization's financial records be conducted each time there is a change in the executive leadership (meaning the president, the treasurer, or both). The internal audit department of the institution may conduct the audit for major student organizations depending on institutional policy. For organizations with a more limited scope, a student majoring in accounting, finance, or a similar discipline could be invited to conduct the audit.

Conducting an audit will serve as a good experience for the student and will be a valuable service for the organization.

Most audits are very simple. The auditor checks receipts against deposits, and expenditures against the disbursement records of the organization. If the auditor identifies a problem, it is more likely the result of an honest mistake than a major conspiracy to defraud the organization of funds. It is best that the audit be conducted as a matter of routine procedure rather than as the result of a disaster. You can be very helpful by insisting that the audit be conducted.

Taxes

We address the topic of taxes with great caution because of the complexity of state and federal tax codes as well as various Social Security regulations. It is possible that a student organization may have to pay sales taxes on items sold (such as T-shirts or food for fundraisers), withhold income taxes and FICA contributions from employees (and make contributions on their behalf), pay worker's compensation insurance, and mail W-2 forms to employees. If the organization is formed as a corporation, it will have to file annual reports with the Internal Revenue Service and perhaps your state's department of revenue, and if it holds real property, it may have to pay real estate taxes on that property. This last item might apply to Greek letter houses, for example. In addition, some states require that other property, such as motor vehicles, be subject to annual taxes. On the other hand, depending on the organization's relationship with its institution, it might be exempt from having to pay sales tax on items purchased. To make this discussion even more complex, an organization requires a tax ID number to establish a checking account, have investments as simple as a passbook savings account, or conduct other financial business.

Obviously the subject of taxes is very complicated and we are not trying to be overly dramatic in describing the potential challenges resulting from the tax status of the organization you advise. Many organizations are very simple and will have no liability resulting from the tax code. For example, the departmental special-interest club that collects modest dues and has a couple of events each semester is unlikely to run afoul of the tax code. But a student organization with products that it sells or employees that it hires is venturing into potentially complicated territory.

Your role is not to serve as a tax consultant to the organization. Rather, you should know that the organization may have tax obligations and you should urge the student leaders to file the necessary documents with the appropriate authorities in order to ensure that the requirements of state and federal law are met. Your institution's chief financial officer (vice president or vice chancellor for finance or business affairs), staff in the bursar's office, or staff in the student government finance office can provide information about these filings. Getting help early on in the fiscal year is a good strategy for avoiding tax problems with one other thing to remember—most institutions operate on an academic year, say August through May. The tax year in most cases runs from January 1 through December 31 so a tax filing is due shortly after the end of the fall academic term.

Fundraising

Fundraising may seem simple at first blush, but such may not always be the case. If it were, most institutions would experience record-breaking success in their advancement activities every year. Fundraising is hard work, with many disappointments along the way. Moreover, some institutions have very tight regulations governing fundraising activities on campus. Fundraising activities may be limited with respect to time, place, and manner.

Exhibit 8.4 provides a list of a few examples of fundraisers. Please remember that all of these fundraisers may not be appropriate for every campus, as regulations vary widely from college to college. Some activities may not even be legal in certain states. In spite of the complexity of fundraising issues, there are some general elements that you should be aware of, if for no reason other than to help you advise the organization when problems arise.

Legality

Although we discuss legal issues elsewhere in this volume, let us assert here that you need to remind the officers of your organization that fundraisers must be legal under state or federal law. Raffles, casino nights, lotteries, and other fundraisers related to games of chance may not be legal in your state or may require a license issued by the appropriate gaming authority. Just because there are casinos or lotteries in your state does not mean that any organization or person can conduct these kinds of activities. Moreover, gaming activities may violate the spirit of your institution. The legality of a fundraiser should be checked either with the student activities office, campus police chief, or the institution's legal counsel. The last thing anyone wants is for a fundraiser to be broken up by the local police as a result of a violation of gaming laws.

EXHIBIT 8.4
Sample Fundraising Ideas

Income Derived from Services Provided
- Vending machines
- Facility rentals
- Jewelry cleaning
- Lawn mowing, leaf raking, snow removal
- Data entry/word processing
- Small machine repair
- Computer software installation and repairs

Income Derived from Sales or Rentals
- Refrigerators
- Lofts
- Carpets
- Buttons
- Final exam support baskets
- Holiday cards or stationery
- Balloons
- College cups or mugs
- Calendars or desk blotters
- Diploma frames
- Birthday baskets

Other Ideas
- Raffles
- Car wash
- Flower sales
- Bake sales
- Recycling
- Sports tournaments
- Casino nights
- Auctions
- Rent-a-person
- Santa grams
- Valentine grams
- Starving artist festival
- Book exchange
- 5K foot race
- Farmer's market space rental
- Car bash
- Penny voting
- Face painting

Food Sales

Another area of concern relates to the sale of food. Selling doughnuts or other pastries has the potential to make a quick profit for a student organization, but the institution may have granted exclusive rights to a commercial company to sell food items on campus. You should recommend that the officers check with the food service director to determine whether or not a proposed activity violates the agreement with the institution. Officers need to do this checking whether the campus has a commercial food contractor or operates its own food service.

It is also important to note that food must be handled appropriately, meaning that hot foods need to be kept hot and cold foods cold. Food handlers may need to undergo a health exam and have a permit from the local department of public health. These factors must be taken into consideration before having a spaghetti dinner, ice cream social, or other event that involves food sales. One simple way to have food provided at organizational events is to have the campus food service cater the event rather than having a pitch-in or potluck dinner where the participants bring food that they have prepared.

Conflict with Campus Fundraising Plans

Another issue related to fundraising is that the organization should avoid contacting potential donors who may be part of the institution's long-range fundraising plan. A student organization might think that a gift of $5,000 from a donor is enormous, and it is substantial in terms of the organization's fiscal circumstance, but the institution may be planning to ask the potential donor for a gift 20 to 50 times that size. Most institutions are very careful in cultivating potential donors. Should a student organization receive a modest gift from a potential benefactor, this act may obviate the potential donor's making a major gift to the institution. Thus, careful coordination with the fundraising office is in order (Schuh 2009). Students may not think about fundraising in the same way your institution does; you can make sure that your group's plans do not get in the way of those of the institution. This caveat applies not only to individual donors but also to corporate donors for the same reasons. To take this a step further, student organizations need to make it clear that they do not represent the institution.

Case Vignettes

Unauthorized Travel

You have just begun your role as adviser to a campus club. Upon beginning your role you find out the two of the club's officers attended a conference for officers of such clubs in the summer and expect to be reimbursed for their travel expenses. In reviewing the minutes of meetings from last year you note that these expenses were never discussed. To make matter worse, the officers drove 1,000 miles to the conference and your institution's policy is that travel over 500 miles in one direction requires the use of a common carrier, not a personal vehicle.

How do you proceed?

An Invitation to the Governor

Your campus club has been known to invite a speaker each year to address the annual awards and officer installation banquet in the spring. In previous years a faculty member from campus has served as the speaker and that process has worked well. The banquet is in two days and you just found out that the governor has been invited by one of the members to address this year's banquet, and has accepted the invitation. The institution's policy is that the Office of the President extends all invitations to the governor or members of the state's Congressional delegation. Something needs to be done, but what?

What are your next steps?

Student Injury

You advise a student organization that raises money each year by shoveling snow at a local apartment complex. The money raised helps defray the annual celebratory dinner at the end of the year. This year your town experienced a particularly heavy snow and one of the organization's members involved in shoveling snow was hurt, requiring surgery to repair a knee injury. The student did not have medical insurance. The resulting medical bills are staggering and could result in the student's having to withdraw from school. The student's parents are talking about suing to recover damages.

What do you do to respond to this circumstance?

No Taxes

You have just begun advising a student organization that by all appearances is well financed and smoothly run. It has a "welcome to campus" event each fall during which it sells T-shirts to students at the institution and the result is net revenue of several thousand dollars. You find out after asking a couple of questions of the organization's leaders that sales tax has never been paid on these transactions and, after asking the institution's legal counsel if sales taxes should have been paid, to your dismay you find out that the organization could be liable for back sales taxes over the six years that the T-shirts have been sold. The state has not asked for payment of back sales taxes due but that does not mean that such will not occur. The organization does not have the funds to make the payment of back taxes.

Now what do you do?

Chapter 9

Legal Issues and Risk Management

THERE MAY BE no aspect of contemporary collegiate life that is more challenging than the legal environment in which institutions of higher education operate. As Pavela (2011) observes, "Legal issues influence institutions of higher education in many aspects of their endeavors from admissions practices to contractual relationships with faculty and staff to oversight for various aspects of student life" (120). Oversight of student life in the context of selected legal issues is the focus of this chapter.

We have not prepared this chapter to scare you away from your assignment. Rather, we believe that advisers have a responsibility to conduct their practice with a rudimentary understanding of the law and risk management strategies so that they can advise student organizations appropriately. We also want to make it crystal clear that we are not attorneys; we are long-time advisers to student organizations who have learned about legal issues through our experiences, and we are avid readers of literature about legal issues involving student groups and their advisers. We want to emphasize that the advice we provide in this chapter will neither make you an expert on the law nor will it serve as a substitute for campus legal counsel. We do believe, however, that we can offer suggestions for practice that are consistent with basic principles of the law as it applies to student organizations so that you can point out potential problems to the members of the organization you advise and minimize risk to the organization and its members. It is important to remember, "The legal environment influencing higher education and student affairs has become increasingly complex over the past three decades. Every indication is that the trend will continue in the future" (Sandeen and Barr 2006, 166). We believe that this definition of risk management is appropriate for this chapter: "Risk Management is the process of advising organizations of the potential and perceived risks involved in their activities, providing education about the guiding boundaries established for organizations, and taking corrective actions and proactive steps to minimize accidental injury and/or loss" (Texas A&M, 2013b).

In this chapter, we look at several fundamental distinctions between public and private institutions and at students' constitutional right to organize. Then we move into issues related to managing risk, which is of significant concern for many student organizations. Finally, we discuss several special legal issues that apply to student organizations, including dealing with alcoholic beverages and transportation.

We also want to offer a word about working with legal counsel. Attorneys whose primary focus is to provide advice to faculty and staff about a myriad of issues are available on many campuses; however, these legal counselors can provide assistance only if you contact them. Ledbetter (2009) advises the following: "Administrators must also be prepared to seek legal advice from their college counsel when needed" (524). There will be times, however, when the group makes a decision, regardless of the advice you or legal counsel provide. Legal counsel can provide advice to you on the ramifications of a certain course of action, but in the end, the choice will be made by the group. For example, should the members of an organization drive fifty miles to attend a speech of an acclaimed world leader if weather forecasters have predicted a sleet storm? Legally they can. What happens if the storm causes unsafe driving conditions during the trip, and an accident results? Counsel can provide various legal scenarios if an accident occurs, but the members have to decide whether or not to make the journey, and in many cases (such as in this example) the appropriate course of action is not clear-cut.

Distinctions between Public and Private Institutions

The difference between public and private institutions is profound in the eyes of the law, although over time the lines between public and private colleges have become a bit blurred. Kaplin and Lee (2013) offer the following distinction between public and private institutions: "structures and processes for public higher education differ from those for private higher education. These variations between public and private institutions exist in part because they are created in different ways, have different missions, and draw their authority to operate from different sources" (24).

This distinction means that private institutions have more latitude to deal with students and their organizations than have public institutions. "State governments usually regulate private institutions less than they regulate public institutions. The federal government, on the other hand, has tended to apply its regulations comparably to both public and private institutions, or, bowing to considerations of federalism, has regulated private institutions while leaving public institutions to the states" (Kaplin and Lee 2013, 45). However, "insofar as the federal Constitution is concerned, a private university can engage in private acts of discrimination, prohibit student protests, or expel a student without affording the procedural safeguards that a public university is constitutionally required to provide" (Kaplin and Lee 2013, 45). This latitude does not imply, however, that private institutions have complete freedom to deal with students and their organizations on a capricious basis. Kaplin and Lee (2013) point out, "The inapplicability of the federal Constitution to private schools does not necessarily mean that students, faculty members, and other members of the private school community have no legal rights assertable against the school. There are other sources for individual rights, and these sources may sometimes resemble those found in the Constitution" (58).

One of the ways that private institutions frame their relationship with students is through contract theory, which holds that the student and the institution engage in a contract that will govern their basic relationship. This relationship is spelled out in various documents, such as the catalog or student handbook that private institutions publish on a regular basis. Presumably private colleges will have rules that are specific enough so that a reasonable person will not have difficulty interpreting what they mean.

Right to Organize

Under the U.S. Constitution, students at public universities have a right to form organizations. "Specifically, students in public postsecondary institutions have a general right to organize; to be recognized officially whenever the school has a policy of recognizing student groups; and to use meeting rooms, bulletin boards, computer terminals, and similar facilities open to campus groups" (Kaplin and Lee 2013, 1243). Consequently, students at state institutions may form clubs, interest groups, teams, and other organizations as they wish.

On the other hand, private colleges do not have to allow students to form organizations. In the strictest sense, a private college may determine that having student organizations is not in the best interest of the college, and consequently may not allow such activity. But what happens if the college accepts federal funds to build a special building, and students, all of whom received federal financial aid, want to form an organization and meet in that building? Lawsuits are made of such circumstances. As a practical matter, the educational benefits of students forming organizations are complementary with what most colleges desire from such experiences, and therefore, in most cases students are allowed to organize.

This does not mean, however, that student groups can do whatever they want, wherever they want, whenever they want. Kaplin and Lee (2013) cite *Healy v. James* as a leading case in this area of law. They conclude that three principles affect student organizations on campus. First, student organizations seeking recognition may be required to adhere to specific campus regulations requiring that their activities be peaceful. Second, administrators may deny recognition of student organizations that have been disruptive. Third, the institution may deny recognition of organizations that advocate violating the law.

In administrative practice, *Healy v. James* (1972) often is cited as providing the tools to administrators to regulate the time, place, and manner in which organizations go about their business on campus. *Healy* also has been interpreted to mean that students may not disrupt the general routine of colleges and universities, such as by their taking over a classroom or making so much noise in a library that patrons cannot read.

From your perspective as an organization's adviser, it will suffice simply to know that students have a right to organize and that institutions can require them to follow a registration or recognition process to use campus facilities and services. The burden of applying regulations fairly and without prejudice falls on the institution. As Kaplin and Lee (2013) conclude, "Administrators should apply the rules evenhandedly, carefully avoiding selective applications to particular groups whose views or goals they find to be repugnant" (1246).

Federal and State Laws

It should go without saying that student organizations must comply with state and federal laws. Some students, however, operate under the assumption that because they are students they are exempted from state and federal laws. Obviously they do not enjoy such immunity. One area of particular importance relates to the possession and use of alcoholic beverages. Evidence is available for us to conclude that alcohol abuse is widespread on some campuses, the proof of which typically can be found in trash receptacles after a weekend of revelry and is of major concern to institutional administrators (Dunkle and Presley 2009). Underage consumers of alcoholic beverages run the risk of arrest; those providing the alcoholic beverages also may be liable to arrest and prosecution.

As we have stated elsewhere, most institutions have a variety of rules and regulations designed to influence the behavior of student organizations; some of the more common regulations prohibit the use of alcoholic beverages on campus and require that student organizations be registered to use space on campus. Some require adherence to policies regarding the display of posters in campus buildings. Many campuses expressly prohibit organizations from hazing new members (some state laws also prohibit this activity).

Even though campus regulations do not carry the force of law, you are obligated to urge the student officers and members in the strongest terms possible to follow the letter and spirit of the regulations. You probably will not want to work with students who wiggle in and out of trouble because they have breached campus regulations on a chronic basis, nor do you want to expose yourself to the penalties of the legal system by condoning the violation of laws. Accordingly, we urge you to explain the law to students and emphatically point out the risks they run when they do violate laws or campus regulations. Organizations that are chronic violators of the law, in particular, should cause you to pause and reflect on whether being associated with them is in your best interest.

Managing Risk

Our discussion of managing risk starts with defining a tort. "A tort is broadly defined as a civil wrong, other than a breach of contract, for which the courts will allow a remedy" (Kaplin and Lee 2013, 213). "The two classic torts that most frequently arise in the setting of postsecondary education are negligence and defamation" (2013, 214). In the case of advising, the most common tort is negligence.

Although the risk of lawsuits centering on negligence is obvious, and you are not immune from being sued, certain elements must be present for litigation to be successful for the plaintiff or claimant. Barr (1988) identifies three elements that must be present in a negligence claim: (1) the defendant owed a duty of care to the claimant, (2) the defendant breached that duty, and (3) the breach of duty was the proximate cause of the injury. The applicable general standard in this situation is that you must behave like a "reasonable person," that is, behave the way a reasonable person would in a similar situation. The standard does not call for extraordinary insight, prescience, or some other quality that an average person normally would not apply to similar circumstances.

College students tend to see themselves as being invulnerable to accidents and injuries, and they may plan events without carefully reflecting on the risks involved. Thus it falls to you to apply the "reasonable person" standard to student events, reviewing activities with officers and other members who are planning programs and making sure that risks have been identified and minimized.

In practical terms, the "reasonable person" standard means that normal precautions should be taken to prevent problems from occurring that a reasonable person would anticipate. You are not expected to foresee that falling space junk will hit a car and cause an accident resulting in injuries to the passengers. On the other hand, wrestling and boxing matches, eating and drinking contests, or long distance running for students who have not engaged in a rigorous physical training regimen are dangerous because the activities potentially involve a great deal of risk. Reasonable people would not schedule such an event.

Job Descriptions

One of the best ways to manage the risks associated with being an organization's adviser is to ensure that this appointment is part of your official assignment at the university. In some cases being the organization's adviser makes perfect sense because advising would follow naturally from your normal work assignment. For example, when a member of the student activities staff advises the union board, that work commonly would be understood to be a part of the person's responsibilities at the college. But suppose a faculty member from the chemistry department coaches and advises the rugby club? Is advising the rugby club part of the faculty member's work at the university, or is it simply a volunteer assignment that has no connection with the person's employment on campus?

We cannot overstate the importance of the advising role's being defined as part of your formal work at the university. If advising a student organization is not seen as part of your role on campus, then such resources as legal counsel or the university's insurance policy may not be available to you. It works to your advantage to make sure that the assignment is within the scope of your employment at the institution.

As a practical matter, most organizations will not be involved in high-risk behavior that could result in tremendous exposure to negligence. Departmental clubs, for example, generally are engaged in fairly benign activities. They have meetings, host speakers, hold banquets, and so on. On the other hand, many campuses have organizations that engage in high-risk activities, such as contact sports, that can result in injuries. The rugby club team in the previous example illustrates our point. Moreover, some clubs take trips by car or van. As a matter of self-protection, advisers to all organizations should have confirmation that advising is part of their institutional assignment. It would be a painful lesson if you were to learn after the fact that university legal counsel and other resources such as insurance would not be available to provide a defense against a negligence claim.

Event Planning

Although things can go wrong even when events are well planned, your keeping the "reasonable person" standard in mind and trying to anticipate problems and provide solutions in advance make excellence sense. Four basic principles apply in event planning that will help minimize risk.

Contracts We start by offering a reminder that unless you have special skills or an education in the area, you ought to get help if you are being asked to sign a contract on behalf of the organization. This contract could cover anything from an agreement with a restaurant to cater a banquet to a purchase from a vendor who will make T-shirts for the organization's members. Depending on your campus's policy, you may need to have contracts reviewed by the institution's legal counsel or senior financial officer. On the other hand, absent a campus policy, you may prefer to consult with the office of student activities and seek advice in terms of the contract that you are being asked to sign, or the contract that an officer of the organization needs to sign before the T-shirts can be ordered. Most contracts are going to be straightforward, meaning that the vendor agrees to provide the T-shirts and the organization agrees to pay a certain amount for them. Bur since most of us don't buy fifty T-shirts at a time, or plan banquets for a hundred people, we think asking for a review from a knowledgeable person makes great sense.

Industry Standards Industry standards should be followed if they are available. For example, whenever equipment is to be used in an event, your group should follow the instructions provided by the manufacturer about how to use the equipment. In addition, governing bodies, such as the National Intramural–Recreational Sports Association (http://nirsa.org/), are sources of information on how to provide for the safety of participants in various activities. Many sporting events require certain kinds of equipment. Fast-pitch softball, for example, should not be played unless catchers wear appropriate protective gear and batters wear helmets. Camping equipment ought to be checked by knowledgeable, well-trained staff before being used on a trip. If people supervising various elements of an event are required to have a certain level of skill, they should be trained in accordance with the industry standards. If an organization is having a swimming event, for example, the lifeguards should be trained to meet Red Cross standards. Similarly, private officers who are hired to provide security for an event need to have appropriate training. Industry standards should never be compromised.

Transportation   Student organizations may want to take field trips that require transportation off campus. These trips may be to a local attraction, but in other cases they can involve trips of considerable distance. The use of private automobiles with student drivers has the potential for tremendous problems.

Clearly, the safest way to travel is to use a common carrier, meaning commercial transportation. When a common carrier is used, the risk associated with the trip is in effect partially transferred to that carrier. This approach assumes that the carrier is licensed to do business, does not have a history of accidents, and has not experienced any other problems such as failing to provide safe equipment. The use of a common carrier is always preferable to having members provide the transportation. Common carriers, unfortunately, are likely to be more expensive than private transportation, so the only practical way to take the trip may be to use student drivers. Alternate precautions will need to be taken to ensure a safe trip.

You certainly cannot ensure that problems will not arise during a trip, but your group should take several steps in advance of the trip to make sure that reasonable precautions are in place. Among these are the following:

- All drivers should have valid operating licenses.
- No drivers should have a history of speeding tickets, reckless driving, driving while intoxicated, or any other problems that would lead one to conclude that they are not prudent operators of vehicles. In short, all drivers should have a clean record of operating motor vehicles.
- All drivers and vehicles should be insured.
- All vehicles should be in good operating condition.
- No vehicles should be operated in a fashion that is not consistent with how the vehicle was designed, for example, overloaded with passengers and luggage, or with passengers riding in the open bed of a truck.
- No driver should be at the wheel for an extended period of time. Drivers should be rotated to avoid fatigue.

- No person should be allowed to drive after consuming alcoholic beverages.

- You need to ask very pointed questions about the safety of the vehicles and the drivers' records. If any questions arise, the trip should be postponed until the problems can be addressed.

At times it may make more sense to use institutional vehicles rather than the members' vehicles. Again, this approach may require additional expense, but presumably vehicles kept in the institution's motor pool undergo routine maintenance and have excellent vehicle service records. If your group does use institutional vehicles, it will have to follow the institution's regulations regarding the use of such vehicles. For example, there may be issues related to insurance and to operator training. Obviously, your group must plan in advance if it intends to use institutional vehicles. We recommend that you call the motor pool administrator far in advance of when transportation will be required to avoid last-minute problems that could cause the trip to be canceled.

As the types of students who attend our colleges continue to diversify (see Renn and Reason 2013), several additional implications arise related to travel. What happens if organization members want to bring their children on a trip because long-term child care is difficult to arrange? May the nonstudent spouse of an organization member come on the trip? May a student who is a minor come on the trip? These scenarios and others illustrate thorny problems for groups, leaders, and advisers. Who will provide oversight for the minor child in the example above when the student is attending a session of a conference? Supposing that the college proscribes alcoholic beverages, may spouses drink if they are of age? What if a student who is a minor suffers an accident and needs medical care? You and your group's leadership should consult with legal counsel on how to proceed in advance of the trip.

Substitute Events Some kinds of activities—such as tugs of war, weightlifting contests, and competitions related to how much people can eat, how fast they can eat a certain amount of food, or the worst of all—both—are inherently risky, and if it is possible, your group should plan substitute events. If an event is planned in which there is some risk, then your group should take steps to ensure that the risk is minimized. The value of risk management strategies is identified by Kaplin and Lee (2013) who assert, "Risk management may be advisable not only because it helps stabilize the institution's financial condition over time but also because it can improve the morale and performance of institutional personnel by alleviating their concerns about potential personal liability. In addition, risk management can implement the institution's humanistic concern for minimizing the potential for injuries to innocent third parties resulting from its operations and for compensating any such injuries that do occur" (169).

Waivers

One common way organizations attempt to minimize risk is by asking participants to sign waiver forms crafted so as to absolve the organization (and its leaders) from any responsibility for injury that may result from participating in the activity. The assumption underlying the use of waivers is that by having students waive their right to hold anyone responsible for their injuries, the institution (and the adviser and officers) will be held harmless from whatever occurs.

The potency of waivers, meaning whether they will be successful in protecting an institution against unfavorable legal action, will depend on the legal environment of the state in which the institution and the legal action taken against it is located. Many institutions have risk management departments that can be helpful in developing appropriate language in developing a waiver or an informed consent document. Examples of these can be found at http://riskmanagement.rutgers.edu/waivers-and -informed-consent-forms or http://orm.uoregon.edu/content/waivers.

Insurance

Another way of minimizing risk is to purchase insurance, including health and accident insurance as well as liability insurance. There are two ways of securing liability insurance. One approach is to make sure that you are covered under the institution's blanket liability insurance. Many institutions have a liability policy that protects employees from judgments against them in the course of their work; the insurance provides monetary compensation in the case of an adverse judgment against the employee. As stated earlier, for insurance purposes it is imperative that you be defined as an institutional employee engaged in an assignment that is part of your work assignment; you cannot be seen as performing this function as a volunteer.

The second method of securing liability insurance coverage is for you to purchase a private policy. Often, professional associations offer this kind of insurance for a fairly modest premium. Some advisers carry liability insurance even if their institution provides coverage as just described. The ultimate decision on purchasing personal liability insurance is yours to make. Our general view is that an adviser without some form of coverage is taking a big risk; a policy providing several million dollars in liability coverage would be very prudent protection.

Your institution should also consider requiring health and accident insurance for student participants in various events. The institution may have a health and accident insurance policy that can be made available to students on an event-by-event basis. If available, students pay (or the organization pays on their behalf) a modest premium in exchange for basic health and accident insurance. The value of this coverage is well worth the cost if a student suffers an injury in the course of the event and requires medical attention. Although it is unlikely that a healthy, traditional-age student will come down with a complex illness requiring hospitalization while on a trip sponsored by the organization, the student might slip and fall suffering an injury and a trip to the emergency room of the local hospital. If this kind of policy is available, the institution's office of risk management can describe the coverage in more detail.

Special Issues

For us to provide you with appropriate background on legal matters, we also need to address six special legal issues. These regard handling money; following the copyright law; hazing; the possession and use of alcoholic beverages; serving people with disabilities; and reporting potential crimes.

Money Chapter 8 is devoted to financial management, but we should also look at the legal context that governs how funds are handled. You do not serve as the organization's treasurer, but you should be keeping a careful eye on the legal aspects of how the organization handles its funds. Obviously, the organization must avoid expending funds in violation of state law or contrary to institutional regulations. If the organization sells products, such as a T-shirt sale, it may have to collect sales tax. If it hires workers, it may have to pay social security tax and even withhold income tax; even the slightest hint of an irregularity demands an intervention on your part, through a direct discussion with the organization's officers, a call to the institution's student activities office, or a conference with the chief financial officer of the institution.

Copyright Laws Faculty members commonly think of copyright laws in the context of their photocopying sections of books and using the resulting material in class, for research, or in some other way related to scholarship.

Organizations are more vulnerable, however, to violating the copyright law as it applies to the use of copyrighted entertainment materials. The fair use doctrine is applied to determine whether or not a violation of the copyright law has occurred. Kaplin and Lee (2013) write:

> Fair use involves a case-by-case inquiry that requires balancing of the following four statutory factors:
>
> *Purpose and character* of the use, including whether the use is for educational versus commercial purposes
>
> The *nature of the copyrighted work*—is it a factual or creative work?
>
> The *amount and substantiality* of the portion to be used in relation to the work as a whole
>
> The *effect or impact* of the use upon the potential market for or value of the work (1588–1589)

Renting a DVD and showing it at a club meeting, a residence hall lounge, or a fraternity house may seem like a harmless, inexpensive form of entertainment. The problem with this scenario, unfortunately, is that it may constitute a public showing of copyrighted work, which is illegal, assuming the material included in the video is copyrighted and those exhibiting the video have not purchased a special license. Without an agreement with the copyright holder, no one can show copyrighted work in a public forum even if no fees or ticket sales are involved. So, unless your organization secures a special license, it will have to seek alternative forms of entertainment or risk exposure to legal penalties. Similarly, copyright laws govern the use of music. When the organization's leaders are proposing programming involving copyrighted materials a conversation between you, the organization's leaders, and legal counsel is in order. A discussion of penalties is available at a "Dear Colleague" letter at http://ifap.ed.gov/dpcletters/GEN1008.html. Your institution's senior technology officer, dean of students, or legal counsel may have ideas about obtaining permission to use copyrighted materials for organizational programs.

Hazing   The Fraternity Insurance Purchasing Group (2013) defines hazing as "any action taken or situation created, intentionally, whether on or off fraternity premises, to produce mental or physical discomfort, embarrassment, harassment, or ridicule" (8). Hazing may have become less common on contemporary college campuses than might have been the case years ago. Nonetheless, it has been known to be a part of the ritual of certain organizations and clubs. Consequently, it is important to point out that many states have passed laws that make hazing illegal. In New York, for example, "A person is guilty of hazing in the first degree when, in the course of another person's initiation into or affiliation with any organization, he intentionally or recklessly engages in conduct which creates a substantial risk of physical injury to such other person or a third person and thereby causes such injury" (Cornell University 2014). Campuses also may have policies that make hazing a violation of institutional regulations. Middlebury College, as an illustration, has the following policy: "College policies include the prohibition of many activities that have traditionally been associated with hazing, such as illegal alcohol use and abuse, vandalism, theft, verbal or physical abuse or threat of harm, sexual harassment, and other forms of harassment" (Middlebury College 2013).

Hazing often is thought of as the exclusive territory of fraternal organizations but such is not always the case. Student military organizations and performance groups have been known to engage in hazing with severe consequences. A notable example is the Florida A&M University marching band (Alvarez 2013). The *FIPG (Fraternal Information & Programming Group)* Manual has excellent material related to hazing prevention. It is available at http://www.fipg.org/ and we recommend this resource to all organization advisers.

Alcoholic Beverages "Abuse of alcohol and other drugs can cause problems of great magnitude involving harm to both students involved in the abuse and others in the educational community" (Sandeen and Barr 2006, 162). Among the problems created by alcohol abuse are physical and emotional problems by those who abuse alcohol, drunk driving citations, traffic accidents, intoxicated students who fall out windows or off roofs, fights and other forms of altercations, and so on. In the worst situations, students die directly or indirectly from alcohol abuse.

"Many states, under Dram Shop statutes, hold persons who negligently furnish liquor to minors vicariously liable for minors' acts. Institutions could be liable to third parties for its students' acts if the university furnishes liquor or authorizes the serving of liquor to minors" (Ledbetter 2009, 514). In other words, an organization and its adviser may be held responsible for what happens as a result of the misuse of alcoholic beverages by a participant in the organization's event.

The best risk management technique regarding alcohol is that it should not be available at student events. If it must be served, at a minimum you should make efforts to ensure that

- Underage people are not served.

- Anyone operating a motor vehicle is not served.

- A limit is placed on the amount of alcohol any single person can consume.

- Nonalcoholic beverages are available.

- Food is served.

- Alcoholic beverages are not served for at least an hour before the activity concludes.

- All those who are of legal age to possess and consume alcoholic beverages wear a wrist band that cannot be transferred to an underage person.

Another strategy that you might want to encourage the organization to employ is to use a commercial vendor (such as a restaurant or club) for events involving alcoholic beverages. Let professional bartenders decide when people have had enough to drink. Participants should also use designated drivers or commercial transportation so that they can get home safely.

Using these strategies will not guarantee that alcoholic beverages won't cause problems—too much can go wrong when college students and alcohol mix—but at least you can provide yourself and the members of your organization with a margin of safety.

People with Disabilities "Two federal laws forbid employment discrimination against individuals with disabilities. The Americans with Disabilities Act (ADA), 42 U.S.C. §§ 12101 et seq., prohibits employment discrimination by employers with fifteen or more employees, and also applies to labor unions, and employment agencies. Section 504 of the Rehabilitation Act, 29 U.S.C. § 794 (also discussed in Section 14.5.4), also prohibits discrimination against individuals with disabilities, but unlike the ADA, there is no threshold number of employees required for coverage" (Kaplin and Lee 2013, 451–452) by Section 504 (*Schrader v. Fred A. Ray M.D.*, 296 F.3d 968 [10th Cir. 2002]). "In combination, these laws have created enormous challenges for student affairs and higher education" (Sandeen and Barr 2006, 160–161). These laws prohibit excluding students from participating in campus organizations and activities. If activities require special accommodations for students with disabilities, those accommodations must be provided. For example, a student who has a hearing impairment may require an interpreter. Meetings and activities must be held in buildings accessible to students who use wheelchairs.

Most campuses have made tremendous progress in making programs and activities accessible, but other issues arise. What happens when the group travels to a conference? What if, because of the unusual circumstances of the trip, a student requires an attendant? Who pays for an interpreter for a student with impaired hearing? If the group is traveling by van, must the vehicle be accessible? These questions can lead to difficult and potentially expensive solutions. Our view, however, is that while there may be considerable expense in arriving at a reasonable accommodation, denying access to participate in organizational activities is far worse for all concerned, whether the denial technically is legal or not. Most accommodations are not as dramatic as what one may surmise from the questions raised in this paragraph. The value of inclusion, in our view, trumps any problems caused by the additional costs that may be associated with providing a reasonable accommodation. If answers are not clear to questions raised by alternative accommodation solutions, taking advantage of campus legal counsel is a logical step; the director of campus services for students with disabilities also is likely to be helpful. Contact these resources for their advice when your group is planning activities that will require special accommodations for students or advisers with disabilities. In some cases the ADA and Section 504 may not apply to the activities of private universities; we recommend that organization advisers check with the appropriate institutional resources to make sure that they and the organization's members understand their obligation to apply the law to circumstances that involve access to organizational programs and services.

Title IX We include just a word about Title IX, which prohibits discrimination on the basis of sex in higher education programs (National Center for Education Statistics 2014). More information about Title IX can be found at http://nces.ed.gov/fastfacts/display.asp?id=93 and we provide this brief reference as a reminder that should anyone suggest that the organization you advise prohibit women from membership or from any of the activities that the organization sponsors, legal problems very well may not be far behind.

Adherence to the Clery Act "The law requires universities to notify the campus community of certain criminal activity and includes a provision giving individuals who bring sexual assault complaints access to information regarding the institution's findings" (Ledbetter 2009, 523). "On

Aug. 14, 2008, the *Higher Education Opportunity Act* or HEOA (Public Law 110–315) reauthorized and expanded the *Higher Education Act* of 1965, as amended. HEOA amended the *Clery Act* and created additional safety- and security-related requirements for institutions" (United States Department of Education 2011, 1). This act potentially applies to organization advisers in that they may be required to report crimes that are reported to you as having occurred on campus or in other areas related to your institution. The University of Florida, for example, has interpreted reporting requirements to include crimes on campus, in property owned by the university or by university-recognized student groups, or on public streets and sidewalks adjacent to campus (Stump 2013, 1).

What this means for advisers and how legal representatives interpret the Clery Act may vary from institution to institution. What is clear is that the federal government takes reporting requirements seriously and that means if an adviser becomes aware of information covered by the act, a call to legal counsel is in order. It is important to note that the Act has many other requirements related to reporting crimes, developing crime statistics, and notifying members of the campus community of potential emergencies.

Case Vignettes

Film Festival

The student organization you advise would like to hold a "classic film festival" and show a series of movies over the course of the semester that are well regarded as classics. The festival would be open to any members of the campus community, including faculty, staff, and students. The members are unsure as to whether or not to charge admission but a preliminary discussion indicated that the admission probably won't be charged. Should you as the adviser worry about this proposed activity?

Rituals

The campus organization you advise has, for years, had a secret initiation ritual. You are not a member of the organization and as such have never witnessed the ritual. While you have no evidence to support your concern, you have heard some "whispers" about members' being forced to engage in activities that could be defined as mild physical abuse. As the adviser, what might you do to allay your concerns?

Secret Bank Account

You are an adviser to an organization with which you've not worked before this semester. Although you have no evidence to confirm this, you are suspicious that the organization has a bank account from which funds are withdrawn to purchase beer for off-campus parties. As you are new to the organization, you've never attended one of these events, but you've heard members talking about end-of-the-year "bashes" and you know that because the organization's funds are deposited with the institution's bursar's office, members must be using some other way to pay for alcohol, if it has been purchased. How might you proceed?

Party Bus

Your organization has a couple of older members who have purchased a dilapidated bus that they park at the off-campus apartment where they reside. You are new to the organization but you've heard some of the members talking about the annual trip they take on the bus to a sporting event where tailgating to excess is the norm. Some of the members who go on this trip are not twenty-one and the rumor is that everyone who goes drinks to the point where the person driving the bus on the return trip may be intoxicated. Because this trip is not an official event, even though most of the members of the organization go on it, should you be concerned? What, if anything, might you do?

Chapter 10

Dealing with Issues and Conflicts

AT VARIOUS TIMES you will have to assist the organization or individual members with issues, conflicts, and other problems. "Successful leaders have come to understand that conflict is not only inevitable in student organizations, but it is also beneficial and healthy, if properly managed. Conflict can stimulate new ideas, clarify elements of an issue, increase task motivation, and lead to better solutions because of increased understanding of opposing perspectives" (Franck 1983, 26). It may be difficult, however, for a student or adviser to perceive the benefit of conflict while committee members are yelling at one another, when a member is in tears, a committee chairperson resigns, or when one executive officer is left out of social functions by the other officers.

Issues and conflicts may be caused by any number of factors, roles, or situations. In some situations, the conflict may be inherent to the structure of the particular student organization. In other situations, conflict may arise from members' and executive officers' inability to communicate, or may be due to members' wanting the organization to get involved in something other than its stated purpose. In this chapter, we categorize the sources of conflict and other problems as organizational structure, politics, funding issues, assumption of power, tradition and culture, communication, personalities, and differing purposes. For each category, we clarify terms, provide examples, and suggest solutions through activities and different approaches.

Organizational Structure

The organizational structure of a student organization may lead to problems. In this section, we look at the adviser's level of authority in relation to the organization, the structure of the executive board, the apportionment of representatives, the members' constituency, and the size of the voting membership.

Authority Level of the Adviser

An organization's president may want to deal directly with a departmental chair or director rather than a graduate student assigned as the organization's adviser. Students may perceive or understand that the graduate student adviser does not possess the authority to make decisions for the department regarding budgets, travel, or policies and procedures. An organization that includes in its purpose attention to divisional or campuswide matters would be best served by an adviser who is placed higher in an academic or student affairs department. Osteen and Tucker (1998) have determined that one of the ingredients leading to success in residence hall associations is the authority level of the adviser. Because residence hall associations work on a systemwide basis, they believe the adviser should be a central office senior staff member. This authority level is one of the key ingredients found at the thirteen institutions that were determined to have the most successful residence hall associations in the United States (Komives and Tucker 1993).

An organization whose purpose includes less than a campuswide matter would be effective with an adviser with fewer years of experience or less authority. A Caving Club may be advised by a geology graduate student interested in karst topography, the Hall Government can be advised by the graduate hall director, the Spanish Club can be advised by a Spanish instructor, or the Puerto Rican Business Club can be advised by a graduate business student.

Structure of the Executive Board

In some organizations, the executive board officers report to the organization's president. Presidents are seen to possess an administration, and they may refer to the executive board as "their administration." The relationships among board members and personality of the executive board may be directed or dictated by the organization's president. The organization's members may approach only the president because they recognize that decisions are made by that person. This executive board structure may distance the executive officers from the organization's membership.

An organization president who is concerned about potential conflicts and problems with the executive board structure can use a few strategies. First, the president might empower the executive board with specific duties and with decision-making authority that works with individuals in the organization's membership. Second, when members give reports during meetings regarding committee work or projects, they should stand and face the membership rather than the president or executive board, so as to give the impression that they are representing the organization. Third, the president should refrain from using such expressions as "my administration," "my executive board," or "I have decided," and should use the more inclusionary "we" or "the executive board." Fourth, executive board members should each have an opportunity during the meeting to report to the membership any work they have completed, programs they are involved in developing, or other responsibility-related work they have performed since the last meeting.

Apportionment of Voting Members

For most student organizations, a number of members will attend the weekly meetings, and if any business is to be conducted, a simple show of hands is the deciding factor. For many larger organizations, however, such as student governments or graduate student councils, the structure of the organization and voting privileges are apportioned. For example, each college on the campus might be provided one voting seat, or each zip code may be allocated a specific number of voting seats. Apportionment is an intentional way of structuring an organization, but it can lead to conflict. To minimize conflicts or problems, how the apportionment is determined should be decided with proper and equitable involvement by all constituencies; otherwise some students may feel as if their voices were not heard. Second, if apportionment is structured by specific colleges or zip codes, it is important for the organization's leadership to ensure that the number of students represented in each bloc is equitable lest a constituency receive a disproportionate number of voting seats. Third, the organization should evaluate the apportionment plan on an annual basis. This evaluation will ensure that as colleges and zip codes change, representation will be adjusted accordingly.

Constituency Served by Voting Members

This issue may be closely related to the apportionment of the student organization, and again is more likely to occur in a large student organization rather than in a special-interest, military, or sports organization. These organizations adopt purposes that typically do not involve serving constituencies with radically different views because they share a common, nonpolitical constituency. However, in the case of student governments, graduate student councils, and residence hall associations, specific constituencies may attempt to secure a majority of the voting rights of the organization. Student government constituencies may be aligned with Greek letter organizations, specific academic units, or a particular political persuasion. Graduate student councils may align with specific academic units. Residence hall association constituencies may be aligned as individual residence halls or as underclass students against upperclass students.

One strategy used by organizations to reduce the likelihood of a constituency's gaining majority voting rights is to include a set of voting guidelines in the organization's constitution that eliminate majority constituency voting. These guidelines would establish a percentage of voting members from each constituency not to exceed 50 percent. For example, a residence hall association could be represented by a percentage of members from individual underclass and upperclass halls, at-large seats, and alumni seats, none of which make up a majority of the voting representatives. For some organizations, this is entirely possible, because the purpose of the organization dissuades members from politicizing their group through constituency management. For student governments, this basic organizational concept is the framework for party control in the organization and is included in the purpose of the organization. You need to recognize the constituencies represented in your organization to foresee the conflicts and problems that might arise among constituencies possessing differing purposes, goals, or objectives.

Size of the Voting Membership

For many organizations, the number of the voting members is never a problem, because the dozen members who attend the weekly or monthly meeting know each other or may have been involved with each other for a number of months or years. For student governments, residence hall associations, Greek letter, or some special-interest organizations, however, the size of the voting membership can be a problem. When a student government holds a vote for student body executive officer positions, many campuses allow the entire student body to vote. For some campuses, setting up a room in the student union with several voting tables is all that is necessary on the day of voting. For other campuses, a successful strategy has been to hire the city or county elections officials to staff multiple voting sites over the course of one or more days. The student government then pays the city or county a fee for administering the process. Other campuses have effectively moved to online voting platforms. The online voting approach eliminates the need for numerous voting poll workers and efficiently and securely provides voting opportunities for large numbers of students.

Similar conflicts or problems may arise in Greek letter and some special-interest organizations that have memberships or representatives in excess of one hundred students. These student organizations similarly employ a voting process that allows only the members of the house or organizational representatives an opportunity to vote. This process restricts the voting to students who have worked with and know the strengths and weaknesses of those running for election. It also eliminates the potential expense or possible involvement of an individual voting or running for office who possesses little knowledge or experience in the organization.

Organizations continue to develop new technological applications to improve the efficiency and accuracy of how they conduct business. Institutions are using database management to allow students online voting via students' personal devices while sitting in their rooms or waiting for a class to start. Although these systems increase the convenience for students, they also open new opportunities for abuse. You will want to monitor these systems closely and call on technology experts to help you understand the system and anticipate potential problems.

Politics

How the members of a student organization choose to work with each other and with other organizations may be best described as politics. Politics is a collective term that for some student organizations serves as the basis of their purpose. For other organizations to function properly over an extended period of time, they must conscientiously refrain from practicing politics in any form. A student organization's involvement in politics may lead to conflict and problems.

Politics can be closely compared to power. (Chapter 4 discusses the seven different power bases.) When students take advantage of their position, their knowledge, their connections to other influential persons, or their ability to provide rewards, they are practicing a form of politics. When students begin to coalesce with similar views toward a specific agenda, they are practicing a lobbying or bloc voting approach. As these groups of students become more organized and intentional in their approaches, they begin to form parties. Some student organizations follow a party doctrine to give purpose to their organization. During campus elections for seats in a student government senate, these organizations may form a ticket of students from their organization to run collectively as a party. This party develops statements or platforms that all members support. Students voting for individual senators may vote for the individual person or may vote all party members in to senate seats.

Throughout these processes the potential exists for conflict and problems; for example, students may feel pressured to vote for a specific person or party, legislation may fail to pass in a student senate because of bloc voting, or budget allocations may be hindered by various pressures or favors needing attention. Most student organizations will never be involved in these types of politics: their interest in political involvement is nonpartisan, or the organization takes a politically neutral stance. The few organizations that are involved in these political practices do so because of their interest in political processes, the legislative system, or campaign issues.

If you are an adviser to one of these types of organizations, you can assist in decreasing the likelihood of misuse of politics by ensuring that policies, guidelines, and proper financial practices are followed. Some additional strategies include meeting with the students involved in the student government executive and legislative branches jointly to discuss the use and misuse of their positions. Forming a student and faculty oversight committee is also a good strategy to prevent an organization or election process from getting involved in politics that create conflict or problems. The organization also can use the campus student conduct and conflict resolution system as an option when the student code of conduct has been violated.

Funding Issues

Although we discuss general financial matters at length in chapter 8, there are a number of funding issues that can lead to conflict and problems that go beyond the general level. In this section we discuss lack of funding, record management, use of funds, budget preparedness, and external influences.

Lack of Funding

Student organizations never seem to have enough funds to accomplish everything they would like. Komives and Tucker (1993) found that multiple-source funding was a common theme in student organizations' success. Unfortunately, most student organizations receive funding from only one source: fundraising.

The major problem arising from a shortage of funds is that the time spent raising funds is time taken away from the enjoyment of fulfilling the organization's purpose. The members of a sailing club, for example, who must spend considerable time raising money through car washes, bake sales, or sponsorships, may find they have little time to practice sailing. Students can become quite frustrated.

Chapter 8 identifies numerous sources of funds that student organizations might pursue. As the group's adviser, you can also stress that fundraising events themselves can provide positive experiences for the members other than just raising money. These events, if handled properly, can provide an opportunity for members to work on a project together, which creates teamwork and a sense of group purpose. Fundraisers also allow the students to get away from campus and have fun relaxing from the pressures of schoolwork, or to assist the community in a common venture through a service learning project. Through creatively planned fundraising events, students can focus their attention away from their frustration over the lack of funds.

Financial Record Management

Students elected or appointed to positions responsible for the financial records have an important responsibility. Conflict and problems arise when the student responsible for the record keeping, typically an organization's treasurer, auditor, or accountant, gets behind in his or her duties. For many student organizations, record keeping may simply be maintaining a checkbook. For larger student organizations, with several students working on financial matters, record keeping may involve a number of different agencies and full-time employees handling several accounts. Regardless of the complexity of the duty, it is important to maintain financial records in a timely fashion. Audit criticisms, returned checks, bounced checks, lost bank statements, or cash lying around can create problems both devastating for the organization and tremendously time-consuming to clear up. Chapter 8 discusses how audits, record keeping, and presentation of records can be best accomplished.

Use of Funds

Private and public institutions allow students to make decisions on the expenditure of funds, as regulated by the policies and procedures of the institution and the laws of the state. Occasionally, executive boards or individual members of student organizations make questionable decisions about how to spend their funds. Some student organizations have purchased vehicles and laptop computers for an individual's use; members have taken personal trips; and one student government even purchased one thousand pink plastic flamingos. In most of these extreme examples the oversight was not in place to cancel these purchases through such techniques as two-party signatures on checks or institutional staff involvement.

The types of conflict and other problems resulting from how funds are used can vary. Negative public reaction to the use of funds to purchase items for personal use is very difficult to overcome. In some instances, when use of funds appears to be out of control, all accounts are frozen while an audit takes place, staff involvement becomes a necessary step in the use of students' funds, or an organization such as a student government may be forced to disband while an assessment and reorganization take place. Advisers who take the time to learn about the student organization's financial practices can assist the organization and its members in developing a sound system of fund use.

One good practice for a student organization is to conduct readings regarding the expenditure of funds, held over the course of two consecutive organizational meetings. An expense reading requires the expense to be proposed, debated, and voted on during a meeting. By using two meetings to discuss the information, members can take the information to their respective constituencies for feedback prior to the second reading. Also, both readings will be recorded in the organization's minutes. By involving membership in spending decisions, these practices help reduce the likelihood that funds will be misused.

Budget Development

The student responsible for preparing and presenting the budget may face conflicts and problems. The duty of the financial officer who prepares the budget is to secure the best information possible using both past and current figures. When a budget is presented to the membership for approval, it is important for the financial officer to be prepared to answer questions regarding how much money was spent on a specific line the previous term; how the amount in each line item was determined; who was involved in providing information for the budget; which items are new and were not included in the past; whether the organization has enough revenues to meet its expenses; what the source of the revenues is; or what difficulties the financial officer foresees in the budget for the given term. The membership can ask many questions related to the budget presentation. A good strategy to employ prior to presenting a budget is to have the financial officer prepare and present the budget to you and the organization's executive board. You and the board then can anticipate the questions that the membership is likely to ask. This "preview" gives the financial officer an opportunity to respond and to secure additional information or make additional copies of appropriate documents to support his or her answers. The more carefully the financial officer prepares the budget, the better able he or she is to make the presentation and to respond to questions from the organization's membership.

External Influences

Individuals representing various companies and agencies will approach a student organization's executive board or financial officer with proposals. On the surface these proposals may look like good arrangements for making additional money for the organization. Student organizations and advisers must take care in the relationship they establish with outside vendors, fundraisers, or individuals.

A number of reputable companies provide fundraising ideas, strategies, and services for student organizations. These companies have had success with institutions for many years by providing a percentage return to the organization for the sale of carpets, refrigerators, pennants, mugs, key chains, diploma frames, birthday boxes, welcome baskets, and so forth. One factor to consider is that on some campuses, student government–funded organizations are not allowed to conduct fundraising. Often businesses are looking for a way to affiliate with your institution to get in front of their target market. Frequently, they have been told no by the institution and therefore view student organizations as a method to get their foot in the door. (Chapter 8 discusses the use of external vendors as a fundraising option.) Many problems can arise from contracts, guarantees, and formal arrangements that student organizations enter into to raise funds. The institutional student activities office or general counsel's office are good resources when a company or individual approaches an organization regarding these ventures.

Assumption of Power

Student organizations have frequent turnover in executive board, committee, and task force members. In addition to this turnover, whenever students are elected, appointed, or assigned responsibilities, they assume a position with new responsibilities and duties. Member and leader turnover may result in role confusion and subsequent conflicts and problems.

As student organization executive boards are elected, several conflicts or problems might arise. The president of the organization may be elected from the membership or may, by constitutional designation, be required to have prior service on the executive board. Similarly, executive board members may have had to satisfy other qualifications in order to be elected. Conflict can arise if, following election, the executive board did not meet to identify and clarify their specific responsibilities and the duties of various board members. You can assist this process by ensuring that the executive board meets to discuss and agree on its responsibilities. Chapter 5 discusses officer duties and the position descriptions of the officers in greater detail.

Role confusion can also interfere with the assumption of power and decision-making authority. For example, the financial officer may understand that decisions regarding finances are the responsibility of the financial officer, but the president, assuming the role of leader of the organization, might believe that any decision regardless of the financial implications should be made by the president. Or the organization secretary, who is responsible for reserving meeting space, does so without the consent of the president, who wants to be involved in all operational decisions. Both examples highlight the need to discuss roles and responsibilities as soon after an election as possible.

Role confusion can also ensue for people serving as advisers, because they "are charged with maintaining fiscal responsibility, yet are also indoctrinated into the philosophy of allowing students to do their own programming. Often these two roles conflict as when students wish to sponsor a program requiring a considerable financial commitment, and it is unclear whether students can make the programming decision or the adviser can make the budget-conscious decision" (Franck 1983, 26). As we have stated elsewhere, it is essential that you and the executive board hold a meeting to clarify and agree to everyone's roles as promptly as possible following the election. It is a good practice to outline the roles and responsibilities of each officer in the organization's constitution and use the constitution as a guide when conflicts arise.

Because students are involved in committees, task forces, and groups other than the executive board, it is important that these students receive a committee charge from the appropriate executive board member. A written committee charge identifies the purpose of the committee, the role of committee members, a timeline the committee should follow to fulfill its purpose, and how the committee should present the information it has worked on. Exhibit 10.1 provides an example of a committee charge. You too may have a role in assisting the executive board to determine or draft the committee charge. Large student organizations may require a separate, designated adviser to work with a committee, task force, or special project.

EXHIBIT 10.1

Committee Charge Example

Committee: Executive Board Organizational Review

Chair: Nicholas Osteen

Members: Brad Langan, Amanda Simon, Yvonne Dooley, Dominick Healy

Timeline: To begin meeting immediately upon receipt of the committee charge. Committee meeting frequency is determined by committee members. Final report due at end of present term.

Purpose: To review the present organizational structure of the executive board. To provide a written report to the president outlining recommendations for organizational change and the rationale for the recommendations. To identify the steps taken and the individuals who provided information to the committee in considering recommendations.

Member role: To participate actively in committee discussion. To represent the constituency that appointed the member. To take information to the bimonthly organizational meetings for feedback.

| _____ | _____ |
| President | Date |

Tradition and Culture

Students join organizations for various reasons, one of which is their interest in the role an organization plays in campus traditions. There are many student organization traditions that are positive or service oriented. Greek letter organizations possess long-standing traditions of tapping members into chapters or using Greek letters and shields to reflect the history of the organization. Recognition and honorary organizations are steeped in tradition, as such organization names as Mortarboard or Cicerones would suggest. Sports organizations such as rugby clubs maintain traditions in the practice of their sport traced back to its European ancestry. Despite all the positive traditions and cultures attached to many student organizations, the potential for conflict or problems still exists. A tradition that is not in line with the educational mission of the institution, or a practice that violates the student code of conduct or state and federal laws are two categories of traditions that you can work to avoid.

Stereotypes and Cliques

When students stereotype an organization or a person who is a member of an organization, they engage in an activity that is not inclusive or accepting of that person or organization. Lack of inclusion or acceptance generally runs against the educational mission of an institution. You can work with student organizations by discussing stereotypes and the negative views associated with them. You can also assist in bringing members of different organizations together to speak on their purposes and programs. This meeting generally provides information that is beneficial to all the student organizations in attendance. For example, if members of an organization are stereotyping members of a computer club as being "geeks," "techies," or "nerds," the adviser of the organization can work to bring his or her members to a meeting with members of the computer club. What may well be discovered is that the two groups can join together in a fundraiser using the club's expertise with computers and the other organization's expertise with publicity. Bringing two organizations together can be mutually beneficial and can work to eradicate stereotypes.

You also need to be aware of the membership cliques that form as members find commonalities. Classes of students entering the organization will have a tendency to form a clique of students with similar academic interests. Cliques can be exclusive and open to stereotyping, or they may begin to organize as separate, smaller entities in order to vote as a bloc during meetings. Together with student leaders, you can work to identify these problems early, associating returning members with new members early in the year or designing programs to combine the talents and skills of returning and new members. These efforts will provide benefits as the year progresses by encouraging open communication, fostering retention of new members, and involving members in programs.

Code or Law Violations

Traditions that violate the campus code of student conduct or state and federal laws clearly are problematic. Traditions such as hazing are associated with a number of organizations. Increasingly, we are observing hazing associated with sports clubs, military organizations, Greek letter organizations, and even honor organizations. As discussed from the legal viewpoint in chapter 9, hazing activities in Greek letter organizations are defined as:

> Any action taken or situation created intentionally, whether on or off fraternity premises, to produce mental or physical discomfort,

embarrassment, harassment, or ridicule. Such activities may include but are not limited to the following: use of alcohol; paddling in any form; creation of excessive fatigue; physical and psychological shocks; quests, treasure hunts, scavenger hunts, road trips, or any other such activities carried on outside or inside the confines of the chapter house; wearing of public apparel that is conspicuous and not normally in good taste; engaging in public stunts and buffoonery; morally degrading or humiliating games and activities; and any other activities that are not consistent with fraternal law, ritual, or policy or with the regulations and policies of the educational institution. (National Interfraternity Conference 1991, I-34)

In the effort to eliminate these practices, campuses and governing bodies of fraternities are actively pursuing chapters that continue to practice hazing. If you discover any signs that your group is planning these types of activities, you should discuss it with organizational leadership immediately. You should remind student leaders that hazing is illegal in all states. In addition, you can develop programs that educate your organization's members about the types of activities that are considered hazing and the rationale for prohibiting hazing activities in an educational setting. Most campuses have excellent resources to help identify hazing activities and provide alternative activities. You can find these resources in student conduct, student activities, or the Greek life office.

Another degrading activity that many student organizations practice is commonly referred to as an auction, during which individuals are auctioned to the highest bidder. The person may be auctioned as a date, to provide a package of gifts or services to the winning bidder, or because they are the best dressed. This type of fundraiser is particularly demeaning to African American students, who commonly view this activity as a continuation of the tradition of the sale of slaves. These auctions are also discouraged due to the objectification of men or women they present, especially date auctions. You can work with your student organization, first, to discuss why the name of the function is inappropriate, and you can work with other students who can in turn communicate information in a peer fashion to help members understand that the activity is demeaning. Second, you can work with the students to reconceive and rename the activity as perhaps a rental of services rather than as an auction. Your actively involving students in these discussions is crucial to students' understanding the problems with this type of activity.

Communication

Communication is the factor most likely to cause conflict and other problems in a student organization. Chapter 5 discusses ways of enhancing various forms of communication on several different levels, and includes examples of agendas, minutes, and resolutions. In this section we discuss the communication conflicts and problems that you may encounter.

Communication can be intertwined with politics, funding issues, organizational structure, and any of the other factors that can cause conflict or problems in an organization. Because communication involves nonverbal, verbal, or written messages, it involves all facets of the student organization. In addition, students' increased use of social media manifests itself in the form of a greater online presence where students represent themselves and their organizations. Refer to Exhibit 10.2 for a case study on the potential conflicts and problems associated with communications.

Nonverbal Communication

A number of problems may result from the nonverbal communication and messages sent by you, the executive board, or members. While a student organization meeting is in session, the individuals who are not currently speaking send strong messages to one another through their nonverbal communication.

Advisers Some student organizations have their adviser sit at the front table with the executive board. Other advisers sit in a front row of the body, and still others sit on the far end of the back row. Where you sit during the meeting will communicate whether you are an active or passive participant. We recommend that you sit in the front row on the side, where members can see you, recognize that you are paying attention during the meeting, and still understand that you are not an active participant in all meeting matters.

Executive Boards In larger organizations, the executive board may be seated at a front table; other groups have more informal meetings where the executive board and members are seated in a circle. Regardless of the level of formality, it is imperative that while a member is speaking the executive board be attentive to the individual. Executive board officers who roll their eyes, shake their heads, or sigh in disgust send strong messages to every other individual in the room, each of whom will interpret the messages differently. You can work with executive board members to increase

EXHIBIT 10.2

Communication Case Study

Directions: You can use the following progressive case study with groups of five or six students or advisers. Pass out the initial case to the participants and allow them time to answer the two questions. When they have completed the questions, take ten to fifteen minutes to discuss their answers. Following discussion, hand out the first update and again allow time to complete the questions that follow; continue with the second and third updates in the same way. To finish, allow the participants time to complete the final questions prior to discussion.

Initial Case

You are an adviser to a Greek letter organization. You have served as adviser for the past six years; you possess a good knowledge of the organization's history and procedures, and are familiar with the members. It is the middle of the fall term, and the organization meets on a weekly basis.

Your executive board is composed of three new members to the board and two who had served in varying positions on the board the previous year. At last night's meeting, the president did not recognize two members who wanted to speak.

1. What are your questions at this point in the situation?

2. What action do you take in the situation?

Update One

You have just met with the president to inquire as to why she did not recognize the two speakers. She tells you that several members approached her prior to the meeting and told her the two members would

(continued)

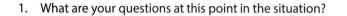

EXHIBIT 10.2 (*continued*)

question why she has not sent a letter to the dean of students requesting an investigation of an alleged hazing activity the two members had witnessed.

1.   What are your questions at this point in the situation?

2.   What action do you take in the situation?

Update Two

The president reluctantly tells you that she was also present at the hazing activity but did not participate. She further explains that the activity caused no harm to anyone and was not meant to be seen by the two members.

1.   What are your questions at this point in the situation?

2.   What action do you take in the situation?

Update Three

You have not told anyone else about your conversation with the president. You have encouraged her to send the letter to the dean of students. During the next meeting, the president allows the two members to speak. They ask the president why the letter was not sent. The president states that she has taken care of the situation and that the situation did not warrant a full investigation. One of the two members reports that she has information that a sexual assault took place as a result of the hazing activity, and asks the president whether she was aware of that information.

1. What are your questions at this point in the situation?

2. What action do you take at this point in the situation?

Final Questions

1. What department, or agencies, or people should have been involved in this situation?

2. What kind of follow-up is necessary in this situation?

(*continued*)

EXHIBIT 10.2 (*continued*)

3.   What other strategies could you have employed in this situation?

---

their understanding of the role of nonverbal communication, not only in meetings but also during individual conversations that executive board officers have with members.

Members Some signals that individual members send during a formal meeting—by getting up to chat with other members, reading newspapers, wearing headphones, playing with phones/tablets/laptops, or holding sidebar conversations—detract from the decorum of the meeting and send a message of being uninterested or of lacking respect for the speaker. The executive board can work with you to conduct a program for members on nonverbal communication and the messages it sends. How members give their reports during meetings is also important, particularly for large formal meetings of student organizations. Members or chairs of committees who stand up and deliver the report to the executive board are sending the message that the report is exclusively for the executive board. To communicate the message that reports are for all the members of the student organization, the member or committee chair should stand in front of the room and turn to give the report to the members of the organization. This reporting procedure takes the emphasis away from the executive board and places it on the members.

A common practice is for students to use their technology during classes, meetings, and the like. For some, people typing, texting, or tweeting while they are speaking is an affront. For others, there is encouragement to use technology to record or represent to others what is being discussed. It will be important as an adviser to spend time with the executive board to discuss the level of technology the executive board will want to allow during meetings.

Verbal Communication

You should take care as an institutional representative to provide appropriate information to the membership of a student organization. Information used in the context of your regular staff or faculty duties may be confidential, or subject to reaction from legal counsel prior to public consumption. Protected information regarding discipline, personnel, academic records, and so forth should be used only in the course of your job, not as part of your advising role.

When you choose to speak during the organization's meeting, you should always take care to avoid siding with one view of the membership. Your role in communicating information is to clarify institutional policies and procedures, to assist the organization's understanding of fiscal responsibility, to provide information on the history of the organization's involvements, and so forth. When you side with a particular subgroup's view, you risk polarizing the membership.

Executive board officers should receive proper training in effectively maintaining the decorum of meetings. Using proper procedure, executive officers can avoid an individual member's using all the available time or getting so emotionally involved as to disrupt the meeting. The organization's president can limit the length of debate, limit the number of times a member can speak about an issue, call a member out of order, or speak to the member following the meeting.

Written Communication

The written materials produced by members of a student organization convey a number of different messages. First, when executive officers produce correspondence, it should be organized and professional. It should not be handwritten on a sheet of notebook paper. The correspondence becomes a part of the history and files of the organization and should be treated professionally.

Similarly, sending copies of the correspondence to other individuals requires attention. When someone in the organization sends a memorandum to the director of the student union and copies are sent to the dean, the vice president for student affairs, and the president of the institution, the memo becomes much more important than a simple file copy. The author of the memo wants the other individuals to be aware of the contents of the memo, to take action, or to ensure that appropriate action is taken. You can assist the authors of correspondence in understanding the implications of copying memoranda to various institutional or state personnel. Occasions will no doubt arise when a student organization will want to send copies of memos or other documents to key administrators, but the authors should understand the potential impact of these communications.

Strengths and Personalities

The personalities of an organization's members, executive officers, and adviser can lead to potential conflict or problems. Understanding individuals' strengths, psychologies, or personality types will allow you not only to assist the student organization through difficult times but also to reinforce the team building of the executive board and membership. There are two programs available to you that we believe are useful in better understanding individuals and how groups can work together. We will briefly summarize StrengthsQuest and the Myers-Briggs Type Indicator.

Taking the Clifton StrengthsFinder assessment will provide users with a prioritized list of thirty-four different strengths. "A strength is the ability to provide consistent, near-perfect performance in a given activity" (Clifton and Anderson 2001–2014, 6). As you understand one another's strengths you are better prepared to work with one another, select a balanced group of students for a committee, and the like. We recommend that you have the executive board take and discuss the StrengthsFinder assessment. The assessment can be facilitated by a certified educator.

One of the most widely used and accepted personality indicators is the Myers-Briggs Type Indicator (MBTI). Because of space restrictions, we will provide only a brief overview of the MBTI.

"C.G. Jung developed one of the most comprehensive of current theories to explain human personality" (Lawrence 1995, 7). Whereas some people saw behavior as random, Jung saw behavior as patterned. The lifelong work of Isabel Briggs Myers "to carry Carl Jung's theory of type . . . into practical applications" (Lawrence 1995, 6) resulted in the Myers-Briggs Type Indicator (MBTI), which Myers developed with her mother, Katherine Briggs.

The personality types identified in the MBTI are categorized by four dimensions: extroversion or introversion, sensing or intuition, thinking or feeling, and judgment or perception. Student organization members can take the MBTI and have the instrument scored to determine individual preferred types. Each individual would possess an identified preferred type in each of the four categories. Understanding the relationships between members who possess one of sixteen different combinations of traits will allow the members to recognize each other's motivations and actions. "If teachers and others in the helping professions were to learn just one thing about psychological types, the thing most important to understand is the power of the dominant process. . . . The most essential thing to know about the motivations of types is that thinking dominant types do their best work when pursuing logical order; feeling types do their best work when their heart is in it; sensing types do their best work when their practical skills are needed and valued; and intuitive types do their best work when pursuing an inspiration" (Lawrence 1995, 16).

We suggest that you have the executive board and the organization's membership take the MBTI. A certified interpreter of the MBTI should present and facilitate a discussion on the MBTI. We find that the MBTI is a very teachable, understandable, and practical tool in developing understanding of personalities among the executive officers and membership of a student organization.

Organization Membership

Public institutions have worked with student organization advisers and students to ensure that membership remains open to any student to participate, become a member, or seek leadership positions. Conflicts arise when a student organization attempts to dissuade or deny students from these opportunities. In the *Christian Legal Society (CLS) Chapter v. Martinez* case (2009), the CLS of the University of California, Hastings College of Law filed suit against the university in a California federal district court. CLS believed their First Amendment rights were violated because the institution held that in order for the CLS to be recognized they must allow any student membership to the organization. The CLS required its members to attest in writing that "I believe in: The Bible as the inspired word of God; The Deity of our Lord, Jesus Christ, God's son; The vicarious death of Jesus Christ for our sins; His bodily resurrection and His personal return; The presence and power of the Holy Spirit in the work of regeneration; [and] Jesus Christ, God's son, is Lord of my life" (Oyez Project 2010, 1). The district court dismissed the case and on appeal, the U.S. Court of Appeals for the Ninth Circuit affirmed. The court held that the school's "conditions on recognizing student groups were viewpoint neutral and reasonable. Therefore, the school's conditions did not violate the CLS's First Amendment rights" (1). This case was then heard by the Supreme Court of the United States who held on June 29, 2010, that "a public college does not violate the First Amendment by refusing to officially recognize a student organization unless it allows all students to join the group, even if that all comers policy requires a religious organization to admit gay students who do not adhere to the group's core beliefs" (Scotus Project 2010).

It is important to work with the campus student activities office when a question arises regarding a student organization's membership practices. There may be greater questions that need to be addressed and in many cases the campus attorneys may be involved.

Differing Purposes

The challenges associated with differing purposes can arise at two levels—the organizational and the individual.

Organizational Level

The purpose statement of the student organization is included in the group's constitution. The student leadership should work with you to regularly review and interpret the purpose statement, which guides the organization as it makes decisions, sets goals for the year, and becomes involved in campus matters. When an organization strays from its stated purpose, the potential for conflict and problems increases.

Problems for an organization may result when it becomes involved in an area where another student organization already works or performs a function; when it takes a political stand or supports a candidate even though the purpose dictates political neutrality; or when it fails to provide the basic programs, services, or funds called for by the purpose statement. In these circumstances you can work with the executive board to assist the organization in clarifying its purpose by holding a roundtable discussion or open forum. If the membership determines that the purpose needs modification, then the organization's constitution should provide the proper steps to modify the purpose.

Individuals involved in a student organization may possess differing attitudes toward its purposes. For example, one or two members of a student organization may strongly believe that the organization should move in a different direction because of religious, political, or philosophical views. It is important for the executive board and organization to allow members the opportunity to express their views. A good strategy is to provide an issue forum as an agenda item at some point during a meeting. The issue forum allows members to address a concern that is of interest to them. The time allowed for an issue forum should be limited; if members desire additional time, a motion to extend the time could be in order. For an organization to prevent a potential problem caused by a member's strong opinion on an issue, it is important to provide the member with an opportunity to speak.

Individual Level

There are occasions when a student organization is considered a university entity (by either the institution or the public) and its existence gives credibility to the institution. For example, the Hispanic-Latino Student Organization may be a student organization; however, its presence on campus allows for Hispanic students to feel as though the institution embraces their culture. This organization may host and fund all the Hispanic Heritage Month events which the public perceives as institutionally driven. Most of the time this process works because the student organization and the institution will strive together to ensure common goals are met. However, there are occasions when the interest of the organization is at odds with those of the institution. For example, if a student organization is responsible for selecting talent at a homecoming event for alumni and they choose a performer the institution knows will be offensive to many, the institution can then be stuck with a public relations issue not necessarily of their making.

Many of the issues and circumstances that lead to conflicts and other problems can be minimized by planning for discussions with the newly elected executive board, possessing documents that clearly identify the organization's purpose, and better understanding and working with one another's strengths and personalities.

Chapter 11

Ensuring Quality in Advising

WHEN DESCRIBING THE challenges that face higher education in the United States, Kuh, Kinzie, Schuh, and Whitt (2005) observed that the future of postsecondary education facing the country was daunting: "The task is to do something at a scale never before realized—to provide a high quality postsecondary education to more than three quarters of the adult population" (xiii). High quality, in our view, extends to all of the experiences of college students, in the classroom, outside of the classroom, in the formal curriculum, the informal curriculum, and so on. Our position is that being a member of one or more student organizations provides an excellent learning opportunity for students, brought to fruition, in part, by high-quality advising provided to the leaders and members of the organization. In addition, our point of view is that all people who play a role in higher education have an obligation to demonstrate that their work is effective and achieves the goals associated with their responsibilities. They need to participate in ongoing programs of assessment so that they can (1) demonstrate accountability to their stakeholders, and (2) improve in their work, along the line crafted by Ewell (2009). Although we do not wish to be overly dramatic in exploring the topic of quality in advising, we are certain that advisers who do not complete their work diligently and competently will not fulfill their obligations to the students with whom they work and to their institution.

There is no point in having individuals advise organizations unless the advice and counsel provided by these individuals are of high quality. But how do we know whether the advising is of high quality? How can we determine whether the organization is benefiting from advising? How does the adviser know whether the organization is functioning at a high level of effectiveness? These and other questions form the basis for this chapter. We propose to address issues related to ensuring quality in advising; to this end, we look at different methodological approaches for assessing advising, briefly describe various methods, and then introduce some techniques that you can use to assess both your group and the job you are doing.

Assessment can be quite complicated, and a number of excellent books have been written on this topic; what we are providing in this chapter is an overview of the process. We realize that most advisers have a full-time work assignment in addition to their work with a student group and, as a consequence, cannot be engaged in highly complex assessment studies. On the other hand, knowing how well one is doing is important to the adviser as well as the organization. In another context, Ed Koch, the dynamic former mayor of New York, was known for traveling around his city and asking citizens this question: "How'm I doin'?" New Yorkers, so the story goes, were not reticent about providing colorful feedback to the mayor. Similar to the feedback provided to Mayor Koch, our view is that the assessment of the adviser and the organization is an ongoing process that may be informal and, at times, anecdotal, but also will require systematic techniques at times, and so we provide information in this chapter that will meet both needs. Our approach will be to introduce some tools that can be used to address the topic of adviser assessment without becoming so burdensome that you will never want to address this issue except in the most cursory way. Although we are not attempting to transform you into an expert on the topic of assessment, we trust that the ideas we present will help you make reasoned judgments about the quality of support you are providing to the organization you advise.

Assessment Defined

Sandeen and Barr (2006) observed the following about assessment: "The curiosity about 'how we are doing,' has become a major force in education at all levels and is now widely known as *assessment*" (132). To establish a common point of departure, we begin with a definition of assessment as "any effort to gather, analyze, and interpret evidence which describes institutional, departmental, divisional, or agency effectiveness " (Upcraft and Schuh 1996, 18). This definition was originally developed to apply to units within student affairs. With just a bit of modification it can be applied to organizations and their advisers. We propose to define assessment for the purpose of this discussion as "any activity designed to determine the effectiveness of the organization or its adviser." Evaluation, for the purpose of this chapter, refers to using assessment data to bring about change and improvement. We believe that advisers can use assessment information to improve their work with student organizations. We recognize that assessment and evaluation have been characterized as different terms in the literature (for example, Schuh and Associates 2009) but because the terms often are used interchangeably we will not draw distinctions between them in this chapter.

Although we are interested primarily in providing tools to help you and your organization determine the effectiveness of your work, it is also important that you are able to measure how well the organization is doing; in short, the assessment process assists in adviser and organizational accountability to various stakeholders. In addition, we see this process as leading to improvement. Hence, we are mixing assessment and evaluation to lead to an environment when accountability and improvement frame the development of the organization and its members.

Types of Assessments and Evaluations

Assessment and evaluation typically occur during the delivery of programs, such as an organization's activities during an academic year, or at the end of an academic year after the organization's activities have been completed. When the assessment or evaluation activity occurs often is referred to as formative or summative. "Formative evaluation refers to the use of evaluation to improve a program during the development phase. It is contrasted with summative evaluation after the completion of the program" (Love 2004, 67). "If the reason for evaluating a program is to decide whether or not to terminate it or to assess which program among several to continue, a summative evaluation will be necessary, and decision makers are likely to be interested in the outcome" (Brown and Podolske 1993, 220). Brown and Podolske (1993) also emphasize that evaluation has a political dimension, although in the context of looking at the effectiveness of an adviser, one would hope that the political nature of evaluation could be kept to an absolute minimum. Nevertheless, "whose interests are served and how interests are represented in an evaluation are critical concerns" (House 1994, 84).

In the context of assessing your work as an organization's adviser, you could have the group's officers or members conduct a formative assessment in the middle of the year to give you feedback about how you are doing. A close relative of formative evaluation is performance monitoring through the use of performance measures. Poister defines performance measures (2004) as "quantitative various aspects of performance of public or nonprofit programs, agencies, or other entities that can be observed on a regular basis" (98). One form of a performance measure is an outcome.

In the case of a student organization, an outcome might be what students have learned from their engagement with the organization. For the adviser, a performance indicator might be satisfaction. Are the organization's leaders satisfied with the work of the adviser? What about the organization's members? Poister's chapter (2004) is a useful reference to these and other performance measures.

You also could be involved in conducting a summative evaluation at the end of the academic year; this very well could be a more formal process that involves the organization's members as well as the officers. The information generated by the evaluation could determine (1) whether or not you would wish to serve for another year, or (2) whether the members would like to invite you to serve again. For small clubs, these evaluations are likely very informal, but for a larger organization, a formal evaluation is in order.

Framing Questions

Before undertaking any assessment, you need to answer a number of questions to help frame the evaluation; resolving these questions now will make the whole process go more smoothly. The following are adapted from the work of Schuh and Associates (2009):

1. Why is the assessment being conducted? Is it routine? Is it because members are dissatisfied with you? Do you want feedback? Are there other reasons? Your group must decide why it is undertaking this process. If those conducting the assessment are not sure why they are doing it, the whole project has the potential to be a colossal waste of time.

2. What will be assessed? Are there specific aspects of your performance that need to be assessed, or is this a comprehensive look at everything you do? If the organization is struggling with its finances through the first semester, will an assessment be conducted that centers on your work with the treasurer? On the other hand, if the year has been deemed to be successful, will the assessment take a comprehensive look at all your work as the organization's adviser?

3. How will you be assessed? Will this be a paper-and-pencil instrument? Will members be interviewed? Will the data be collected electronically? These questions address the techniques your group will employ. We provide a brief overview of assessment techniques later in this chapter.

4. Who will conduct the assessment? Will the officers conduct the evaluation? How will you be involved in the collection of information? Should your group use an external person such as a person from the student activities office or someone who is known to possess strong assessment skills, such as a faculty member from the sociology department? Will a single person or a committee conduct the process? How much expertise is needed? The matter of who will do the work is a thorny problem, potentially full of controversy. Although advisers who work with service organizations or honorary societies may not encounter controversial issues, those who advise student government, Greek letter organizations, political clubs, and the like can face very difficult situations that may require unpopular decisions on the part of the adviser, such as how money may be spent. If some of the organization's members have been openly critical about your work, completing an assessment that appears to be honest and accurate may be quite challenging because of concerns about anonymity and confidentiality.

5. How will the results be analyzed? Who gets to decide what the data mean? What is the context for the analysis? If you take issue with interpretations of the data, will the group provide an opportunity for rebuttal?

6. How will the results be communicated, and to whom? Will the data be handled informally, or will someone write a report? Will the information go only to you? Will the officers get the results? What about the members? If the results are sensitive, just how far does the group go? Nobody wants to be embarrassed by the findings of an assessment, so the officers may need to communicate the results to you privately in the case of a very unfavorable evaluation, rather than hanging you out to dry.

Again, we want to emphasize that your role as adviser and the nature of the organization will have a great deal to do with how you are evaluated. In a small departmental club, the assessment may be very informal and could involve everyone in the organization sitting down with you and visiting over refreshments. If you are the student government association adviser, on the other hand, you may need to be evaluated much more formally and on a regular basis because this assignment very well could be part of your full-time job assignment at the institution. In this case, your evaluation could be tied to salary adjustments, a continuing appointment, and career advancement.

Assessment Techniques

We can categorize assessment techniques as either quantitative or qualitative; each method employs different techniques for generating information. Linda Suskie (2009) provides excellent examples of both assessment techniques. With respect to quantitative methods, she observes, "*Quantitative* assessments use structured, predetermined response options that can be summarized into meaningful numbers and analyzed statistically" (32). Among the examples of quantitative assessments she provides are rubric scores, survey ratings, and performance indicators. Suskie indicates, "*Qualitative* assessments use flexible, naturalistic methods and are usually analyzed by looking for recurring patters and themes" (32). Some examples of qualitative methods, according to Suskie, are reflective writing, notes from interviews, focus groups, and observations.

Both methods require considerable rigor to be done well. Simply setting out to conduct an assessment without considerable background and experience using either approach would be unwise because you very well could wind up with data that are neither valid nor reliable. If you or your group are inexperienced with assessment techniques, we suggest that you seek help from the student activities office, the dean of students' office, or perhaps a colleague in one of the social sciences who is knowledgeable about these techniques.

Evaluating the Adviser

To begin evaluating your work, you might first consider thinking broadly about how your interaction with the organization is progressing. Kearney (1993) provides a series of questions that are particularly appropriate for creating this general framework.

- What are your accomplishments?

- What are your current strengths?

- What are your uncertainties and misunderstandings?

- What obstacles are in your way?

- Are there any specific goals or action steps that you would like to formulate as a result of your self-appraisal?

We provide several tools in this chapter to help you and your organization conduct evaluations. First, there is the Adviser's Self-Evaluation

Checklist (Exhibit 11.1), which you can self-administer at almost any point during the academic year. You answer the questions yes or no based on your opinion of yourself and your work. You or your organization can add other questions, and you can skip any questions that you believe do not pertain to your work.

The Adviser's Log (Exhibit 11.2) illustrates a way for you to keep a record of your interactions with members of the organization over a period of time. This log, in which you can note the purpose of the interaction, what resulted from the interaction, and what the student(s) learned, will provide a record of your work with the organization over the course of an academic term or year. The log also provides a space where you can note assistance or advice you might have received in addressing the situation. Most circumstances can be handled without assistance but occasionally help is needed and it is useful to keep a record of who was helpful to you if for no other reason than to send that person a thank-you note at the end of the academic year.

The Adviser's Evaluation Checklist (Exhibit 11.3) is a tool similar to the self-evaluation in Exhibit 11.1; the organization's officers, members, or both can complete it. As is the case with the self-evaluation, you or the group can add or delete items, and you can administer the checklist during the academic year or at the end.

The purpose of each of these tools is to give you feedback regarding activities and traits that are central to your relationship with the organization. If you or your organization seek to conduct a more formal evaluation, you can use these instruments in conjunction with other strategies, but only after you and the group have answered the questions introduced earlier in this chapter (Why is the assessment being conducted? What will be assessed? and so on).

If your organization would prefer to conduct the assessment using a discussion format, you can use some or all of the questions in Exhibit 11.4. These questions pertain to the heart of your relationship with the organization and its members. Depending on the needs of the group, you or the members might add or delete questions. Because leading such a discussion requires considerable skill, your group might prefer to have a person external to the organization lead the discussion. Whether or not you are present depends on the nature of the evaluation. Once again, you and the group should address the framing questions so as to avoid making embarrassing mistakes.

EXHIBIT 11.1

Adviser's Self-Evaluation Checklist

Please answer the following questions as they relate to your role as an organization adviser:

Item	Yes	No
I actively provide encouragement to members.	___	___
I know the goals of the organization.	___	___
I know the group's members.	___	___
I attend regularly scheduled executive board meetings.	___	___
I attend regularly scheduled organizational meetings.	___	___
I meet regularly with the officers of the organization outside of formal meetings.	___	___
I assist with the orientation of new members and participate as needed.	___	___
I attend the organization's special events.	___	___
I assist with the orientation and training of new officers.	___	___
I help provide continuity for the organization.	___	___
I confront the negative behavior of members.	___	___
I understand principles of group development.	___	___
I understand how students grow and learn.	___	___
I understand the principles that lead to orderly meetings.	___	___
I have read the group's constitution and by-laws.	___	___
I am knowledgeable about the organization's history.	___	___
I recommend and encourage without imposing my ideas and preferences.	___	___
I review the organization's financial records with its financial officer.	___	___
I understand the principles of good fundraising.	___	___
I understand how issues of diversity affect the organization.	___	___
I attend conferences on and off campus with the organization's students.	___	___
I know the steps to follow in developing a program or event.	___	___
I know where to find assistance when I encounter problems I cannot solve.	___	___
I can identify what members learn by participating in the organization.	___	___
I work with the organization's members in conducting assessments and evaluations.	___	___

EXHIBIT 11.2
Adviser's Log

Date	Name of Student(s)	Purpose of Interaction	What Resulted	Follow-up Needed	What Student(s) Learned

EXHIBIT 11.3

Adviser's Evaluation Checklist

Item	Yes	No
The adviser provides encouragement to members.	____	____
The adviser knows the goals of the organization.	____	____
The adviser knows the organization's members.	____	____
The adviser attends regularly scheduled executive board meetings.	____	____
The adviser attends regularly scheduled organizational meetings.	____	____
The adviser regularly meets with the officers of the organization outside of formal meetings.	____	____
The adviser participates in the orientation of new members.	____	____
The adviser attends the organization's special events.	____	____
The adviser assists with the orientation and training of new officers.	____	____
The adviser helps provide continuity for the organization.	____	____
The adviser confronts the negative behavior of members.	____	____
The adviser understands principles of group development.	____	____
The adviser understands how students grow and learn.	____	____
The adviser understands the principles that lead to orderly meetings.	____	____
The adviser has read the group's constitution and by-laws.	____	____
The adviser knows the organization's history.	____	____
The adviser provides advice and encouragement without imposing his or her ideas and preferences on the organization.	____	____
The adviser reviews financial records with the organization's financial officer.	____	____
The adviser understands the principles of good fundraising.	____	____
The adviser understands how issues of diversity affect the organization.	____	____
The adviser attends on and off campus conferences with the organization's students.	____	____
The adviser knows the steps to follow in developing a program.	____	____
The adviser can identify what members have learned by participating in the organization.	____	____
The adviser works with the organization's members in conducting assessments and evaluations.	____	____
Others items specific to your organization:		
_____	____	____
_____	____	____
_____	____	____
_____	____	____

EXHIBIT 11.4

Discussion Questions for Assessing the Adviser

The following questions can be explored as a part of a group discussion.

1. How well do you know the adviser, and in what context?

2. Do you know how to contact the adviser other than at meetings?

3. Does the adviser attend your events?

4. Is the adviser interested in your organization? How do you know this?

5. For officers: Is the adviser approachable? Is the adviser available to provide advice and counsel to you when you have problems?

6. Does the adviser know the purpose and goals of the organization? What evidence do you have to support this?

7. Does the adviser seem to know the history of the organization? How do you know?

8. What does the adviser do at meetings? Is the adviser an active participant in discussions or a passive observer?

9. Does the adviser help clarify what you have learned by participating in the organization? In what ways?

10. What role does the adviser play in the financial management of the organization? What advice has the adviser provided about fundraising?

11. When it is clear that the adviser has ideas that differ from those of the group about how to handle something, what happens?

12. What do you like best about your adviser?

13. If you could change everything about your adviser's performance, what would the one aspect you would not change?

Assessing the Organization

In addition to evaluating your own work, you might want to employ one or more tools available to you to evaluate how well the organization is functioning. Obviously, you can answer several questions for yourself at any time:

- Is the organization meeting its goals?
- Is the number of members consistent with what is desired?
- Is the organization healthy in a financial sense?

- What are students learning?

- Are students having fun?

You and the group need to consider these and other questions periodically.

Although we did not intend this chapter to provide a comprehensive approach to program assessment, it is useful to include one example of an approach to evaluating specific programs, such as a speaker, a workshop, or a social activity. Exhibit 11.5 is based on an all-purpose evaluation form that was developed by M. Lee Upcraft, assistant vice president emeritus at Penn State University; it can be used with a wide variety of programs. In addition to the statements included in Exhibit 11.5, basic demographic information about program participants could be included in the questionnaire you use in addition to their opinions about the program. The form not only elicits student opinions but also asks questions related to how the student was affected by the program. Your group can develop a similar generic evaluation form to meet the specific needs of individual campuses. We think a generic form is far more useful than a specific one developed on a program-by-program basis. Hence we think it would be a good idea to develop a generic form to collect participant assessments about programs if your organization conducts programs regularly, such as a club in an academic department that sponsors monthly programs.

Organizational Goals and Objectives

One of the best ways to look at an organization is to review its stated goals and objectives. These are articulated in the constitution and by-laws and should be used to frame the activities of the group. Is the group concerned with governance, such as a student government association, residence hall association, or Women's Panhellenic Association? Is the group primarily a special-interest group that provides programs for members, such as a departmental club, or sports club? Perhaps the group provides programs for others, such as a dance performance group, musical ensemble, or drama club. Does the organization have a service function such as service clubs and some honorary societies? You can measure the activities of the organization against its goals and objectives and determine, in a general sense, whether the organization is engaged in activities consistent with its purpose. For example, a service club whose members spend most of their time having parties and social events may have strayed from its stated purpose. You can then ask, Why is this occurring? Or, if a performance group

EXHIBIT 11.5

Generic Statements for Program Evaluation

Please indicate the extent to which you agree or disagree with the following statements:

Item	Strongly Disagree	Disagree	Neutral	Agree	Strongly Agree
The purpose of the program was clearly identified.	☐	☐	☐	☐	☐
The purpose of the program was achieved.	☐	☐	☐	☐	☐
My expectations for this program were met.	☐	☐	☐	☐	☐
I have learned new skills as a result of attending this program.	☐	☐	☐	☐	☐
I can apply what I have learned from the program.	☐	☐	☐	☐	☐
I anticipate that my behaviors will change because of the program.	☐	☐	☐	☐	☐
I have greater knowledge of the organization because of the program.	☐	☐	☐	☐	☐
Different points of view were encouraged during the program.	☐	☐	☐	☐	☐
The material presented in the program was well organized.	☐	☐	☐	☐	☐
The presenters were well informed about the material presented.	☐	☐	☐	☐	☐
I found the presenters to be interesting.	☐	☐	☐	☐	☐
The information presented was communicated well.	☐	☐	☐	☐	☐
The handouts were well done.	☐	☐	☐	☐	☐
The visual aids enhanced the program.	☐	☐	☐	☐	☐
The facilities were adequate for the program.	☐	☐	☐	☐	☐
Other statements:	☐	☐	☐	☐	☐
	☐	☐	☐	☐	☐
	☐	☐	☐	☐	☐

Source: Adapted from N. W. Dunkel and J. H. Schuh, *Advising Student Groups and Organizations* (San Francisco: Jossey-Bass, 1998), 220.

does not conduct any programs for a year, it is reasonable to raise questions related to its viability. Still another example could be that Greek letter organizations may assess themselves using standards adopted by the Greek community.

Breadth of Participation

The appropriate size of an organization will vary dramatically with the organization's goals and objectives, but regardless of its purpose, for an organization to be viable over time, it must have an adequate number of members who participate regularly in events. A water polo sports club, for example, does not need one hundred members, but it certainly needs enough members to enable participants to practice and play games. On the other hand, a club that offers performances will need sufficient members to have enough people to be in the performance and to provide technical support during the performance.

Beyond having enough members, organizations should also have wide participation so that not just two or three people are doing all the work, particularly when they need help from many members. The officers should not have to handle all the organizational responsibilities, plan and deliver various events, arrange for transportation, and so on. One of the best ways for you to measure the health of your organization is to determine whether enough people are members of the organization and whether the responsibility for keeping the organization going is spread among the members. In addition, when programs or events are held, do enough members attend to make the effort of those planning and delivering the program worthwhile?

Finances

We have discussed financial issues elsewhere in this book, but let us indicate in this chapter that if the organization experiences chronic financial problems, these problems will distract the members from the primary goals of the group. Thus a quick review of the organization's balance sheet will help you evaluate the organization's success in terms of its financial well-being. Without question, well-being can be defined in various ways but several questions that can be employed to determine an organization's financial well-being include the following:

- From one year to the next is the organization's balance sheet stable, that is, is the fund balance the same or greater year after year?

- Have any programs that require an admission fee or participation charge, such as a performance or a retreat, lost money? Did the organization plan to lose money on the activity?

- If the organization charges membership dues, are these charges the same year after year or have they been increased dramatically from one year to the next? If so, has a decline in membership occurred, and if so, can it be attributed to the dues increase?

- Is keeping the organization solvent, such as by having many fundraisers or other forms of activities designed to raise money, detracting from the purpose of the organization? Keep in mind that if philanthropy is a central purpose of the organization, then the members may spend what seems to be an inordinate amount of time on fundraising, which is not a problem.

Learning

Perhaps the most important criterion of organizational success for you to consider is what the members are learning as a result of their participation in the group. Are officers learning management skills? Is leadership being developed? Are members learning to work cooperatively? Is creativity being encouraged? Do routine tasks, such as preparing financial statements, become easier over time? You can consider these questions and others idiosyncratic to the group as part of an informal evaluation. We have listed a few questions that you could ask group members as part of a discussion held after a program or at the end of the membership year (which may coincide with the end of the academic year but also could be at another time when the terms of the leaders have concluded and new leaders are appointed or elected):

- What did you learn from the experience?
- How did the experience affect your thinking about ___?
- What have you done as a consequence of the experience?
- What did you do well? What would you have done differently?
- Have you applied what you learned in other situations? If so, please give an example or two.
- What do you plan to do in the future as a result of the experience?
- What would you tell your friends about the experience?
- Would you want your sibling to participate in the experience? Why?
- Knowing what you know now, would you have participated in the experience?

Indicators of Organizational Success

We think an effective approach to determining organizational success is to use dashboard indicators. Mitchell and Ryder (2013) indicate, "A dashboard is a performance management system that allows users to track and respond to organizational or institutional activities based on key goals- and objectives-based metrics or indicators" (73). Operational dashboards, defined as "most often (being) used for monitoring processes and situations that demand a timely response" (Mitchell and Ryder 2013, 74), have particular applicability to student organizations. In the case of a student organization, dashboard indicators, broadly defined, can be used to monitor the organization's progress and can be reported on the organization's website. Dashboard indicators also can be referred to as key performance indicators, or KPIs (Mitchell and Ryder 2013).

We think that these indicators can yield useful information that the organization's adviser, leaders, and members can use to determine at any given time the level of success that the organization is experiencing.

Exhibit 11.6 provides a list of selected indicators of a successful organization. Some of the characteristics are dashboard indicators, such as membership data, whereas others are yardsticks for success, such as keeping the organization's constitution and by-laws current. The responses to each of the indicators are "yes," "no," or "maybe." For example, if the organization's officers were devoting a portion of executive board meeting in October to the organization's finances, the first item on Exhibit 11.6 dealing with the organization's finances has to do with the timely payment of dues. The officers could ask the treasurer, "Have the members paid their dues for the fall semester?" If the treasurer responds that 98 percent of the members have paid their dues, then the answer is "yes," but if only 35 percent have paid their dues, the response is "No." "No" or "maybe" responses then lead to further questions and perhaps action plans to rectify the situation. After they have provided their responses, we invite the adviser, officers, or others to follow up with an answer to this question, "How do you know?" In this example, the response will be based on the treasurer's records, thus providing evidence that supports the conclusion.

We invite advisers in particular to use these characteristics of your organization to measure the group's effectiveness. Not all of the items will apply to your group, and you can add other measures, but in general the list will help you get a sense of the group's level of health. If some of the areas appear to be weak, they might provide the basis for discussion with the officers or members. Areas of strength should generate notes of congratulations or affirmative comments in meetings. These items are a quick

---

EXHIBIT 11.6

Indicators of Student Organization Success

Goals and Objectives

- Members understand the purpose of the organization.
- The constitution and by-laws are current.
- Members have read the organization's constitution and by-laws.
- Members understand how to amend the constitution and by-laws.

Membership

- Membership is stable or growing.
- Few members drop out.
- Recruitment of new members is well organized.
- Recruitment of new members is shared by the membership and is not only the responsibility of the membership chair.
- Members know what is going on in the organization.

Meetings

- Meetings are held regularly.
- Meetings are run using Robert's Rules of Order or a similar approach.
- Members attend the meetings regularly.
- Officers attend the meetings regularly.
- Organization business is discussed and members are engaged in the conversation.

Leadership

- Students have learned leadership techniques.
- A variety of people provide leadership for the group.
- Officers complete their terms.
- Elections are contested.
- Officers have read the organization's constitution and by-laws.
- Communication mechanisms, such as a newsletter or website, have been established and are used regularly.

Finance

- Dues are paid on time.
- Financial reports are accurate and produced with regularity.

(*continued*)

EXHIBIT 11.6 (*continued*)

- Long-term debt is kept to a minimum.
- Self-financing events are successful.
- Multiple sources of financing exist.

Special Events

- Special events are planned with the needs of the members in mind.
- Special events are self-financed.
- Special events are well attended.
- Members have an opportunity to suggest and plan special events.

Learning

- Members can identify what they have learned by participating in the organization.
- Members learn to work cooperatively.
- Members' leadership skills have improved over time.
- Members can identify skills that are transferable to their careers after college.

yet effective way of measuring success and reporting them to those who are interested in the organization's progress.

Other Assessment Techniques

Three additional techniques for evaluating the organization are the exit interview, observations by a third party, and document review. Palomba and Banta (1999) provide an example of exit interview by describing interviews with seniors that have led to an improved understanding of student learning styles. Kuh, Kinzie, Schuh, and Whitt (2010) also identified the value of exit interview with seniors, in this instance with graduating seniors at the University of Kansas. Whether the adviser employs a systematic approach, as was the case in the examples provided earlier, or a more informal conversation with graduating seniors, the adviser can get a sense of how well the organization has functioned and what might be done in the future to improve the members' learning experiences.

Another approach is to collect information through observation. Merriam (2002) indicates that the involvement of observers can range from "being a complete observer to an active participant" (13). We think that a particularly useful approach is to have a third party who has no connection to the organization observe informally for a period of time, perhaps several meetings or a combination of meetings and events. A third party presumably can offer an unbiased opinion about the group, which is a real strength of this approach. This outsider's view can often yield unexpected insights into how your group is functioning. But it is possible that third parties can be biased or that they can misinterpret the activities of the organization and thus the selection of the observer needs to be done with care. Not just anyone can be helpful as an observer. Merriam concludes, "Observation is the best technique when an activity, event or situation can be observed firsthand, when a fresh perspective is desired, or when participants are not able to willing to discuss the phenomenon under study" (13). Still, these two alternatives can be useful.

Finally, another major source of data according to Merriam (2002) is documents that can take the form of "written, oral, visual (such as photographs) or cultural artifacts" (13). Merriam points out, "The strength of documents as a data source lies with the fact they already exist in the situation; they do not intrude upon or alter the setting in ways that the presence of an investigator might" (13). Typically, a protocol for analyzing documents is developed by which more than one person might analyze the documents individually and then get together with any other persons doing the same analysis to compare findings. Documents that should be readily available for review include web pages, meeting agendas and minutes, financial records, and photographs of events or activities. In addition, if the officers prepare annual reports these documents also would be available to review.

Conclusion

We finish this chapter with the observation that ensuring quality in advising is a central element in the advising process. We have tried to provide a number of ideas and techniques in this chapter that will help the advisers conduct assessments and evaluations of their work so that they demonstrate accountability in working with student organizations as well as continue to improve their work with students.

Chapter 12
Training

WHEN A STUDENT asks someone to serve as their student organization adviser, that person is likely to agree without necessarily knowing all of what he or she is committing to. Many are unaware of what they signed up for until they receive that first notice from an activities office that says something like, "Thank you for serving as the adviser to the Forensic Scientists club. After you have signed the following eighty pages and promised to attend the thirty events hosted by the organization over the next year, please take the training modules found on our website. It should only take the next seventy-five hours to complete. The organization is not eligible to register until you have completed training." Although this is clearly an exaggeration, being an effective adviser can often take more time and energy than expected and often advisers, whether new or veteran, realize at some point in the journey that they were ill prepared for a particular component of the job. As the level of accountability, liability, and focus on cocurricular learning increases, so does the emphasis on advising students and student organizations. And with these increases comes the institution's need to ensure appropriate and adequate training for student organization advisers.

In this chapter we will discuss the training expectations for student organization advisers: what is expected of advisers, what adviser training may look like, and how training for advisers and student leaders overlap and diverge. Examples of comprehensive training programs will be shared, as well as different methods of delivery.

Student Organization Adviser Training

It is important to remember that most student organization advisers are volunteers. They have "a day job" and agreed to serve in the role for a variety of reasons. With that said, it is appropriate for an institution to publicize the expectations it has for someone who is willing to serve in this capacity. The Council for the Advancement of Standards in Higher Education (CAS 2012) gives a useful list of expectations advisers need to be prepared to meet prior to accepting the responsibility:

- Be knowledgeable of student development theory and philosophy to appropriately support students and also encourage learning and development.

- Have adaptable advising styles in order to be able to work with students with a variety of skill and knowledge levels.

- Have interest in the students involved in the organization.

- Have expertise in the topic in which the student group is engaged.

- Understand organization development processes and teambuilding (95).

Like a job description outlining required skills, clarifying expectations can help frame the work of an adviser in a simple, straightforward way. This also helps to avoid the unfortunate situation of an adviser simply thinking he or she is just a signature on a piece of paper. Iowa State University Memorial Union's Student Activities Center (www.sac.iastate .edu) does an excellent job of explaining expectations on their website and they also include the university's philosophy on advisers which, unfortunately, may not be as readily shared by all institutions.

Using the CAS, advisers and those who train advisers can determine the baseline expectations of advising. CAS (2012) states that "although students' efforts are the backbone of campus activities, campus activity advisers serve as the catalysts of these efforts" (92). Although this statement was written with professional staff of student activities in mind, it correlates to the work of student organization advisers no matter their "real" job because without the presence of an adviser organizations do not have the support they need to achieve their goals. And even though there is a clearly articulated expectation of CAS that student activities offices "must provide information and training opportunities for advisers" (95) there is not necessarily a prescribed curriculum. Therefore, each college and university, usually through the student activities office, will develop a training program based on what student organizations, advisers, and the institution needs to be successful. All student organization advisers have the student activities staff as a resource to consult and help with problem solving, but having exposure to certain topics will be to everyone's benefit. What follows is a list of potential training topics for student organization advisers along with a brief explanation of their significance.

Hazing

Hazing can be a part of any student organization's culture. Advisers will do well to be familiar with state law regarding hazing, what signs to look for if a student is being hazed or if the organization you advise is hazing, alternatives to hazing, and what to do if you suspect hazing is happening.

Recognizing Students in Crisis

This is the most critical responsibility for a student organization adviser. Because advisers have a great deal of contact with students it is important that they recognize indicators of distress, psychological disorders, and risky behavior (Junco and Mastrodicasa 2007). Advisers need to be trained on identifying indicators, and when and how to take action. Your campus counseling center will have resources available to help identify at-risk students.

Clery Act

The Clery Act requires the compilation and disclosure of campus crime statistics, which, in the most recent *Handbook for Campus Safety and Security Reporting* (2011), indicated that there are four types of campus security authorities, one of which is university personnel who have significant responsibility for students and campus activities. Therefore, institutions interpreted this to mean that student organization advisers are considered campus security authorities and must therefore be trained on the Clery Act, what is considered a crime and how to report.

Title IX

In April 2011, the U.S. Department of Education's Office of Civil Rights issued the *Dear Colleague Letter* which addresses student on student sexual harassment and sexual violence as well as the school's responsibility to take immediate and effective action (U.S. Department of Education Office of Civil Rights 2011). This, coupled with the Violence Against Women Reauthorization Act of 2013, has made campuses rethink many of their practices. There are a few implications for student organization advisers worth noting. First of all, advisers, as university employees, are required to report any written or oral report of sexual harassment to the institution's Title IX coordinator. Second, institutions are mandated to provide training to students with the purposes of prevention and education. Third, some institutions have added language in the constitution requirements for student organizations stating that they agree that the organization will not engage in unwelcomed conduct of a sexual nature and will not create a hostile environment.

Protecting Minors

The 2011 Penn State sexual abuse scandal gave institutions a wakeup call regarding the presence of minors on campus. In many states school officials are now required by law to report the suspicion of sexual abuse or neglect of a minor. Many schools have developed scope documents explaining requirements and best practices for any institutional activities involving minors. Because some student organizations have events, camps, or work-shops with minors as primary participants, advisers need to be aware of their institution's opinion about whether student organizations and their activities are within the scope of institutional responsibility. Regardless, as a best practice, we recommend that all student organizations follow the campus protocol any time minors are involved.

Understanding Student Identities

According to Junco and Mastrodicasa (2007), the Net Generation is the most diverse generation in US history as the 2000 Census found that more than 31 percent of students are from non-White families. The changing demographics of who is going to college allows students to increase their exposure to people of different religions, races, ethnicities, socioeconomic statuses, sexualities, and genders. This does not necessarily mean our students are equipped with multicultural competency nor does it mean that student organization advisers are either. Junco and Mastrodicasa (2007) cite Keeling (2003) who states, "advisers need to understand minority populations and their needs" (158).

Communicating with Students

As simple as this may sound, the generational difference between most advisers and the students with whom they work will often lead to communication challenges. For example, this generation of student is looking for instant gratification, expecting an immediate response on Facebook, text message, or an e-mail. Today's students are not necessarily equipped to hear "no" and are more apt to ask an adviser for an answer than to search for it on their own (Junco and Mastrodicasa 2007). Junco and Mastrodicasa (2007) recommend that advisers ask direct questions to students which should help them articulate their purpose and goals. They also have the capacity to communicate with vast amounts of their peers very quickly.

This has implications for advisers as they help student organizations plan events or mobilize students around a cause.

Vanguri performed a study in 2010 which looked at why advisers take on these roles and how those experiences influence further involvement. A finding from this research indicated that advisers believe they could be more effective if they better understood what resources are available to student organizations. Also, there was a mixed response on the method of training. Some advisers preferred a structured, formalized workshop whereas others, especially seasoned advisers, felt that training could be tailored to their level of involvement and responsibility (Vanguri 2010). This tells us that when approaching training, one method of delivery will not be effective. The content, in addition to the audience's experience and size, should be considered when determining the training methodology. Exhibit 12.1 illustrates in-person adviser trainings on a variety of topics.

EXHIBIT 12.1

Sample Adviser Training Schedule

Student Organization Adviser Orientation

Friday, September 28, 2012, 12:00–1:30 P.M., Memorial Union TITU

Wednesday, October 17, 2012, 4:00–5:30 P.M., TITU (Red Gym)

Tuesday, January 15, 2013, 12:00–1:30 P.M., Memorial Union TITU

This workshop is designed for anyone who advises student organizations. We will discuss student organization adviser's roles and expectations and student organization adviser resources. You also learn about the new Wisconsin Involvement Network (WIN) and how the groups you advise can make the best use of this software! There will be time for questions and discussion.

Student Organization Adviser Risk Management Workshop

Wednesday, December 5, 2012, 2:30–4:00 P.M., Memorial Union TITU

Let's hear from the experts! A representative from UW Risk Management, UW Legal Services, and a seasoned Student Organization Adviser will be on hand to guide us in a discussion of common risk management issues encountered by Student Organizations and their Advisers . . . and how to successfully prepare for and handle risk.

(continued)

EXHIBIT 12.1 (*continued*)

Student Organization Adviser Round Table

Monday, March 4, 2013, 12:00–1:30 P.M., Memorial Union TITU

There is a wealth of knowledge, experience, and great ideas in our own community. This session gives you a chance to share your wisdom and ask questions of each other in an informal setting. Whether you have been advising an organization for ten years or you just began, please come and share your ideas.

Transitions and Technology

Friday, April 12, 2013, 12:00–1:30 P.M, Memorial Union TITU

Led by students currently in student organizations, this workshop is designed to help advisers understand how students are using technology, especially to improve the transition of leadership from one year to the next. Come prepared with questions for the students. We will also hear from a representative from DoIT on the technology resources available for RSOs. Participants should walk away with ideas about how to better engage students using technology and some ideas to ease transition of leaders and members from one year to the next.

Source: University of Wisconsin-Madison Center for Leadership and Involvement, http://www.cfli.wisc.edu/advisors_resources.htm.

One of the benefits of technology is that the method by which these training modules are shared with advisers can be varied, which makes the training process much more convenient and efficient. Previously, sharing occurred only through in-person printed handbooks and paper assessments. Today, there are options for sharing information, testing knowledge, and receiving feedback. Here are a few examples of models used for adviser training:

- The Ohio State University's Ohio Union includes a mandatory in-person adviser training session that must be done every two years and online resources on a variety of topics from top ten tips for advising to group development (www.ohiounion.osu.edu).

- Penn State University's office of Student Activities hosts multiple brown bag lunches for advisers on topics ranging from adviser roles to how to hold ethical elections. They also have archived a number of useful PowerPoint presentations (www.studentaffairs.psu.edu/hub/studentactivities).

- Guilford Technical Community College's Office of Student Life provides all advisers with a PowerPoint presentation every semester covering pertinent topics, and offers in-person training twice a year and at the request of the adviser (Cross, personal communication, February 10, 2014).

An issue that every institution needs to address is whether or not training for student organization advisers should be mandatory. There is consensus that training for student organization officers is necessary and most institutions require proof of participation prior to an organization's completing the registration process. However, due to the "volunteer" nature of the role advisers have, coupled with their faculty status, it is rare for training to be mandatory. The approach the institution has in its relationship with student organizations will dictate training requirements as well.

Advisers Training Students

Student leaders of organizations are often subject to numerous training programs. Most campuses have a prescribed training regimen that includes topics like program planning, financial accountability, hazing prevention, roles and responsibilities, and university policy. Some institutions, such as Oregon State University's Center for Leadership and Involvement (http://oregonstate.edu/sli), provide supplemental training to leaders and members alike who are interested in improving their skills. In addition, some campuses have a peer education program where students train other students on such topics as how to run a meeting, how to motivate your peers, effective marketing methods, and partnering on programs. See Exhibit 12.2 for an example of what a peer education program can offer student leaders.

EXHIBIT 12.2

Sample of Peer Educator Workshops

Group Guidance

The Involvement Team will work with individual executive boards, committees, or student groups to discuss best practices for organizational management. ITeam consultants have been trained to offer guidance on a number of issues including:

Student Involvement

- Successful Programming and Event Coordination
- Creating Dynamic Student Groups
- Teamwork and Membership Motivation
- Structuring Student Groups
- Managing Effective Meetings

(continued)

EXHIBIT 12.2 (*continued*)

Retreats

In conjunction with a student's organization, the Involvement Team will help plan a retreat for organizations and will facilitate the activities planned. Retreats will be customized and presented by trained members of ITeam, allowing you to relax and enjoy the benefits of your new and improved organization.

Workshops

The Involvement Team offers all student organizations a number of different presentations with suggestions, tips, and advice on how to improve or successfully manage their organization. If you are interested in ITeam putting on a workshop or presentation for your organization please e-mail us and ITeam will be in contact with you about scheduling your presentation.

Workshop topics presented by the Involvement Team:

Advising	Anger Management	Assertiveness
Burning Out	Cohesiveness	Communication Skills
Conflict Resolution	Confrontation	Decision Making
Delegating	Event Planning	Goal Setting
Group Dynamics	Icebreakers	Low Ropes Initiatives
Officer Transitions	Organizational Structuring	Parliamentary Procedures
Presentation Skills	Running an Effective Meeting	Teamwork
Time Management	UF Resources	AND MANY MORE!!

Source: University of Florida Department of Student Activities and Involvement, https://www.studentinvolvement.ufl.edu/GetInvolved/InvolvementTeam/GroupServices.

Just as it has with adviser training, technology has allowed for large numbers of students to be trained online and at their convenience. However, many institutions have opted for a mixed approach to training students because of the value of face-to-face interaction even though that can mean hours of time spent in training sessions, depending on the number of student organizations and the requirements of the institution. For example, the University of Florida registered almost a thousand student organizations in 2012–13 and trained nearly four thousand student leaders in person. In addition to this, training modules were available online for general members and advisers. Also, most training sessions for organization leaders are held within a specific registration time frame. This means that training is scheduled near the end of the registration period to capture the majority of student organizations as they register and prepare for their first meetings and events. Some campuses have a continuous registration process, so training opportunities must be available all year long.

Although officers of student organizations receive training by student activities offices, the general members of student organizations are often not included. Therefore, advisers have the ability to fill those gaps. Also, advisers are often the first to identify that an organization is struggling around an issue or is ready to be challenged to learn something new. It is a benefit to have advisers who are prepared to either run a training program themselves or assist in finding resources like those found from a peer education group as mentioned previously or from existing departments on campus, such as the office for leadership and civic engagement. The following topics are popular issues which either organizations will look to advisers for guidance on, or which advisers may identify as something that needs a structured intervention.

Conflict Mediation

Occasionally advisers find themselves in the middle of a bad soap opera where the purpose of the organization is continually hijacked by student leaders who cannot get along. Warranted or not, conflict within the group can be destructive if not addressed. Many times advisers will be asked to play the referee which can be an awkward position for them. Using existing resources on campus, such as those found in the student conduct office, or referring the organization to a student activities professional may be helpful.

Ethical Decision Making and Problem Solving

The responsibility of an adviser is not to simply tell students what decisions to make or how to solve a problem, but to help students "identify choices and take responsibility for the choices they make" (Love and Maxam 2011, 413). Advisers will have more wisdom and experience to illuminate the "bigger picture" more clearly for student leaders. And it is sometimes much simpler for an adviser to make a decision, but every time that happens it chips away at the opportunities students have to think critically, take responsibility, and develop self-confidence. Though it is easy to get caught up in your passion for the organization, it is not yours. The good and the bad truly belong to the students. If you always make decisions, you fail as an adviser because you negate student learning.

University Policy

As an adviser, you could read the student organization handbook numerous times before feeling confident in your knowledge of policies and regulations. With the annual transition of student leaders it is obvious that organizations will benefit from an adviser who has a working knowledge of policy and an understanding of where to find assistance when needed. It is recommended that advisers attend training on this topic and, if it is not offered directly to advisers, to participate in one for student officers.

Team Building and Motivation

A common problem plaguing many organizations is how to develop a sense of team and translate that into action. Advisers are frequently asked to help in this regard. Usually the first idea that comes to mind is "we need a retreat!" Retreats can be effective at team building and motivating students, but occasionally the level of engagement felt immediately following a retreat may not carry through for the rest of the year. Exhibit 12.3 provides questions to determine whether a retreat is necessary and how to organize it appropriately. We discussed group dynamics in chapter 4 and motivation in chapter 5, but there is value in restating the need for advisers to be prepared to assist students with team-building exercises and to discuss how students can motivate their peers. There are a multitude of team-building activities, including those found on the Student Activities Involvement Leadership website of Eastern Washington University (www.ewu.edu/student-activities), and Exhibit 12.4 offers a list that advisers can share with student leaders of ways to motivate members of student organizations to succeed.

EXHIBIT 12.3

Determining the Necessity of a Retreat

Directions: Have the executive board answer the following questions individually. Once the students have completed this worksheet, discuss their responses to determine if there are common themes.

1. Why should your organization have a retreat?

2. What would be the main purpose of your retreat (circle one)?

    Team Building   Skills Training   Communications   Goal Setting

    Problem Solving   Planning   Learning   Leadership Transition

    Socializing   Orientation   Revitalization   Conflict Resolution

3. Who is the retreat for?

4. What type of facility do you need?

5. What do you expect the organization to provide for participants?

6. How much are you willing to spend of the organization's budget on the retreat and/or have members pay themselves?

7. What is the best format (circle one)?

    Workshops presented by experts (i.e., advertising, program planning, public speaking, fundraising, etc.)

    Experiential Exercises (i.e., teambuilding, brainstorming, communications skills, ropes course, etc.)

    Recreational Exercises (i.e., skiing, hiking, canoeing, biking, etc.)

8. Who would facilitate or present (circle one)?

    Organization Officers   Organization Members

    Student Organization Adviser   Other University Administrators

9. Who is responsible for planning the retreat?

(continued)

EXHIBIT 12.3(*continued*)

10.   What is the outcome for the organization you would like to see as a result of the retreat?

11.   How do you plan on measuring that outcome?

Source: Adapted from the *ACPA Commission of Student Involvement Advisor Manual* retrieved from http://www.uc.edu /content/dam/uc/sald/docs/acpaadvisormanual.pdf.pdf.

EXHIBIT 12.4

Tips on Motivating Students to Take Action

People Need to Feel Important: See people as worthwhile human beings loaded with untapped potential; go out of your way to express this attitude.

Give Praise: Reinforce for continual achievement. All people need praise and appreciation. Get into the habit of being "praise-minded." Give public recognition when it is due.

Give People Status: The more status and prestige you can build into a committee or an organization, the more motivated the members become. There are many status symbols you can use to make others feel important. For example, develop a "Member of the Week/Month" Award or "Committee Chairperson of the Month" Award. In addition, simply treating people with courtesy is a way of giving them status.

Communicate: People like to know what is going on in the organization. They want to be told about problems, objectives, and "inside information." They feel recognized and important when they are kept informed. Two-way communication within the organization is necessary in order to achieve a mutual understanding. Mutual understanding leads to motivation!

Give Security: People need more than financial security. People will look to you for intrinsic security. For example, they must know that you like them, respect them, understand them, and accept them not only for their strong points, but also for their weaknesses.

People Need You and People Need People: They need you to give them what they want and need: intrinsic satisfaction. When you give them what they want, they will give you what you want. This is what motivation is all about. It is not something you do to other people, but something they do for themselves. You give them the reasons and that makes you the motivator—a person who gets things done through others.

Develop Purpose: Always explain why. Instill in the members that their assistance is vital for success. Share ways that participation can encourage personal growth.

Encourage Participation in Group Goal Development: Include all members when planning goals. Consider and follow through on members' suggestions. Remember that we support that which we help to create.

Develop a Sense of Belonging: People like to belong. Those who feel like they belong will more likely invest themselves.

Source: Reprinted from the *ACPA Commission of Student Involvement Advisor Manual* retrieved from http://www.uc.edu/content/dam/uc/sald/docs/acpaadvisormanual.pdf.pdf.

Diversity and Inclusion

Advisers should emphasize the institution's values around diversity, inclusivity, and multicultural competency. The campus community can offer the environment students need to place themselves "in positions to explore, reflect, examine, and challenge our ways of seeing and being in the world" (Pope and Mueller 2011, 346). Advisers can challenge students to take the risk of expanding their multicultural experience and learn how to appreciate all the identities our students have. Further, advisers are uniquely positioned to challenge students not to simply tolerate each other but to celebrate all of their uniqueness. For example, you could take the organization you advise to a cultural event like the Muslim Students Association's Fastathon which is celebrated after the end of Ramadan to educate non-Muslims about the religious practice of fasting while raising money for the hungry. Debriefing this experience will allow students to reflect on personal beliefs, prejudices, and assumptions. This is an example of a safe way students can be challenged to develop interpersonal competency.

Something you have probably noticed as you have read this chapter is that there are more similarities than differences between the training for advisers and the training for students in leadership roles within organizations. In many ways the delivery methods used by campuses are the same and there is overlap within the topics of training. However, we would like to point out one specific difference. Advisers need to have a basic understanding of a number of issues, as do organizations, not so they can do the work, but so they can guide students through the process. The advising relationship is a great example of one where the process by which you advise has a greater bearing on the successful development of a student than the product, or output, of a student organization. The approach to training advisers should embrace this difference.

Chapter 13

Developing and Increasing Personal Effectiveness

IN THIS FINAL chapter, we address three issues related to the practice of advising student groups: additional recommendations for professional practice, some thoughts about keeping advising activities rewarding, and suggestions for continuing education.

Recommendations for Professional Practice

Four areas of professional practice are worthy of additional comment. These are developing a philosophy of advising, emphasizing learning, securing administrative support for advising activities, and forming coalitions on campus.

Philosophy

The focus of this book has been on the technical side of advising student organizations. From time to time we have referred to institutional philosophy, values, and beliefs. We want to emphasize that you too need to develop your own philosophy of advising and advising style, within the philosophical frameworks of the campus.

Student affairs professionals can influence the learning environment. They prepare students to function in a democratic society and advance issues of social justice (see Reason and Broido 2011). In describing student affairs practitioners, Young (1996) quite perceptively states: "More comfortable with practice than philosophy, members of the profession spend a great deal of time developing programs, services, and procedures and much less time musing about values that support all those activities" (83). We use Young's observation as a point of departure in suggesting that you develop a philosophy about working with student groups that will then guide your practice.

No one can tell you that there is one best way to go about working with student organizations. Some advisers are more comfortable taking a very active role with their organization—attending all the organization's meetings and events, having frequent meetings with the officers, and visiting with members regularly. Others prefer to take a more passive role with the organization—waiting to be contacted for advice, attending events on an irregular basis, and spending little time with individual members or officers.

Either approach can work, depending on the needs of the campus, the needs of the officers and the members, the nature of the organization, and the degree of comfort you feel in establishing a relationship with the organization. Our view is that you need to develop an advising style that fits best with all these factors. We recognize that there will be areas such as the organization's finances and legal issues that will need your knowledge and attention. Although advising style is important, the values and philosophy that undergird it are the critical factors in developing relationships with students.

Commitment to Learning

Why do colleges and universities have student organizations? This question can be answered in a variety of ways, all of which could be right. Students need to have fun, they need to learn to work within complicated organizations, and, at public institutions, they could not be prohibited from forming organizations even if the institution wished to do so. Perhaps the most crucial reason for student groups is that student learning is enhanced by membership in campus organizations.

In looking at issues of the future, Komives and Woodard (1996) suggest that student affairs staff "must become experts at identifying the developing and learning experiences inherent in student employment, community service, cooperative education and other forms of experiential learning and link those to students' academic experience" (549). Obviously, we believe that students have much to learn from their experiences as members and leaders of organizations, and you can play an important role in making sure that these experiences are meaningful.

You can expedite the learning process by asking key strategic questions through the course of the academic year. Among these are: What have you learned as a result of [a specific experience]? What have you learned in class that you can apply to that situation? If you were to summarize for an employer what you have learned from this experience, what would you say? If you were faced with this situation in the future, what would you do differently? There are many other questions you can ask of students that will help them think reflectively about their experiences, apply their classroom experiences in the out-of-class environment, and grow as learners.

Administrative Support

We have described a variety of very difficult situations that have significant ramifications not only for the organization and its students but for the institution as a whole. Make a mistake about how best to plan and supervise a trip, and the consequences could be dramatic and perhaps tragic. Fail to provide adequate oversight for the student treasurer, and all kinds of problems can arise. Do not spend adequate time reading and understanding a contract, and there can be legal and financial ramifications.

It is therefore essential that you know administrative support is available and where to obtain that support; we have provided suggestions throughout this book about where to find legal advice (chapter 9), help with financial matters (chapter 8), and assistance from various units throughout the institution.

Early in your advising experience, you need to make sure that such support is available. Having to function without it would put you in an untenable position. If support is not available, we question quite seriously whether you should accept an invitation to serve as an adviser; in our view, administrative support is essential to your success. No adviser should ever have to deal with problems, large or small, without some level of help and assistance.

Forming Partnerships and Coalitions

Another key form of support comes from your relationships with colleagues who can provide you assistance and counsel. Among these colleagues are student affairs professionals, those who provide administrative support on campus, and other advisers.

Partnerships (see Whitt 2011) between academic and student affairs can improve student access and retention, provide evidence of learning outcomes, cope with financial constraints, and meet the needs of changing student populations. Kuh et al. (2005) as stated in Whitt (2011) mentions "effective partnerships among those who have the most contact with students—faculty and student affairs professionals—fuel the collaborative spirit and positive attitude of these campuses" (486).

Coalitions can be beneficial in a number of ways (see Komives and Woodard 1996). They bring out the best thinking on issues of mutual interest and tend to result in stronger voices on campus. A coalition with those who provide administrative support makes the interchange between you and the support person natural and easy, and helps break down whatever barriers may exist. People begin to develop rapport, anticipate each other's needs, and freely exchange ideas and information.

Times may arise when those who provide administrative support to you will need your help, because as an adviser you will get to know students and their needs. As was pointed out in chapter 7, students are frequently called on to participate in institutional activities, and there are times when those who provide administrative support will need your help in arranging student involvement. If the legal counsel, for example, were to host a meeting on campus for colleagues throughout the state to discuss legal issues related to students, how better to find student panelists for a discussion session than through student group advisers?

Another coalition is that of advisers themselves. As institutions continue to grow in complexity, and faculty and staff become more specialized, it becomes increasingly difficult for people from disparate disciplines to get to know each other well on campus. But advisers who work with student groups—whether the geology club, the wakeboarding club, the marketing club, or the association of future accountants—share common issues and experiences. One effective way to meet informally to discuss these common concerns is to organize (with the help of the student activities office) a monthly advisers' forum.

Keeping the Work Rewarding

Having offered some thoughts about improving your professional practice as an adviser, we now move on to discussing several ideas about how to keep your work as an adviser rewarding. Experiences with students can be both exhilarating and discouraging, and it is very important to develop ways to stay enthusiastic about working with student groups.

Watching Students Grow

As cited by Pascarella and Terenzini (1991), Sanford (1962) describes how students grow by facing and responding to challenges, and students' being involved in campus organizations is undoubtedly one of the best ways for them to experience such growth. For this reason, we urge you to remind yourself that the work is highly rewarding and will pay off in the long run as students learn and grow. Knowing that students grow and learn from their organizational experiences should be a strong incentive for you in difficult moments.

It was no accident that we decided to identify rewards and benefits for advisers in the very first chapter of the book, because you need to remind yourself that in spite of all the tough moments, long hours, and challenges you face, working with students individually and in groups as part of the advising experience is thoroughly rewarding. You may find it useful to reread the section on the rewards of advising from time to time, particularly when in challenging situations.

Enjoying Students

Barr (1993) also reminds us to enjoy our students. She writes, "It would behoove all of us to take time to enjoy the wonder of learning that many students experience and appreciate their enthusiasm" (526). Too often we can find it all too easy to fall into the trap of characterizing students as doing not much more than creating problems. At times students make uninformed decisions, poor choices, or silly commitments, all of which result in the adviser having to intervene to "clean things up." In some ways, this cleanup work is what our job is about: when our organizational leaders make mistakes, it is our job to work with students so that they can learn from their errors and not repeat these mistakes in other circumstances where the ramifications could be far more serious. Most of us decided to pursue careers in higher education, whether in teaching, research, or administration, because we wanted to be associated with students. Serving as organizational advisers allows us to develop ongoing relationships with our students, and in that respect we are quite fortunate to have such an opportunity.

In your day-to-day work as an administrator, faculty, or staff member, you may have few opportunities to participate in and observe student culture and fads. Student organization advisers are typically the first to understand the latest in fashion trends, dance steps, music, tattoos, body piercings, and the like. Advisers can understand the use of social media (i.e., Facebook, Twitter, Instagram, and so forth) as a communications tool used by students. These insights can lend to the discussions when considering programs, activities, events, and services for students.

Maintaining Perspective

It is also important for you to maintain your perspective about your organization and your students. For many of the students, the roles they play within their organizations will be their first as leaders. They will undoubtedly make mistakes. One of the best ways to think about this aspect of advising is to remember that the college theater troupe, newspaper staff, or track team will not perform nearly as well as what you would expect from professional actors, the working press, or professional athletes.

Members of our organizations are students preparing for fulfilling lives as citizens, and only a few may move into positions directly related to their student organizational experience. Advisers need to realize that organizations will bounce along with imperfections and challenges; problems large and small are the natural order of the day but they also give students experience and an opportunity to reflect on their own growth. As Komives, Wagner, and Associates (2009) state, "the best way to learn . . . [is] through experience and reflection. The experience half of the equation refers to taking action, having the courage to get in there and try—testing out new skills, approaches, tactics, and ways of doing things. Reflection, on the other hand, refers to thinking about what happened, what can be learned from it, and how to go about it next time" (421).

Recommendations for Continuing Professional Education

In order to stay active professionally and learn more about working with students, we conclude this chapter with some thoughts about continuing professional education. The three main ways to pursue your professional education are by becoming involved with professional organizations, reading, and attending training workshops and seminars.

Professional Organizations

Several professional associations provide good opportunities for in-service education for organization advisers. The National Association for Campus Activities (NACA), an organization of individuals whose careers tend to be focused on student organizations and their activities, would be a natural affiliation for you. The NACA online portal includes archived materials (i.e., articles, magazines, and so on) that are readily accessible. In addition, College Student Educators International (ACPA), which has a committee (technically called a commission—Commission for Student Involvement) devoted to student activities, would be a logical affiliation for you. The Student Affairs Administrators in Higher Education (NASPA) and its six regions and numerous state associations offers professional development opportunities through its Knowledge Communities, conferences, and publications. The National Association of College and University Residence Halls (NACURH) has established an Adviser Recognition and Training Program. The American Student Association of Community Colleges (ASACC) provides an Adviser Certification program. You will also find state associations providing adviser training such as the Florida College System Student Government Association (FCSSGA) Adviser Training. The Association of College and University Housing Officers-International (ACUHO-I) has a program committee that includes leadership development and working with residence hall associations. The Association of College Unions-International (ACUI) has a student programs component that is concerned in part with leadership development, student organizations, and advisers.

Advisers of Greek letter organizations will have resources available through individual fraternities and sororities as well as the Association of Fraternity/Sorority Advisors (AFA). The North American Interfraternity Conference (NIC) is also a useful resource.

All these organizations have annual conferences, and in some cases they offer regional conferences as well. The challenge is to find an organization that best meets your specific needs, which obviously will vary depending on your level of expertise as an adviser, your interest in the association, and other factors that encourage your active involvement. Nuss (1993) observes that "there is no one best association, and you should feel comfortable exploring alternatives at various points in your career" (376). She adds, "Whether you are a new professional, someone who has made a recent career change, or a senior student affairs officer, associations should play a meaningful and significant part in your development. It is never too early or too late to consider and reconsider the variety of associations and the forms of participation and involvement available" (377).

Professional Reading

In addition to sponsoring conferences, the associations we just mentioned publish materials on a regular basis, and at times these materials include information for organization advisers. We also recommend the *NASPA Journal of Student Affairs Research and Practice*, published by the Student Affairs Administrators in Higher Education, the *SACSA Journal*, published by the Southern Association for College Student Affairs, and the *Journal of College Student Development* published by the College Student Educators International (ACPA).

The World Wide Web (WWW) and the ERIC CASS (Educational Resources Information Center, Counseling and Student Services Clearinghouse) document repository are both valuable tools for locating published materials about student organizations. The Web and ERIC will have such materials as unpublished campus reports and training materials, which you may find useful throughout the course of your work. Exhibit 13.1 includes the addresses of the resources we have mentioned in this chapter.

EXHIBIT 13.1

Additional Resources

American Student Association of Community Colleges (ASACC) Adviser Certification

2250 North University Parkway #4865

Provo, UT 84604

www.asacc.org/advisor-network/certification-requirements

College Student Educators International (ACPA)

One Dupont Circle, NW, Suite 300

Washington, DC 20036-1110

www.acpa.nche.edu

Association of College and University Housing Officers-International (ACUHO-I)

1445 Summit Street

Columbus, OH 43201-2105

www.acuho-i.org

Association of College Unions-International (ACUI)

1 City Centre, Suite 200

120 W. 7th Street

Bloomington, IN 47404-3925

www.acui.org

Association of Fraternity/Sorority Advisors (AFA)

PO Box 1369

Fort Collins, CO 80522-1369

www.afa1976.org

ERIC-CASS

Counseling and Student Services Clearinghouse

School of Education

201 Ferguson Building

University of North Carolina at Greensboro

Greensboro, NC 27412

www.uncg.edu/~ericcas2/

Florida College System Student Government Association (FCSSGA) Adviser Training

www.fcssga.org/fcssga-advisors-training-program.html

Jossey-Bass Inc., A Wiley Brand

1 Montgomery, Suite 1200

San Francisco, CA 94104

www.josseybass.com/highereducation

National Association for Campus Activities (NACA)

13 Harbison Way

Columbia, SC 29212-3401

www.naca.org

Student Affairs Administrators in Higher Education (NASPA and *NASPA Journal of Student Affairs Research and Practice*)

111 K Street NE, 10th Floor

Washington, DC 20002

www.naspa.org

North-American Interfraternity Conference
(NIC)

3901 W. 86th Street, Suite 390

Indianapolis, IN 46268–1791

www.nicindy.org

SACSA College Student Affairs Journal

Aaron Hughey or April Heiselt

Senior Editors

www.sacsa.org/

csajournal@gmail.com

Training Opportunities

Professional organizations, such as those we have listed here, and individual campuses provide a variety of workshops, short courses, and other training opportunities for advisers. Frequently, professional associations offer online training opportunities or preconference workshops that explore various issues in depth. Regional and statewide professional associations offer one-day "drive-in" conferences that can be very helpful to your professional development. It is also common for the student activities office, the residence life office, or other campus agencies to sponsor weekend, half-day, and other types of intensive workshops for advisers.

A Final Word

We conclude this book where we began, with a word about students, reminding you that student growth and learning is a fundamental part of organizational membership. We referred to the work of Astin, Pascarella, and Terenzini, and others who consistently have pointed out how valuable organizational membership is for students. We think that the time, effort, and energy you put forth in working with student organizations enriches students' experiences substantially.

We dedicate our book to the tens of thousands of advisers on college campuses throughout the world who are committed to enhancing the lives of students. Whether you are a beginning adviser or seasoned with many years of experience with student groups, we hope that this book will help you advance your work. Your students will be the beneficiaries of your efforts.

References

Alvarez, L. 2013. "A University Band, Chastened by Hazing, Makes Its Return." *New York Times*, September 6. Retrieved from http://www.nytimes.com/2013/09/07/us/a-university-band-chastened-by-hazing-makes-its-return.html.

American College Personnel Association. 1994. *The Student Learning Imperative*. Washington, DC: American College Personnel Association.

American Student Government Association (ASGA). 2014. http://www.asgaonline.com.

Anson, J. L., and R. F. Marchesani, Jr. 1991. *Baird's Manual of American College Fraternities*. 20th ed. Indianapolis: Baird's Manual Foundation.

Archer, J. 1992. "Campus in Crisis: Coping with Fear and Panic Related to Serial Murders." *Journal of Counseling and Development* 71: 96–100.

Army ROTC. 1996. *Cadet Handbook*. Gainesville: Army ROTC, University of Florida.

Army ROTC. 2013a. *Cadet Handbook*. Gainesville: Army ROTC, University of Florida.

Army ROTC. 2013b, June 9. *U.S. Army Cadet Command*. Retrieved from www.cadetcommand.army.mil/.

Association for the Promotion of Campus Activities. 2014. *Regional APCA Advisory Committee Overview*. Retrieved from http://www.apca.com.

Association of American Colleges and Universities (AAC&U). 2002. *Greater Expectations: A Vision for Learning as a Nation Goes to College*. Washington, DC: Author.

Association of Fraternity/Sorority Advisors. 2013. *Welcome to AFA*. Retrieved from http://afa1976.org.

Astin, A. W. 1984. "Student Involvement: A Developmental Theory for Higher Education." *Journal of College Student Personnel* 25: 297–308.

Astin, A. W. 1985. *Achieving Educational Excellence: A Critical Assessment of Priorities and Practices in Higher Education*. San Francisco: Jossey-Bass.

Astin, A. W. 1993. *What Matters in College? Four Critical Years Revisited.* San Francisco: Jossey-Bass.

ASU PRSSA. 2013. *ASU PRSSA Purpose.* Retrieved from www.prssa.appstate .edu/index.php.

Barr, M. J. 1988. "Institutional Liability: What Are the Risks and Obligations of Student Services?" In *Student Services and the Law: A Handbook for Practitioners,* edited by M. J. Barr and Associates. San Francisco: Jossey-Bass.

Barr, M. J. 1993. "Becoming Successful Student Affairs Administrators." In *The Handbook of Student Affairs Administration,* edited by M. J. Barr and Associates. San Francisco: Jossey-Bass.

Barr, M. J. 2009. "Budgeting and Fiscal Management for Student Affairs." In *The Handbook of Student Affairs Administration,* 3rd ed., edited by G. S. McClellen, J. Stringer, and Associates, 481–504. San Francisco: Jossey-Bass.

Baxter Magolda, M. B. 2001. "Enhancing Learning." In *The Professional Student Affairs Administrator: Educator, Leader, and Manager,* edited by R. B. Winston, Jr., D. G. Creamer, T. K. Miller, and Associates, 287–308. New York: Brunner-Routledge.

Baxter Magolda, M. B., and P. M. King. 2004. *Learning Partnerships: Theory and Models of Practice to Educate for Self-Authorship.* Sterling, VA: Stylus.

Bayless, K. G., R. F. Mull, and C. M. Ross. 1983. *Recreational Sports Programming.* North Palm Beach, FL: Athletic Institute.

Beabout, G., and D. J. Wenneman. 1994. *Applied Professional Ethics.* Lanham, MD: University Press of America.

Beck, R. C. 1983. *Motivation Theories and Principles.* Englewood Cliffs, NJ: Prentice Hall.

Benne, K. D., and P. Sheats. 1948. "Functional Roles of Group Members." *Journal of Social Justice* 42: 41–49.

Bethany College. 2013. *Benefits of Joining a Student Organization.* Retrieved from http://www.bethanywv.edu/students/student-involvement/.

Biotechnology Club. 2013. *Club Purpose.* Retrieved from https://sfcollege .collegiatelink.net/organizations/biotech.

Blake, R. R., and J. R. Mouton. 1985. "Don't Let Group Norms Stifle Creativity." *Personnel* 628: 28–33.

Blanchard, K., and N. V. Peale. 1988. *The Power of Ethical Management.* New York: Morrow.

Blank, M. A., and C. Kershaw. 1993. "Promote School Renewal: Plan a Retreat." *Clearing House* 66: 206–208.

Blocker, H. G. 1987. *Fundamentals of Philosophy.* New York: MacMillan.

Boatman, S. A. 1986. "Astin's Theory of Student Involvement: Implications for Campus Activities." Paper presented at the National Association for Campus Activities national convention, Washington, DC.

Boatman, S. A. 1988. "Strong Student Governments . . . and Their Advisement." *Campus Activities Programming* 209: 58–63.

Boyer, E. L. 1987. *Campus Life: In Search of Community.* Princeton, NJ: Carnegie Foundation.

Boyer, E. L. 1990. *Scholarship Reconsidered: Priorities of the Professoriate.* Princeton, NJ: The Carnegie Foundation.

Brown, M. T. 1990. *Working Ethics: Strategies for Decision Making and Organizational Responsibility.* San Francisco: Jossey-Bass.

Brown, R. D., and D. L. Podolske. 1993. "A Political Model for Program Evaluation." In *The Handbook of Student Affairs Administration,* edited by M. J. Barr and Associates. San Francisco: Jossey-Bass.

California State University San Marcos. 2013. *Student Life and Leadership.* Retrieved from http://www.csusm.edu/sll/studentorgs/.

Career Resource Center University of Florida. 2013. *Resumes and Cover Letters.* Retrieved from www.crc.ufl.edu/students/studentResumesCoverletters.html.

Carr, J. 1995. "The Art of Supervision." Presentation at the National Housing Training Institute, Gainesville, Florida.

Cartwright, D. 1951. "Achieving Change in People: Some Applications of Group Dynamics Theory." *Human Relations* 4: 381–392.

CAS. 2012. *CAS Professional Standards for Higher Education,* 8th ed. Washington, DC: Author.

Center for Leadership and Service. 2013. *Annual Report 2011–2012.* Gainesville, Florida: Author.

Christian Legal Society Chapter v. Martinez, No. 08–1371, 9th Cir., 2009.

Clifton, D. O., and E. Anderson. 2001–2004. *StrengthsQuest.* Washington, DC: Gallup.

Coleman, J. K., and N. W. Dunkel. 2004. *50 Years of Residence Hall Leadership: NACURH, Inc.* Columbus, OH: National Association of College and University Residence Halls.

College of Charleston. 2014. *Student Organization Review Board.* Retrieved from http://sga.cofc.edu/senate/committees/index.php.

Cornell University. 2014. *NY State Penal Law, Chapter, 716, Section 1.* Retrieved from http://www.hazing.cornell.edu/cms/hazing/issues/laws/index.cfm.

Corporation for National and Community Service. 2014, March 4. *Five Colleges and Universities Earn Presidential Honor for Community Service.* Retrieved from http://www.nationalservice.gov/newsroom/press-releases/2013/five-colleges-and-universities.

Country Kickers Dance Club. 1997. *The Constitution of the Ball State University Country Kickers Dance Club.* Muncie, IN: Country Kickers Dance Club.

Cowley, W. H. 1937. "The Disappearing Dean of Men." Paper presented at the 19th annual conference on the National Association of Deans and Advisors of Men, Austin, Texas.

Craig, D. H., and T. R. Warner. 1991. "The 'Forgotten Majority' of Student Organizations and Campus Activities." *Campus Activities Programming* 239: 42–46.

Creamer, D. G., R. B. Winston, Jr., and T. K. Miller. 2001. "The Professional Student Affairs Administrator: Roles and Functions." In *The Professional Student Affairs Administrator: Educator, Leader and Manager,* edited by R. B. Winston, D. G. Creamer, T. K. Miller, and Associates. New York: Brunner-Routledge.

Cuyjet, M. 1985. "Student Government: The Nature of the Beast." *Programming* 18: 25–31.

Cuyjet, M. 1994. "Student Government as a Provider of Student Services." In *Developing Student Government Leadership*, edited by M. C. Terrell and M. J. Cuyjet. New Directions for Student Services, no. 66. San Francisco: Jossey-Bass.

DeCoster, D. A., and R. D. Brown. 1982. "Mentoring Relationships and the Educational Process." In *Mentoring-Transcript Systems for Promoting Student Growth*, edited by R. D. Brown and D. A. DeCoster, 5–17. New Directions for Student Services, no. 19. San Francisco: Jossey-Bass.

Dickinson, G. H. 2005. "Pledged to Remember: Africa in the Life and Lore of Black Greek-Letter Organizations." In *African American Fraternities and Sororities: The Legacy and the Vision*, edited by T. L. Brown, G. S. Parks, and C. M. Phillip, 11–36. Lexington: The University Press of Kentucky.

Dugan, J. P., and S. R. Komives. 2011. "Leadership Theories." In *The Handbook for Student Leadership Development*, 2nd ed., edited by S. R. Komives, J. P. Dugan, J. E. Owen, C. Slack, W. Wagner, and Associates, 35–58. San Francisco: Jossey-Bass.

Dungy, G., and S. A. Gordon. 2011. "The Development of Student Affairs." In *Student Services: A Handbook for the Profession*, edited by J. H. Schuh, S. R. Jones, and S. R. Harper, 61–79. San Francisco: Jossey-Bass.

Dunkel, N. W. 1996. "Supervision: Creating a Relationship for Advancement, Progressivity, and Education." Presentation at the annual meeting of the Association of College and University Housing Officers-International, Providence, Rhode Island.

Dunkel, N. W., K. Bray, and A. Wofford. 1989. *Training and Raising Awareness in Career Knowledge TRACK.* Gainesville: Division of Housing, University of Florida.

Dunkel, N. W., and J. H. Schuh. 1998. *Advising Student Groups and Organizations.* San Francisco: Jossey-Bass.

Dunkle, J. H., and C. A. Presley. 2009. "Helping Students with Health and Wellness Issues." In *The Handbook of Student Affairs Administration*, 3rd ed., edited by G. S. McClellan, J. Stringer, and Associates, 265–287. San Francisco: Jossey-Bass.

Eastfield College. 2014. *Service Learning*. Retrieved from http://www.eastfieldcollege.edu/ServiceLearning.

El-Khawas, E. 1996. "Student Diversity on Today's Campuses." In *Student Services: A Handbook for the Profession*, 3rd ed., edited by S. R. Komives, D. B. Woodard, Jr., and Associates, 64–82. San Francisco: Jossey-Bass.

Ewell, P. T. 2009, November. "Assessment, Accountability, and Improvement: Revisiting the Tension." NILOA Occasional Paper no. 1. Urbana: University of Illinois and Indiana University, National Institute for Learning Outcomes Assessment.

Fincher, J. 2009. "Consciousness of Self. In *Leadership for a Better World*, edited by S. R. Komives, W. Wagner, and Associates. San Francisco: Jossey-Bass.

Fine, S. A. 1985. *Benchmark Tasks for Job Analysis: A Guide for Functional Job Analysis FJA scales*. Hillsdale, NJ: Erlbaum.

Florida Agricultural and Mechanical University. 2014. *Clubs and Organizations Review Board*. Retrieved from http://studentactivities.famu.edu/m.

Florida Association of Residence Halls. 2013. *Constitution of the Florida Association of Residence Halls*. Gainesville: Florida Association of Residence Halls.

Franck, B. 1983. "Conflict: Is It Tearing Your Organization Apart?" *Campus Activities Programming* 165: 26–29.

Fraternity Insurance Purchasing Group. 2013. *FIPG Risk Management Manual*. Indianapolis: Author.

Fried, H. J. 1989. "Teaching and Training." In *Student Services: A Handbook for the Profession*, edited by U. Delworth, G. R. Hanson, and Associates, 353–370. San Francisco: Jossey-Bass.

George Mason University. 2013. *Moving On: A Guide for Career Planning and Job Search*. Fairfax, VA: George Mason University.

Gilligan, C. 1982. *In a Different Voice*. Cambridge, MA: Harvard University Press.

Grand Valley State University. 2014. *Student Organization Review Board*. Retrieved from http://gvsu.edu/studentorg/student-organization-review-board-25.htm.

Greenleaf, R. K. 2002. *Servant Leadership*, 25th Anniversary ed. Mahwah, NJ: Paulist. Originally published 1977.

Harding, T. S. 1971. *College Literary Societies: Their Contribution to Higher Education in the United States, 1815–1876*. New York: Pageant.

Healy v. James, 408 U.S. 169 (1972).

Hersey, P., and K. H. Blanchard. 1988. *Management of Organizational Behavior*. Englewood Cliffs, NJ: Prentice Hall.

Higher Education Research Institute. 1996. *A Social Change Model of Leadership Development Guidebook. Version III*. Los Angeles: Author.

Horowitz, H. L. 1987. *Campus Life: Undergraduate Cultures from the End of the Eighteenth Century to the Present*. Chicago: University of Chicago Press.

House, E. R. 1994. "Trends in Evaluation." In *Assessment and Program Evaluation*, edited by J. S. Stark and A. Thomas, 79–86. New York: Simon & Schuster.

Hughes, R., and C. R. Pace. 2003. "Using NSSE to Study Student Retention and Withdrawal." *Assessment Update*, July-August, 154: 1.

Hunter, M. S., and E. R. White. 2004. "Could Fixing Academic Advising Fix Higher Education?" *About Campus* 9, no. 1: 20–25.

Hutley, K. 2003. *Alexander Astin's Theory of Involvement*. Retrieved from http://archive.today/vAKk#selection-28.1–53.50.

Independent Sector. 2013. *Independent Sector's Value of Volunteer Time*. Retrieved from http://www.independentsector.org/volunteer_time.

Jacoby, B. J. 1996. "Service-Learning in Today's Higher Education." In *Service-Learning in Higher Education: Concepts and Practices*, edited by B. J. Jacoby and Associates, 3–25. San Francisco: Jossey-Bass.

Jacoby, B. J. 2003. *Building Partnerships for Service Learning*. San Francisco: Wiley.

Jardine, C. 1996. "Staff Supervision and Appraisal." Presentation at the National Housing Training Institute, Gainesville, Florida.

Johnson, D. W., and F. P. Johnson. 2013. *Joining Together: Group Theory and Group Skills*, 11th ed. Boston: Pearson.

Junco, R., and J. Mastrodicasa. 2007. *Connecting the Net Generation: What Higher Education Professionals Need to Know about Today's Students*. Washington, DC: National Association of Student Personnel Administrators.

Kaplin, W. A., and B. A. Lee. 2013. *The Law of Higher Education*, 5th ed., vols. 1 and 2. San Francisco: Jossey-Bass.

Kearney, P. A. 1993. "Professional Staffing." In *Student Housing and Residential Life: A Handbook for Professionals Committed to Student Development Goals*, edited by R. B. Winston, Jr., S. Anchors, and Associates, 269–291. San Francisco: Jossey-Bass.

Keeling, R. P., Ed. 2006. *Learning Reconsidered 2: A Practical Guide to Implementing a Campus-Wide Focus on the Student Experience*. Washington, DC: American College Personnel Association, Association of College and University Housing Officers-International, Association of College Unions-International, National Academic Advising Association, National Association for Campus Activities, National Association of Student Personnel Administrators, and National Intramural Recreational Sports Association.

Keeling, S. (2003). Advising the millennial generation. *NACADA Journal,* 23 (1–2), 30–36.

Keppler, K., and J. Robinson. 1993. "Student Governments: What Are the Issues of the Day?" *Campus Activities Programming* 259: 36–46.

Kimbrough, W. M. 2003. *Black Greek 101: The Culture, Customs, and Challenges of Black Fraternities and Sororities*. Cranbury, NJ: Farleigh Dickinson University Press.

King, P. M., and M. B. Baxter Magolda. 2011. "Student Learning." In *Student Services: A Handbook for the Profession*, 5th ed., edited by J. H. Schuh, S. R. Jones, S. R. Harper, and Associates, 207–225. San Francisco: Jossey-Bass.

Kitchener, K. S. 1985. "Ethical Principles and Ethical Decisions in Student Affairs." In *Applied Ethics in Student Services*, edited by H. J. Canon and R. D. Brown, 17–30. New Directions for Student Services, no. 30. San Francisco: Jossey-Bass.

Kohlberg, L. 1984. *The Psychology of Moral Development.* New York: HarperCollins.

Kolb, D. A. 1984. *Experiential Learning: Experience as the Source of Learning and Development.* Englewood Cliffs, NJ: Prentice Hall.

Komives, S. R. 2011a. "Advancing Leadership Education." In *The Handbook for Student Leadership Development*, 2nd ed., edited by S. R. Komives, J. P. Dugan, J. E. Owen, C. Slack, W. Wagner, and Associates, 1–64. San Francisco: Jossey-Bass.

Komives, S. R. 2011b. "Leadership." In *Student Services: A Handbook for the Profession*, 5th ed., edited by J. H. Schuh, S. R. Jones, S. R. Harper, and Associates, 353–371. San Francisco: Jossey-Bass.

Komives, S. R., J. P. Dugan, J. E. Owen, C. Slack, W. Wagner, and Associates. 2011. *The Handbook for Student Leadership Development*, 2nd ed. San Francisco: Jossey-Bass.

Komives, S. R., and G. L. Tucker. 1993. "Successful Residence Hall Government: Themes from a National Study of Select Hall Government Structures." In *Advice for Advisers: The Development of an Effective Residence Hall Association*, edited by N. W. Dunkel and C. L. Spencer, 27–44. Columbus, OH: Association of College and University Housing Officers-International.

Komives, S. R., W. Wagner, and Associates. 2009. *Leadership for a Better World: Understanding the Social Change Model of Leadership Development.* San Francisco: Jossey-Bass.

Komives, S. R., and D. B. Woodard Jr. 1996. "Building on the Past, Shaping the Future." In *Student Services: A Handbook for the Profession*, 3rd ed., edited by S. R. Komives, D. B. Woodard, Jr., and Associates, 536–558. San Francisco: Jossey-Bass.

Kouzes, J. M., and B. Z. Posner. 2008. *The Student Leadership Practices Inventory.* Retrieved from http://www.studentleadershipchallenge.com/Assessments.aspx.

Kouzes, J. M., and B. Z. Posner. 2012. *The Leadership Challenge*, 5th ed. San Francisco: Jossey-Bass.

Kowalski, G. J., and J. A. Conlogue. 1996. "Advising and Supervising: A Comparison of Unique Job Elements." Program presented at the annual meeting of the Association of College and University Housing Officers-International, Providence, Rhode Island.

Kuh, G. D. 1991. "Characteristics of Involving Colleges." In *The Role and Contribution of Student Affairs in Involving Colleges*, edited by G. D. Kuh and

J. H. Schuh, 11–29. Washington, DC: National Association of Student Personnel Administrators.

Kuh, G. D., T. M. Cruce, R. Shoup, J. Kinzie, and R. M. Gonyea. 2008. "Unmasking the Effects of Student Engagement on First-Year College Grades and Persistence." *The Journal of Higher Education* 795: 540–563.

Kuh, G. D., J. Kinzie, J. H. Schuh, E. J. Whitt, and Associates. 2005. *Student Success in College: Creating Conditions That Matter.* San Francisco: Jossey-Bass.

Kuh, G. D., J. L. Kinzie, J. H. Schuh, and E. J. Whitt. 2010. *Student Success in College,* 2nd ed. San Francisco: Jossey-Bass.

Kuh, G. D., and J. P. Lund. 1994. "What Students Gain from Participating in Student Government." In *Developing Student Government Leadership,* edited by M. C. Terrell and M. J. Cuyjet, 5–18. New Directions for Student Services, no. 66. San Francisco: Jossey-Bass.

Kuh, G. D., J. H. Schuh, and E. J. Whitt. 1991. *Involving Colleges: Successful Approaches to Fostering Student Learning and Development Outside the Classroom.* San Francisco: Jossey-Bass.

Lawrence, G. 1995. *People Types and Tiger Stripes.* Gainesville, FL: Center for Applications of Psychological Type.

Ledbetter, B. E. 2009. Legal Issues in Student Affairs. In *The Handbook of Student Affairs Administration,* 3rd ed., edited by G. S. McClellan, J. Stringer, and Associates, 505–525. San Francisco: Jossey-Bass.

Lifton, W. 1967. *Working with Groups: Group Process and Individual Growth.* New York: Wiley.

Love, A. 2004. "Implementation Evaluation." In *Handbook of Program Evaluation* 2nd ed., edited by J. S. Wholey, H. P. Hatry, and K. E. Newcomer, 63–98. San Francisco: Jossey-Bass.

Love, P., and S. Maxam. 2011. "Advising and Consultation." In *Student Services: A Handbook for the Profession,* 5th ed., edited by J. H. Schuh, S. R. Jones, S. R. Harper, and Associates, 413–432. San Francisco: Jossey-Bass.

Lucas, C. J. 1994. *American Higher Education: A History.* New York: St. Martin's Griffin.

Magee, K. 1994. "To Pay or Not to Pay: The Questions of Student Stipends." *Campus Activities Programming* 276: 30–33.

Magolda, P., and S. J. Quaye. 2011. "Teaching in the Co-Curriculum." In *A Handbook for the Profession,* edited by J. H. Schuh, S. R. Jones, S. R. Harper, and Associates, 385–398. San Francisco: Jossey-Bass.

McCarthy, M. D. 1996. "One-Time and Short-Term Service Learning Experiences." In *Service-Learning in Higher Education: Concepts and Practices,* edited by B. J. Jacoby and Associates. San Francisco: Jossey-Bass.

McCluskey-Titus, P., and J. W. Paterson. 2006. "Traditional and Alternative Organizational Models for RHAs." In *Advice for Advisers: Empowering Your Residence Hall Association,* 3rd ed., edited by N. W. Dunkel and C. L. Spencer,

97–121. Columbus, OH: Association of College and University Housing Officers-International.

McKaig, R., and S. Policello. 1987. "Group Advising—Defined, Described and Examined." In *A Handbook for Student Group Advisers*, edited by J. H. Schuh, 45–70. Alexandria, VA: American College Personnel Association.

Medieval Recreations. 1997. *The Constitution of the Ball State University Medieval Recreations*. Muncie, IN: Medieval Recreations.

Merriam, S. B. 2002. "Introduction to Qualitative Research." In *Qualitative Research in Practice*, edited by S. G. Merriam and Associates, 3–17. San Francisco: Jossey-Bass.

Merriam-Webster Dictionary. 2013. Retrieved from www.merriam-webster.com /dictionary.

Mezirow, J., Ed. 2000. *Learning as Transformation: Critical Perspectives on a Theory in Progress*. San Francisco: Jossey-Bass.

Middlebury College. 2013. *Middlebury College Hazing Policy*. Retrieved from http:// www.middlebury.edu/about/handbook/student_policies/hazing.

Mitchell, J. J., and A. J. Ryder. 2013. "Developing and Using Dashboard Indicators in Student Affairs Assessment." In *Selected Contemporary Assessment Issues*, edited by J. H. Schuh, 71–81. New Directions for Student Affairs, no. 143. San Francisco: Jossey-Bass.

Mitchell, S. E. 1993. Motivation of Paid and Volunteer Students." In *Advice for Advisers: The Development of an Effective Residence Hall Association*, edited by N. W. Dunkel and C. L. Spencer, 55–62. Columbus, OH: Association of College and University Housing Officers-International.

Montelongo, R. 2002. "Student Participation in College Student Organizations: A Review of Literature." *Journal of Indiana University Student Personnel Association*, 61–62.

Mueller, K. 1961. *Student Personnel Work in Higher Education*. Boston: Houghton Mifflin.

Munschauer, J. L. 1986. *Jobs for English Majors and Other Smart People*. Princeton, NJ: Peterson's Guides.

Murray, H. A. 1938. *Explorations in Personality*. New York: Oxford University Press.

Napier, R. W., and M. K. Gershenfeld. 1989. *Group Theory and Experience*. Boston: Houghton Mifflin.

National Association for Campus Activities. 2013. *NACA's Mission, Purpose, Values, and Strategic Plan*. Columbia, SC: National Association for Campus Activities.

National Association of Student Personnel Educators and the American College Personnel Association. 2004. *Learning Reconsidered*. Washington, DC: Author.

National Center for Education Statistics. 2014. Fast Facts: Title IX. Retrieved from http://nces.ed.gov/fastfacts/display.asp?id=93.

National Interfraternity Conference. 1991. "Risk Management Policy." In *Baird's Manual of American College Fraternities*, edited by J. L. Anson and R. F. Marchesani, I-34. Indianapolis: Baird's Manual Foundation.

National Multicultural Greek Council. (2008). *About*. Retrieved from http://nationalmgc.org/about.

National Panhellenic Conference. (2011). *Mission Statement*. Retrieved from https://www.npcwomen.org/about.aspx.

National Pan-Hellenic Council. (2014). *Mission*. Retrieved from http://www.nphchq.org/mission.

National Survey of Student Engagement (NSSE). 2001. *2001 NSSE Viewpoint: Improving the College Experience: Using Effective Educational Practices*. Bloomington: Indiana University Center for Postsecondary Research.

National Survey of Student Engagement (NSSE). 2012. *Promoting Student Learning and Improvement: Lessons from NSSE at 13*. Bloomington: Indiana University Center for Postsecondary Research.

Navy–Marine Corps ROTC. 2013. *Navy–Marine Corps ROTC: College scholarships bulletin*. Arlington, VA: Navy–Marine Corps ROTC.

NIRSA. 2013a. *NIRSA Vision*. Retrieved from www.nirsa.org.

NIRSA. 2013b. *Who We Are*. Retrieved from www.nirsa.org.

NROTC. 2013. *History of NROTC*. Retrieved from www.nrotc.navy.mil/history.aspx.

North American Interfraternity Conference. 2013. *Title IX*. Retrieved from http://www.nicindy.org/about/resolutions/#Single%20Gender%20Membership.

Nuss, E. M. 1993. "The Role of Professional Associations." In *The Handbook of Student Affairs Administration*, edited by M. J. Barr and Associates, 364–377. San Francisco: Jossey-Bass.

Odiorne, G. S. 1985. "Mentoring—an American Management Innovation." *Personnel Administrator* 30, no. 5: 63–70.

Osteen, J. M. 1988. "Advising Model for Residence Halls." Unpublished manuscript, Student Activities, University of Maryland, College Park.

Osteen, J. M., and G. L. Tucker. 1998. "Authority, Accountability, and Advice: Understanding the Unique Roles of Residence Life Staff and Hall Government Leaders." *Journal of College and University Student Housing* 271: 34–40.

Owen, K. C. 1991. "Reflections on the College Fraternity and Its Changing Nature." In *Baird's Manual of American College Fraternities*, edited by J. L. Anson and R. F. Marchesani, Jr., I-1–I-7. Indianapolis: Baird's Manual Foundation.

Oyez Project. 2010. *Christian Legal Society Chapter v. Martinez*, No. 08–1371, 9th Cir., 2009. Retrieved from http://www.oyez.org/cases/2000–2009/2009/2009_08_1371.

Palomba, C. A., and T. W. Banta. 1999. *Assessment Essentials*. San Francisco: Jossey-Bass.

Pascarella, E. J., and P. T. Terenzini. 1991. *How College Affects Students: Findings and Insights from Twenty Years of Research.* San Francisco: Jossey-Bass.

Pascarella, E. J., and P. T. Terenzini. 2005. *How College Affects Students, Vol. 2: A Third Decade of Research.* San Francisco: Jossey-Bass.

Pavela, G. 2011. "Selected Legal Issues." In *Student Services: A Handbook for the Profession,* 5th ed., edited by J. H. Schuh, S. R. Jones, S. R. Harper, and Associates, 120–134. San Francisco: Jossey-Bass.

Poister, T. H. 2004. "Performance Monitoring." In *Handbook of Program Evaluation,* 2nd ed., edited by J. S. Wholey, H. P. Hatry, and K. E. Newcomer, 98–125. San Francisco: Jossey-Bass.

Pope, R. L., and J. A. Mueller. 2011. "Multicultural Competence." In *Student Services: A Handbook for the Profession,* 5th ed., edited by J. H. Schuh, S. R. Jones, S. R. Harper, and Associates, 337–352. San Francisco: Jossey-Bass.

Public Relations Student Society of America. 2011. *PRSSA National Bylaws, Policies, and Procedures.* New York: Author.

Radford University Clogging Team. 2013. *Constitution of the Radford University Clogging Team.* Radford, VA: Author.

Reason, R. D., and E. M. Broido. 2011. "Philosophies and Values." In *Student Services: A Handbook for the Profession,* 5th ed., edited by J. H. Schuh, S. R. Jones, S. R. Harper, and Associates, 80–95. San Francisco: Jossey-Bass.

RedbusUS. 2013. *8 Reasons Why You Should Join Student Organizations in US Universities.* Retrieved from http://redbus2us.com

Renn, K. A., and R. D. Reason. 2013. *College Students in the United States: Characteristics, Experiences, and Outcomes.* San Francisco: Jossey-Bass.

Rest, J. 1983. *Moral Development: Advances in Research and Theory.* New York: Praeger.

Robert, H. M. 2011. *Robert's Rules of Order.* Glenview, IL: Scott, Foresman.

Ross, Jr., L. C. 2001. *The Divine Nine: The History of African American Fraternities and Sororities.* New York: Kensington.

Rudolph, F. 1962. *The American College and University: A History.* New York: Knopf.

Rutgers New Brunswick. 2013. *Student Life New Brunswick.* Retrieved from http://getinvolved.rutgers.edu/organizations/register-an-organization/.

Saddlemire, G. L., and A. L. Rentz, Eds. 1988. *Student Affairs Functions in Higher Education.* Springfield, IL: Thomas.

Sandeen, A. 1985. "Legacy of Values Education." In *Promoting Values Development in College Students,* edited by J. Dalton, 1–16. Washington, DC: National Association of Student Personnel Administrators.

Sandeen, A. 2003. *Enhancing Student Engagement on Campus.* Lanham, MD: University Press of America.

Sandeen, A., and M. J. Barr. 2006. *Critical Issues for Student Affairs.* San Francisco: Jossey-Bass.

Sanford, N. 1962. "The Developmental Status of Entering Freshmen." In *The American College*, edited by N. Sanford, 253–282. New York: Wiley.

Santa Fe College. 2014. *Golf Club*. Retrieved from http://www.sfcollege.edu /athletics/?section=clubs/golf.

Saunders, S. A., and D. L. Cooper. 2001. "Programmatic Interventions: Translating Theory to Practice." In *The Professional Student Affairs Administrator: Educator, Leader and Manager*, edited by R. B. Winston, Jr., D. G. Creamer, T. K. Miller, and Associates, 309–340. New York: Brunner-Routledge.

Sauk Valley Community College. 2014. *What Does Student Government Do?* Retrieved from http://www.svcc.edu/students/student-government.

Scheuermann, C. D. 1996. "Ongoing Curricular Service-Learning." In *Service-Learning in Higher Education: Concepts and Practices*, edited by B. J. Jacoby and Associates, 135–155. San Francisco: Jossey-Bass.

Schuh, J. H. 1991. "Making a Large University Feel Small: The Iowa State University Story." In *The Role and Contributions of Student Affairs in Involving Colleges*, edited by G. D. Kuh and J. H. Schuh, 30–41. Washington, DC: National Association of Student Personnel Administrators.

Schuh, J. H. 2009. "Fiscal Pressures on Higher Education and Student Affairs." In *The Handbook of Student Affairs Administration*. 3rd ed., edited by G. S. McClellen, J. Stringer, and Associates, 81–104. San Francisco: Jossey-Bass.

Schuh, J. H. 2011. "Financing Student Affairs." In *Student Services: A Handbook for the Profession*, 5th ed., edited by J. H. Schuh, S. R. Jones, S. R. Harper, and Associates, 303–320. San Francisco: Jossey-Bass.

Schuh, J. H., and Associates. 2009. *Assessment Methods for Student Affairs*. San Francisco: Jossey-Bass.

Schuh, J. H., and W. Carlisle. 1991. "Supervision and Evaluation." In *Administration and Leadership in Student Affairs*, 2nd ed., edited by T. K. Miller, R. B. Winston, Jr., and Associates, 495–531. Muncie, IN: Accelerated Development.

Scotus Project. 2010, June 28. *Christian Legal Society Chapter v. Martinez*, Retrieved from http://www.scotusblog.com/case-files/cases/christian-legal-society-v -martinez.

SKIFFY: The Science Fiction and Fantasy Club of the College of William and Mary. 2013a. *Constitution of the Science Fiction and Fantasy Club*. Retrieved from http://web.wm.edu/so/.sci-fi/constitution.html.

SKIFFY: The Science Fiction and Fantasy Club of the College of William and Mary. 2013b. *Officers 2009–2010*. Retrieved from http://web.wm.edu/so/sci-fi /officers09.html.

Smalls, M. M., and B. Gee, Eds. 2009. *NAPA Guide*. Association of Fraternity /Sorority Advisers. Retrieved from http://www.afa1976.org/portals/0 /membership_intake_guide_nphc.pdf.

Smalls, M. M., and R. A. Hernandez, Eds. 2009. *NALFO Guide*. Association of Fraternity/Sorority Advisers. Retrieved from http://www.afa1976.org /Portals/0/Publications/NALFO_Guide_FINAL.pdf.

Southeast Missouri State University Campus Life and Event Services. 2011, March 15. *Officer Training and Transition Guide.* Retrieved from http://www.semo .edu/pdf/old/Lead_SOResource_OfficerTransition_Long_2011.

Stage, F. K., and P. Muller. 1999. "Theories of Learning for College Students." In *Enhancing Student Learning: Setting the Campus Context,* edited by F. K. Stage, L. W. Watson, and M. Terrell, 25–42. Lanham, MD: University Press of America.

St. John, W. D. 1985. "You Are What You Communicate." *Personnel* 64, no. 10: 40–43.

Stoner, K., K. Berry, L. Boever, and B. Tattershall. 1998. "History and Services of the National Association of College and University Residence Halls, Inc." In *Advice for Advisors: The Development of an Effective Residence Hall Association,* edited by N. W. Dunkel and C. L. Spencer, 181–206. Columbus, OH: Association of College and University Housing Officers-International.

Student Government. 2010, August. *Constitution and Statutes of the University of Florida Student Body.* Gainesville: Author.

Stump, L. J. 2013. *Dear Colleague Letter.* Gainesville: University of Florida.

Super, D. E. 1980. "A Life-Span, Life-Space Approach to Career Development." *Journal of Vocational Behavior* 16: 282–298.

Suskie, L. 2009. *Assessing Student Learning,* 2nd ed. San Francisco: Jossey-Bass.

Texas A&M University. 2013a. *Membership Selection Outcomes.* College Station: Texas A&M University. Retrieved from http://sllo.tamu.edu.

Texas A&M University. 2013b. *What Is Risk Management?* College Station, TX: Texas A&M University Office of Student Activities. Retrieved from http://studentactivities.tamu.edu/risk.

Torbenson, C. L. 2005. "The Origin and Evolution of College Fraternities and Sororities." In *African American Fraternities and Sororities: The Legacy and the Vision,* edited by T. L. Brown, G. S. Parks, and C. M. Phillips, 37–66. Lexington: The University Press of Kentucky.

Tucker, G. 2006. Residence Hall Government Effectiveness. In *Advice for Advisers: Empowering Your Residence Hall Association,* 3rd ed., edited by N. W. Dunkel and C. L. Spencer, 60–96. Columbus, OH: Association of College and University Housing Officers-International.

Tuckman, B. 1965. "Developmental Sequence in Small Groups." *Psychological Bulletin* 63: 384–399.

Tuckman, B., and M. Jensen. 1977. "Stages of Small Group Development Revisited." *Group and Organizational Studies* 2: 419–427.

Turk, D. B. 2004. *Bound by a Mighty Vow: Sisterhood and Women's Fraternities, 1870–1920.* New York: New York University.

UCLA Bruins Leaders Project. 2013. *Social Change Model.* Retrieved from http://www.bruinleaders.ucla.edu/default.htm.

United States Air Force. 2013. *Air Force Reserve Officer Training Corps Fact Sheet.* Retrieved from http://www.af.mil/AboutUs/FactSheets/Display/tabid/224 /Article/104478/air-force-reserve-officer-training-corps.aspx.

United States Department of Education Office of Civil Rights. 2011. *Dear Colleague Letter.* Retrieved from http://www2.ed.gov/about/offices/list/ocr/letters /colleague-201104.html.

United States Department of Education, Office of Postsecondary Education. 2011. *The Handbook for Campus Safety and Security Reporting.* Washington, DC: Author.

University of Florida Geomatics Association. 2013. *UF Geomatics Association Constitution.* Retrieved from http://sfrc.ifas.ufl.edu/gsa/GSA_bylines.htm.

University of Michigan Women's Rugby Club. 2013. *Mission Statement.* Retrieved from www.umwrfc.wordpress.com.

University of Minnesota. 2014. *Community Service Learning Center.* Retrieved from http://www.servicelearning.umn.edu/info/reflection.html#Ideas.

University of Nebraska at Omaha. 2013. *Student Organizations and Leadership Programs.* Retrieved from http://studentorgs.unomaha.edu/.

University of Tennessee. 2013. *One Campus. One Community. Celebrate the Differences.* Retrieved from http://leadershipandservice.utk.edu.

University of Wisconsin-LaCrosse American Marketing Association Collegiate Chapter. 2013. *AMA Purpose and Constitution.* Retrieved from www.uwlax .edu/ama.

Upcraft, M. L., and J. H. Schuh. 1996. *Assessment in Student Affairs: A Guide for Practitioners.* San Francisco: Jossey-Bass.

Van Dusen, W. R. 2004. *FERPA: Basic Guidelines for Faculty and Staff: A Simple Step-by-Step Approach for Compliance.* Retrieved from the NACADA Clearinghouse of Academic Advising Resources website: http://www.nacada.ksu.edu /Resources/Clearinghouse/View-Articles/FERPA-overview.aspx.

Van Etten, S., M. Pressley, D. M. McInerney, and A. D. Liem. 2008. "College Seniors' Theory of Their Academic Motivation." *Journal of Educational Psychology* 1004: 812–828.

Vanguri, D. 2010. "Student Organization Advisor Involvement and Retention." *The Bulletin, 85.* Bloomington, IN: Association of College Unions International.

Verry, B. 1993. "The Organizational Structures of RHAs." In *Advice for Advisors: The Development of an Effective Residence Hall Association,* edited by N. W. Dunkel and C. L. Spencer, 45–54. Columbus, OH: Association of College and University Housing Officers-International.

Wagner, W. 2011. "Considerations of Student Development in Leadership." In *The Handbook for Student Leadership Development,* 2nd ed., edited by S. R. Komives, J. P. Dugan, J. E. Owen, C. Slack, W. Wagner, and Associates, 85–108. San Francisco: Jossey-Bass.

Whitt, E. J. 2011. "Academic and Student Affairs Partnerships." In *Student Services: A Handbook for the Profession*, 5th ed., edited by J. H. Schuh, S. R. Jones, S. R. Harper, and Associates, 482–496. San Francisco: Jossey-Bass.

Wingspread Group on Higher Education. 1993. *An American Imperative: Higher Expectations for Higher Education*. Racine, WI: Johnson Foundation.

Winston, R. B., Jr., W. C. Bonney, T. K. Miller, and J. C. Dagley. 1988. *Promoting Student Development through Intentionally Structured Groups: Principles, Techniques, and Applications*. San Francisco: Jossey-Bass.

Young, R. B. 1996. "Guiding Values and Philosophy." In *Student Services: A Handbook for the Profession*, 3rd ed., edited by S. R. Komives, D. B. Woodard, Jr., and Associates, 83–105. San Francisco: Jossey-Bass.

Index

Page numbers in italics refer to exhibits and figures.

Want to connect?

Like us on Facebook
http://www.facebook.com/JBHigherEd

Subscribe to our newsletter
www.josseybass.com/go/higheredemail

Follow us on Twitter
http://twitter.com/JBHigherEd

Go to our Website
www.josseybass.com/highereducation

WILEY